Up from the Underground

POST-COMMUNIST CULTURAL STUDIES SERIES

Thomas Cushman, General Editor

The Culture of Lies
Antipolitical Essays
Dubravka Urgrešić

Burden of Dreams
History and Identity in Post-Soviet Ukraine
Catherine Wanner

Gender Politics in the Western Balkans
Women, Society, and Politics in Yugoslavia and the Yugoslav Successor States
Sabrina P. Ramet, ed.

The Radical Right in Central and Eastern Europe Since 1989
Sabrina P. Ramet, ed.

The Culture of Power in Serbia
Nationalism and the Destruction of Alternatives
Eric D. Gordy

Russia's Liberal Project
State-Society Relations in the Transition from Communism
Marcia A. Weigle

Revolt of the Filmmakers
The Struggle for Artistic Autonomy and the Fall of the Soviet Film Industry
George Faraday

The Denial of Bosnia
Rusmir Mahmutćehajić

Tundra Passages
Gender and History in the Russian Far East
Petra Rethmann

Up from the Underground

The Culture of Rock Music in Postsocialist Hungary

ANNA SZEMERE

The Pennsylvania State University Press
University Park, Pennsylvania

Library of Congress Cataloging-in-Publication Data

Szemere, Anna.
Up from the underground : the culture of rock music in postsocialist Hungary / Anna Szemere.
p. cm. — (Post-Communist cultural studies series)
Includes index.
ISBN 0-271-02132-2 (cloth : alk. paper)
ISBN 0-271-02133-0 (pbk. alk. paper)
1. Rock music—Hungary—History and criticism. 2. Popular culture—Hungary—20th century. 3. Music—Social aspects. I. Title. II. Post-Communist cultural studies.

ML3534 .S97 2001
306.4′84—dc21

2001021592

Printed in the United States of America
Published by The Pennsylvania State University Press,
University Park, PA 16802-1003

It is the policy of The Pennsylvania State University Press to use acid-free paper for the first printing of all clothbound books. Publications on uncoated stock satisfy the minimum requirements of American National Standard for Information Sciences—Permanence of Paper for Printed Library Materials, ANSI Z39.48–1992.

contents

illustrations

acknowledgments

In writing this book I was fortunate to be guided by an outstanding group of individuals. Chandra Mukerji gave depth and direction to many of my raw ideas. Martha Lampland's ability to move effortlessly between two languages, cultures, and academic traditions added tremendously to the sophistication of my research. Dick Madsen's insightful and sensitive manner of critiquing and advising was crucial to the success of this project, while Bud Mehan sustained me with his intellectual brilliance, humor, and persistent curiosity about Hungarian culture and politics. George Lipsitz's immense knowledge of popular culture and thorough criticism of my ideas improved my work considerably. I benefited greatly from the interest, enthusiasm, and insightful comments of the following mentors, colleagues, and friends at various stages of my work: Edit András, Katalin Balog, Natalie Bookchin, Tom Cushman, Ana Dević, Simon Frith, Jeffrey Goldfarb, Larry Grossberg, Eric Gordy, Judit Hersko, Laura Miller, Ágnes Román, Ákos Róna-Tas, David Stark, and Christena Turner.

I am especially indebted to my informants—the musicians, journalists, and rock entrepreneurs in Hungary—for their time, concern, and delightful ideas, which inform this research. Several of them shared intensely personal aspects of their lives with me; I sincerely appreciate their generosity. Several friends in Hungary assisted me during my field trips. András Pál and Zsuzsa Kis set up meetings and interviews for me with their artist friends in Szentendre; András Gerő was generous with his advice and provocative ideas to orient my study. Katalin Kovalcsik made participant observation more fun and convenient for me. Tamás Ligeti Nagy provided fresh information and great photos for me. I am most grateful to János Maróthy of the Hungarian Academy of Sciences for his contribution to the intellectual foundation of this research as my former mentor and an exceptional scholar.

I received several forms of institutional help for this work. At the early stages, a Resident Fellowship from the Humanities Research

Institute of the University of California provided support for participation in an inspiring workshop on retheorizing music. The Sociology Department at the University of California, San Diego, offered grant aid for my research trips to Hungary. The Mellon Postdoctoral Fellowship for the Sawyer Seminar "Mass Media and New Democracies" at the New School for Social Research was helpful in my later revisions of the book. I also thank the Joint Committee on Eastern Europe of the American Council of Learned Societies for its generous financial support. Peter Potter, his editorial staff at Penn State University Press, and my copyeditor, Barbara Salazar, did an excellent job of preparing the manuscript for publication.

I am grateful for my family's many contributions to this work. My relatives in Hungary kept me well informed about local pop and rock by a steady supply of cassette tapes and other sources of information. My daughter, Nora, shared with me her knowledge of American youth idioms as we translated Hungarian rock'n'roll lyrics into English. Her genuine and far from uncritical interest in this entire project meant very much to me. So did the numerous forms of long-term support and instant technical help offered by my spouse, András. I also thank him for making it possible for me to work long hours by taking on more than a fair share of household chores and child care. Finally, this book would not have been written without the selfless efforts of my parents, Livia and György Szemere, to ensure a fine education for me.

abbreviations

Alliance of Free Democrats (Szabad Demokraták Szövetsége [SZDSZ])	AFD
Control Group [Kontroll Csoport]	CG
Europe Publishing House [Európa Kiadó]	EPH
Federation of Young Democrats (Fiatal Demokraták Szövetsége [FIDESZ])	FYD
Galloping Coroners (Vágtázó Halottkémek [VHK])	GC
Hungarian Democratic Forum (Magyar Demokrata Fórum [MDF])	HDF
International Federation of the Phonograph Industry	IFPI
Kampec Dolores	KD
Magyar Hanglemezgyártók Szövetsége (Federation of the Hungarian Phonograph Industry)	MAHASZ
Recommended Records	RR
Trottel Records	TR
Ultra Rock Agency (Ultra Rock Hírügynökség [URH])	URA
Young Artists' Club (Fiatal Müvészek Klubja [FMK])	YAC

Up from the Underground

Introduction

As I was strolling along a street in Budapest's inner city in the summer of 1999, I spotted a large billboard inviting me to tour Hungary, to go mountain climbing, even to explore caves. Two lines at the top immediately caught my attention: "What can a tourist do? She's[1] just happy to be here!" (Fig. 1). As a regular tourist in Budapest since 1987, the year I relocated to the United States, I was just happy to be there each time I visited. But I must have been one of the few tourists who knew that the enigmatic lines are from a classic local underground song dating back to 1982, by the group Európa Kiadó (Europe Publishing House or Europe for Rent).

The song called "The Tourist" has little to do with tourism. An allegory of estrangement, it reflected and shaped the sentiments of a sizable group of young people who felt powerless, frustrated, and bored under the soft dictatorship of late socialist Hungary. Over the song's laid-back and intoxicating reggae-like rhythm, the singer's voice is alternately desperate and sarcastic. Like most other underground rock pieces of the time, this one could be heard only at con-

1. The Hungarian language does not mark gender in personal pronouns.

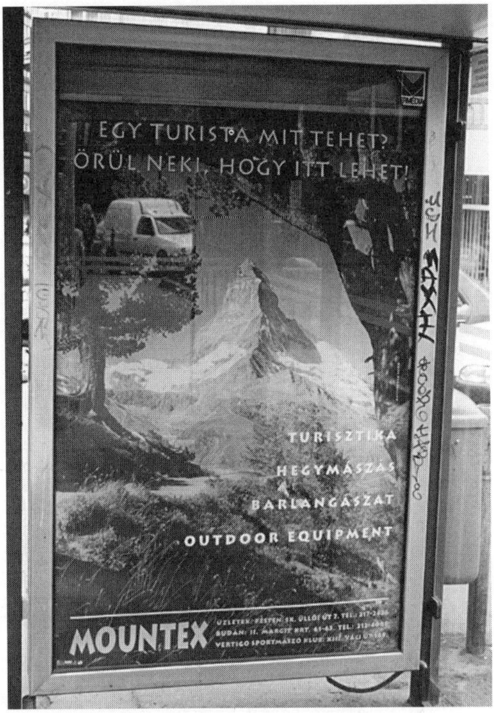

1
Street advertisement for tourism. Photo by Dániel Szemere.

certs and on noncommercially (read: illegally) produced and circulated tape recordings.

The dissident song's afterlife in an ad for tourism some fifteen years later epitomizes the profound transformation that the counterculture of state socialism underwent after Central and Eastern Europe's transition to capitalism. Interpreting this transformation in line with current theories of transition-as-commodification (Merkel 1994, Klíma 1994, Bohlman 2000), one could say that the change in regime spawned the excessive commercialization of culture that now pokes fun at its predecessor, the high-minded and subversive underground. A very different approach would see in the resurfacing of the song's lines the nostalgic value of this music to a generation now in middle age who exploit the memories of their youth to sell products and services. Nostalgia and its complex manifestations is another favored theme of investigations of postsocialist society. related to the emergent commodity culture of the region. From this perspective, underground rock looks the same as the Trabant, the pollution-spewing "people's car" manufactured in the German Democratic Republic, which has become a pricey collector's item in the reunified Germany (Anderson n.d.). The commercialization of nostalgia in Hungary is seen again in the rebirth of the past regime's pompous official marches, hymns, and labor songs as they were repackaged and published under the catchy, tongue-in-cheek title *The Best of Communism.*[2]

Is there indeed nothing more than commerce and nostalgia underlying the images and aphorisms of underground rock in the broadly understood popular culture of postsocialist Hungary? Why the continued attraction of this musical subculture in what has become a different country since the music's heyday? How can the story of this movement—one of unique creativity, courage, crisis, and recuperation—address this question? My book is an in-depth inquiry into the fifteen-year collective history of underground rock musicians (from the movement's inception in 1980 through its complete realignment in 1995) with a focus on how they anticipated, precipitated, and responded to the fall of the Wall in 1989. Investigating the community's musical activities, texts, discourses, and inter- and in-group struggles in their social contexts, I aim to provide a unique account of the transition grounded in an ethnography of everyday life. In doing so, I challenge one-dimensional representations of the politics of popular culture and transition in Eastern Europe and address more general questions about expressive culture and social change. More specifically, I am interested in the ways the producers and consumers of art and popular culture use them to build and rebuild their identities and give direction to their personal trajectories.

The 1990s saw the polarization of the region into a Central and an Eastern Europe. Central Europe includes Poland, the Czech Republic, Hungary, Slovenia, and the Baltic states, characterized by relative economic prosperity and political stability and looking forward to membership in the European Union. At the same time, many countries in Eastern Europe, such as Romania, the former republics of the Soviet Union, Serbia, and Albania, have experienced various degrees of economic stagnation or chaos, autocratic political

2. *The Best of Communism: Selection of Revolutionary Songs*, Gong MK37898.

rule, and severe ethnic strife or war. No postcommunist country has managed to evade altogether an increase in poverty and unemployment and a growing income gap between the haves and have-nots, flare-ups of xenophobia and ethnic hatred, and corruption and the abuse of the democratic institutional system by the ruling elite.

Despite the tumultuous and contradictory history of the region, the tenth anniversary of the fall of the Berlin Wall reminded many people throughout the region of both the importance and the intensity of the cathartic moments of the late 1980s and early 1990s. The demise of the party-state was preceded and precipitated by wide-ranging and arduous social activism, which in Central and Eastern European countries grew into a "velvet revolution." However ephemeral the sense of release as the outgoing regime's central institutions came to be disarmed, abolished, or restructured; however soon the problems of daily living overpowered the satisfaction people felt as the political taboos of a sclerotic system were expunged from public communication; and however distressing the political struggle among previously allied counterhegemonic forces, the empowerment drawn from experiencing a momentous historical change was nonetheless real and pervaded everyday life. Come with me to an underground show in Budapest held shortly before the change in regime and see this elation in the wry humor of the pop artist who opened the show with his perception of "miraculous" social change:

> Well, here we are in Budapest, where miraculous things are taking place—in the past—like the ones we're witnessing now. . . . Let me tell you, though . . . that the claim I made earlier about Marx being my relative was entirely unfounded. Let me revoke it. He happens to be the namesake of my great-grandfather's brother-in-law, as I just found out in a book. So the assumption was grossly mistaken. Marx is off the agenda. And he will remain so. We will only talk about stars,[3] peace, and healing tonight and I hope you enjoy the show.[4]

3. "Csak csillagokról és sztárokrol lesz szó," a bit of wordplay: the Hungarian word for "star," meaning celestial body, is *csillag; sztár* is an English loan word for celebrity.

4. Amateur tape recording, n.d., Zichy Castle, Budapest.

Bidding farewell to Marx was analogous to the hurried removal of his statues, along with those of Engels and Lenin, the renaming of streets, and other symbolic actions dramatizing the change in regime. Unlike the critical discourse of the late 1960s and early 1970s in Eastern Europe generally and Hungary in particular, which offered a rereading of Marx in pursuit of societal reform and renovation, its counterpart in the late socialist period attributed no redeeming qualities to the Marxian teaching.[5] Marx's name became a metaphor for the ideology and practice of state socialism, for the debased "woodenspeak" of Marxism departments in the universities and official discourse in general.[6]

It was all the more surprising, then, to witness, shortly after the change in regime, the rise of anticapitalist rhetoric on the margins of cultural and political life, mostly without explicit reference to the Great Man. The following verse is from a rap song of 1992 by the group whose concert was introduced by the disclaimer of a family connection to Marx:

> You think they're givin' when they're taking away
> It's not things that are sold to you but you're sold to things.[7]

Who could set in rhyme more succinctly the essence of the Marxian notion of commodification? Even more anger was reflected in the discourse of those young experimental filmmakers who bestowed on the first democratically elected government the nasty label "money fascism" for its total indifference to the predicament of the arts. The state-socialist bureaucracy merely banned some art on political grounds, whereas postsocialist officialdom prevented it from being made.[8]

Much has been made of the disillusionment with the economy

5. Theories of self-limiting revolution and civil society were developed by the democratic opposition in Eastern Europe as an alternative to the neo-Marxist critique of Sovietized society (Cohen and Arato 1992, Arato 1993: ix–xiv).

6. The Orwellian phrase is borrowed from Downing 1996: 75.

7. "Itt kísértünk" [Here we're haunting], Európa Kiadó (EPH), in *Itt kísértünk—Love '92*, EMI Quint QUI906019.

8. Tibor Bakács Settenkedő, "Exhumálás: Beszélgetés a BBS vezetőségével" [Exhumation: A discussion with the management of Balázs Béla Studió], *Magyar Narancs*, Apr. 18, 1991, p. 10.

and politics in the wake of the transition, made evident by persistent voter indifference and the reelection in the early 1990s of reform communists—renamed as socialists—throughout Eastern Europe, from Lithuania through Poland to Hungary (Downing 1996: 183–84, Verdery 1996: 10–11, Comisso 1997: 7). It nonetheless seems unjustified to join the chorus of complaints that postsocialist cultural production has been victimized more by the draconian rule of the marketplace than it ever was by political repression. While the contention that economic domination took the place of political repression is not unfounded (Cushman 1995, Klíma 1994), that perspective captures only one side of a complicated picture.[9] It downplays the contradictions and dilemmas involved in redefining individual and collective identities amidst cataclysmic social change. It brackets the paradoxical effects of the shifting status of art and artist in response to the breakdown of the authoritarian political system. The exorcism of Marx's ghost and his rapid reappearance in public discourse is a symptom of rupture not only of the political economy of culture but also of people's consciousness in Central and Eastern Europe, and a reminder of the very intricate ideological and emotional work invested in understanding and accommodating to a new social system.

In the study of societies in transition, the most intriguing question is how social change has empowered or disempowered individuals and collectivities. Before I map the specific sociocultural space the Hungarian rock underground created and occupied in the 1980s and its transfiguration after the system's collapse, let me cite musicians' own interpretations of this momentous transition. This is how László (Laci) Kiss, once a bassist in the band Európa Kiadó (EPH), contrasted music making before and after the change: "[In the state-socialist era] making music was exhilarating because everything was burning hot, everything had three more meanings added to it, and they all congealed into one gesture. Everything had a context to it.

9. Its overemphasis plays into the hands of those who, having celebrated or accepted state socialism as an alternative to the capitalist world order, made scarcely any effort to make sense of its day-to-day realities, its structural shortcomings, and its eventual downfall. On the morally and politically harmful effects of left orthodoxy with regard to a critique of "existing socialism," see Beilharz 1992. At the same time, a debate with doctrinaire leftism should not justify any superficial or apologetic stance toward the newly established and more consolidated regimes of the region.

Now this is kinda gone. You may now attend to other things, to the subtleties of the sound, for example. . . . But it's far less exhilarating. . . . And when it is exhilarating, it's less so to others [than to ourselves]." Music, which had been produced and consumed as a form of resistance, became, in a sense, a private matter after 1989. While rock'n'roll musicians could easily adjust to their expanded cultural and political freedom, they had a harder time coming to terms with the deflation of their social prestige. The shamans and rebels of the previous era now found themselves, to borrow Leonard Cohen's phrase, "workers in song." Attila Grandpierre of the shaman-punk group Vágtázó Halottkémek (Galloping Coroners [GC]) complained to me that with the onset of democracy, not only the police but local music critics too ceased to attend their performances: "They write far less about us than during the communist era. It seems journalists pay less attention to this issue these days. Or perhaps GC's existence doesn't amount to much of a sensation any more. Or they don't care about us that much. Perhaps it wasn't us they really cared about. . . . Today politics and the economy may be much more important [than this music]." It is indeed not GC's musical qualities that changed but the social and political context in which these qualities gained their significance.

A woman musician, Ágnes Kamondy, used the metaphor of the ghetto to relate a whole community's dilemma: "A self-contained culture, or rather a subculture, has disappeared. The ghetto and, along with it, the ghetto existence has ended. We step out and ask: Where shall I live now? I may move in here or move in there or try to obtain a place somewhere else. . . . Stepping out of the ghetto, you seek your place in the wider community." The image of the ghetto and its disappearance captures the controversial realities and implications of the change in regime for former resisters, whose cultural practice in an important sense became void of substance. The underground community was held together primarily by its enemy, an overbearing state and its apparatuses. László Kistamás, a former actor and singer who reorganized alternative pop culture in the 1990s, formulated this idea in the language of social scientists: "What existed [as a subculture] at the time asserted itself in relation to a distinct political constellation. As of now [1993], a subculture reconstituting itself with regard to money has not yet formed. And the culture that shaped its system of values in opposition to a dictatorship and state-run monopolies fell to pieces because a wholly new set of relations developed." And while the toppling of the dictatorship and the collapse of state-run monopolies brought a cathartic moment of liberation, it simultaneously produced a new kind of existential insecurity, the threat or actual experience of isolation and a loss of meaning.

Ruptures in the mode of social existence and in popular culture offer unique opportunities for the study of the many dimensions of autonomy. The major theoretical questions I wish to address are these: What is the nature of popular culture's autonomy and how is it related to cultural actors' autonomy? What aspects of autonomy are at play under conditions of structural social change, and how are they played out by cultural actors? But why is autonomy such a crucial concept in the study of the Hungarian popular music scene? Musicians, critics, concert organizers, record label owners, and music audiences struggled for autonomy through a range of cultural practices: primarily through their music—that is, through textual production; then by establishing their own underground or alternative infrastructure; and finally by their discourse about their art—that is, through the ways in which they interpreted the meaning and significance of rock as a cultural form.

Rock became increasingly contested: viewed as high art by some people, as entertainment by others, or as a surrogate form of political self-expression. The discourse about rock thus involved a confrontation of diverse aesthetic approaches within the community as well as between the musicians and the cultural officials, media personnel, grant-awarding agencies, and others outside the music scene whose decisions affected it. This struggle for autonomy under a changing set of possibilities and constraints constitutes the politics of cultural activity.

I differentiate between two dimensions of these means of striving for autonomy. First, cultural or artistic autonomy may be seen as an aesthetic ideology that claims the independence and separation of the arts from other domains of social life, especially that of politics. Rooted in classical and Romantic philosophies of art (Baumgarten, Hegel, etc.), this ideology has been reappropriated in the social-scientific theories of Max Weber, Pierre Bourdieu, György Lukács, and Theodor Adorno. The most eloquent proponent of art's autonomy in contemporary social theory is Jürgen Habermas. Drawing primarily on Weber and Talcott Parsons, Habermas theorizes the arts as a separate value sphere embodying an aspect of cultural rationalization and of societal complexity and differentiation. Modernity, the argument goes, saw the rise of religion and art, politics and science, ethics and law as independent and often competing systems of values, which practitioners of any one field could experience and represent as standing apart from the social world (Habermas 1984: 159–64, 176–78).

Whereas from a modernist stance the boundaries of autonomous art tend to coincide with traditional high culture, theorists of popular culture have noted the reemergence and reappropriation of this ideology in a wide array of popular forms, especially rock music and jazz (Frith 1981, Vulliamy 1977, Walser 1992, Lopes 1996). The art-versus-mass-culture argument, which assigns the superior qualities of originality and complexity or merely hipness to certain styles while denigrating others, serves a double function. First, it transforms previously neglected or disparaged cultural forms into symbolic capital, thereby imputing higher status and prestige to its practitioners and consumers. Second, in social contexts where art connotes cultural capital and social distinction, the aspiration of popular musicians to be reclassified as artists constitutes a strategy of resistance to the state's attempt to colonize and control cultural production. In state-socialist Hungary, for instance, the politics of aesthetic autonomy pursued by artists, both high and low, served as a form of self-defense that helped them take advantage of as well as further the broader process of cultural and societal rationalization.[10]

Related to autonomy as aesthetic ideology is the political-economic idea of autonomy. This understanding is closer to a commonsensical or everyday idea of cultural freedom and producers' control over the creative process. Pop artists in Western capitalist society, unlike their colleagues in one-party systems, strive for this type of autonomy without even thinking of denying the political contents or implications of their activities (think, for instance, of the working-class social commentary of Bruce Springsteen, the contentious feminist politics of Ani DiFranco, or the militant oppositional stance of

10. I thank Richard Madsen for helping me formulate this line of thought.

the rap group Public Enemy). I aim to disentangle the changing relationships, common features, and disjunctions between these two forms of cultural autonomy in the study of a subcultural community in Hungary, organized around rock music and avant-garde art.

The shifting, often reciprocally accentuated dimensions of autonomy, so central to the self-understanding and day-to-day struggles of popular musicians, constitute a narrative of cultural change in Hungary. Its retelling in this book is predicated on three main assumptions. On the most fundamental theoretical level, I argue for the constitutive role that symbolic forms play, under structural constraints, in macrosocial processes. More specifically, I contend that in state-socialist Eastern Europe, certain brands of rock music and other arts contributed to the formation of a quasi-autonomous public sphere and thus to the dismantling of the party state's legitimacy (Ryback 1990, Ramet 1991: 212–40, Tismaneanu 1992: 161, Mitchell 1992, Kürti 1994, Cushman 1995, Downing 1996). Finally, breakdowns and realignments in marginal culture are indicators of broader processes of disorientation and reorientation in postsocialist society. Studying an art-based community in a state of upheaval and consolidation has the theoretical advantage of allowing distinctions between cultural and political resistance, political ferment and cultural efflorescence, moral crisis and political renewal.

I intend this book to contribute to two major strands of research: to Eastern European studies, including the theorization of postcommunist social change, and to cultural studies, especially the cultural study of popular music. While the respective bodies of literature do not coincide, in recent years researchers across disciplines (Downing 1996; Verdery 1991; Kennedy 1994: 1–45; George Marcus 1993; Cushman 1991, 1995; Gordy 1997) have grown aware of the important theoretical insights to be gained from combining their perspectives, analytical methods, and empirical knowledge.

Popular Music and Social Transition in Eastern Europe

Several authors concerned with state socialism and postsocialist transformation have remarked on the conspicuous lacuna of existing studies with regard to the cultural dimension of social change in the formerly socialist societies (Downing 1996: 16–17, Gordy 1997: 20–21). This gap became even more problematic with the downfall of Soviet socialism, the dilemmas and pains of consolidation, and the rise of and tragic events associated with ethnonationalism in various parts of the region.

Pop and rock culture provides an exciting terrain to study processes of change associated with the transformation of Soviet-style societies, and rock music has been particularly mistreated as a form of cultural and political expression by scholars of Eastern Europe. Before 1989, the very presence of rock music in this region threw into sharp relief the antagonisms between socialist cultural policies and institutions, on the one hand, and markets and consumerism, on the other; between East and West, as well as between the state and civil society (for reviews, see Ryback 1990, Robinson et al. 1991: 69–83). Few scholarly accounts of youth culture in the Soviet bloc emerged during the communist era.[11] Academics' and journalists' avid but ephemeral fascination with the rock and popular music of the former communist countries was bound up with disputes about the music's effects on social transition. While neo-Gramscian theories of hegemony in Western cultural studies attempted to explain why certain forms of cultural recalcitrance had not led to major social change (see especially Willis 1979, Downing 1996: 230–31), the Eastern European landslides suggested that cultural resistance, while seemingly contained for extended periods, may have been instrumental in eroding the state's power by "shifting the terms of discourse," in Sabrina P. Ramet's (1991: 238) words. Questions about the role of music in demolishing the Berlin Wall, however, can't be adequately answered without an understanding of how state-socialist cultural policies, politics, and institutions worked and what spaces pop and rock music occupied in those societies.

The political economy of rock under socialism is complex. From the mid-1970s, mainstream rock music in Hungary was a lucrative business, and as such it highlighted and exacerbated the tensions between socialist values and policies, on the one hand, and the profit orientation of the state-run entertainment industry, on the other.

11. Some of the most informative and insightful sociological studies of popular music in the Soviet bloc were written by Starr (1983) and Troitsky (1987) on the Soviet Union/Russia and by Leitner (1983) on East Germany.

When the record companies turned down dissenting or unconventional styles, they referred to economic rather than political considerations: the "alternative" sounds called *rétegzene* (literally "stratum music," meaning music catering to elite or minority tastes) were found lacking in profit potential. The entire music industry consisted of massive monopolies, with no network of small independent ventures, as in the West, where new sounds could be tried out without substantial economic risk (as for the latter, see Gray 1988). The marginalization of certain styles, then, was neither wholly arbitrary nor necessarily motivated by political factors. Certainly, the monopolistic state-run system of cultural production and dissemination presupposed a political logic that preferred less visible, softer forms of oppression to censorship and exclusion. In other words, the economic argument in the music industry, which promoted only music that was sure to sell, indirectly served political purposes by favoring admittedly well-established, safe, depoliticized entertainment rather than more socially aware, dynamic, and creative forms and styles.

The diversity of social, political, and historical contexts in which the various styles and sounds of pop and rock music were produced and consumed, promoted, and repressed, used and abused over three decades in countries as culturally and politically different as Albania and Poland, Slovenia and Romania, the Soviet Union (itself extremely varied) and Hungary, certainly defies easy generalizations. A number of critics believe that, while rock helped to delegitimize and dismantle the communist regime, nonetheless musicians, especially professionals, proved vulnerable to the crudest forms of selling out to the state, to manipulative cultural policies that pitted some of them against their colleagues or their fans (Leitner 1994, Szőnyei 1992: 379–80). According to a widely held belief among Leningrad/St. Petersburg rockers, the first club in their city was organized by the KGB to incite conflict and intolerance. Even though the club encouraged a measure of independent expression, it also censured what it deemed inappropriate (Cushman 1995: 203–18). And at a 1981 meeting with professional rock musicians in Budapest, Hungary's deputy minister of culture indignantly demanded that the established performers expel underground groups such as the Committee (Bizottság) and Ultra Rock Agency (URA). Members of the professional rock elite took offense at being lumped together with the underground. Never mind that the two tiers of rock culture existed quite separately, and the rock professionals had no means to discipline the maverick musicians (Szőnyei 1992: 379). Jolanta Pekacz (1992: 205) chronicles similar political maneuvering in Poland.

Now how did youth music experience the change in regime and how has it been faring ever since? In most postsocialist countries the withdrawal of the state from the management of cultural matters,[12] the capitalist pluralization of the pop music industry, and the presence of the transnational mass media have completely transfigured the possibilities, expectations, and everyday strategies of actors in popular music, be they musicians, media people, entrepreneurs, critics, or music fans.

Despite the diversity of socioeconomic and political rearrangements that have shaped the experiences and strategies of young cultural actors in the region, I argue that the transition posed the most challenge for those musicians and artists whose identity and politics had been molded by their dissent from the communist state (Ramet 1994, Pekacz 1992, Cushman 1995: 263–327).[13] The severity of this rupture may legitimately be compared to the existential blow suffered by the official ideologues of state socialism, such as instructors of Marxist–Leninist doctrine. Not only were their academic departments shut down by the first postcommunist government, but the kind of knowledge in which their professional identity had been rooted was proclaimed invalid.[14] Both maverick rockers and the authorized propagators of Marxism-Leninism were faced with the task of reinventing their public identities. The rockers were additionally

12. With the important exception of the mass media until the new media legislation of 1995. For accounts of power struggles for the control of the mass media in the early 1990s, see Jenkins and Gorman 1994 and Downing 1996: 159–64.

13. The novelist Péter Esterházy expressed the plight of many artists whose understanding of what it meant to engage in art in Central and Eastern Europe was bound up with the ethos of opposition: "A writer is allowed to engage in politics only when it isn't a must. One may, however, engage in politics even if it's not permitted. But to engage in politics is a definite must when it's forbidden" (quoted in Fráter 1994). What seems to be wordplay is actually a very accurate formulation of the dilemmas and paradoxes artists face when democratization opens up an undivided public space for politicking yet engaging in politics is no longer a moral duty for intellectuals.

14. In reality, though, an increasing number of instructors of Marxism-Leninism, especially the younger ones, had digressed from the canon and taught "secularized" versions of philosophy, economics, and history.

afflicted by long-term deprivation of technology and information; decades of isolation and relative poverty made most Eastern European rock groups conspicuously poor competitors of their Western counterparts (Mitchell 1992).

Thomas Cushman (1995) construed the music of the Leningrad/St. Petersburg rock community as a response to the experience of socialist industrial modernity. If people were disenchanted with the social world, countercultural art provided a means by which that social world became reenchanted. How does the spirit of capitalism affect a cultural form that served to reenchant the bleak realities of Soviet industrial modernity? What happens when the contradiction itself—countercultural art—becomes contradicted? Cushman concludes that the logic of capitalism is discordant with the state of mind and culture of state socialism. Despite their disenfranchisement, dissident artists used to enjoy a specific form of freedom, which he terms existential to distinguish it from political freedom. Artists could sustain themselves at a subsistence level because of the extensive welfare services of the socialist state (cheap housing and utilities, subsidized food, transportation, and so forth). They could afford to maintain their carved-out subcultural space and devote all their energies to music making—what is more, to music of the kind they thought engaging and valuable. With the breakdown of the party-state, they lost this unique form of existential freedom even as they gained political freedom. With the dissolution of the state's welfare net, they could no longer set themselves apart from the "real world," now totally regulated by commerce. Similar views were voiced by my Hungarian interviewees as well.[15]

Cushman considers this development detrimental to the chances that a truly democratic society may emerge from the ruins of the old one. With some help from John Dewey and Habermas, he construes what he terms sociological democracy as reliant on a vibrant public

15. The former musician and club organizer László Kistamás, for example, emphasized that even to ensure an income at the subsistence level, musicians need to think of their music's marketability. László Kiss, a fellow musician who at the time of my inquiry was making a living as a computer expert, talked about the tempting opportunities to grow wealthy offered by the postsocialist market. The lure of such opportunities threatens to distract musicians not only from making music but also from a lifestyle they would find more fulfilling.

culture on which capitalist (or, by the same token, state) forces do not impinge (324–27).

From Underground to Alternative: The Transformation of Rock Culture in Postsocialist Hungary

In Hungary the shift to capitalism took place much more rapidly in popular music than in heavy industry or agriculture. The pace of cultural adaptation, however, was slower than that of institutional reorganization. The oppositional subculture of the 1980s dissolved into a fragmented and conflict-ridden alternative music scene in the 1990s. Such a process replicated typical trends in Western popular music on the margins (Straw 1991, Fornäs 1995, Negus 1992: 16–19).

The sociology of alternative music culture is not well served by subcultural theories. The idea of a musical subculture assumes structural correspondence and cohesion among a specific musical style, verbal and visual images, and patterns of behavior, including ways of speaking, fashion, and uses of mass media (Willis 1978, Hebdige 1979). For both theoretical and historical reasons, which I cannot detail here, subcultural theories no longer capture the dynamics of the youth-and-music phenomenon in our era. Lawrence Grossberg (1992) proposed to regard music-based and often virtual collectivities as affective alliances: relatively loosely organized and socioculturally heterogeneous formations that music fans slide into in their youth and out of as they enter adult life. No structural homology (for a critical review, see Middleton 1990: 159–66) is presumed among the various aspects of expressive behavior exhibited by the people who share a liking for a specific musical group or style. The concept of a music scene, however, has been more widely adopted in academic and journalistic discourse. A scene, according to Will Straw, is "a cultural space in which a range of cultural practices coexist, interacting with each other within a variety of processes of differentiation, and according to widely varying trajectories of change and cross-fertilization" (373). Holly Kruse (1993) argues that young people in the United States today who regard themselves as "alternatives," unlike the countercultural baby boomers, do not emphasize authenticity or commitment to a particular cause. While local tradition seems to shape alternative cultural scenes, those scenes lack stability and a staunch historical awareness. They are glued together by a shared taste for the musically unique. Finally, scenes form part of a translocal network. In regard to the growing importance of globally created (sub)cultural communities, Simon Reynolds aptly stated: "A noise band in Manchester can have more in common with a peer group in Austin, Texas, than with one of its 'neighbors' two blocks away" (quoted in Kruse 1993: 34; see also Lipsitz 1994, Slobin 1993).

How has the musicians' community reorganized itself after its release from the ghetto? Journalists often use the terms "underground" and "alternative rock" interchangeably, but in local popular music discourse "alternative rock" was more frequently used to describe the marginal musical styles of the 1990s. In the context of the societal transition in Hungary, this discursive shift indicates the locally and globally reconfigured status of noncommercial rock'n'roll, since the two terms refer to cultural spaces located and organized differently. The underground culture of the 1980s emphasized recalcitrance toward the dominant (official) culture. The metaphor "underground," widely used by the musicians as a self-reference,[16] suggested a position underneath a more powerful and more visible entity. The political connotation of the term was obvious. "Alternative," by contrast, refers to spaces that are horizontally rather than hierarchically structured. It implicates choice rather than the force or compulsion connoted by "underground."

The local underground of the 1980s formed a close-knit and cohesive social world, an art world with solid boundaries.[17] The alternatives' social world in postcommunist Hungary, by contrast, is fragmented and its boundaries are porous. Neither its position within the public realm nor its aesthetic ideology marks it clearly as the "other" of mainstream popular music. For some musicians, alternative music is a default category. Tamás Kocsis of the formerly underground group Sexepil, for instance, represents such a position:

16. The band Bizottság (Committee) coined a hilarious Hungarianized version, *undorgrund,* a compound of *undor*, "disgust," appropriate to the punk aesthetic of ugliness, and *grund*, "playground."

17. My use of the term "art world" draws on Howard Becker's (1982) study of artistic and cultural communities as professional groups.

"This is precisely why I don't like this word 'alternative' very much: if we played the same kind of music that we played [in the 1980s] now, it wouldn't be 'alternative' anyway. Alternatives are in fact those who can't find any other niche for themselves." The media scholar Miklós Sükösd (1993) offers a distinction between two types of cultural alternative: one defined by the (peripheral) structural position of the medium/artifact and another by the values and contents of the disseminated material. According to this categorization, the semifascist/nationalist skinhead subculture, which has a distinct presence in the Hungarian rock scene, is alternative only in the first sense of the term. It is the most obviously marginalized subculture, yet its politics is spurned by those who proclaim themselves "alternatives" with a definite (left-liberal) political emphasis. The journalist Tibor Bakács Settenkedő[18] (1995) states, correctly, that disturbing as it may sound, the domestic skinhead subculture[19] of the 1990s had a more pronounced "alternative" (read: resistant) identity than the left-leaning alternative culture communities, which he sees as being systematically co-opted by the mass media. Bakács therefore suggests replacing the term "alternative culture" with "parallel culture." This perspective reinforces my view that the postsocialist alternative culture, unlike the underground of the socialist era, is more of a partner of the mainstream culture apparatus than the suppressed other.[20]

The alternative music scene in Hungary thus comprises affective alliances and subcultures built around musical styles that reflect swiftly changing fads and fashions, most of them imported from the West.[21] How do these changes translate into day-to-day practice? For many actors in the field, the transition has opened up new terrains of

18. The comic effect of the journalist's pseudonym, Settenkedő (Sneaking), exemplifies the fresh new voice of *Magyar Narancs* in Hungarian public discourse.

19. Even though the nationalist skinheads have their own British-based fashion store, a few venues where they perform regularly, and sponsors from ultraright political parties, most groups depend on very small-scale self-publishing in the absence of a record label of their own. Their recordings are distributed via mail order or in specialist punk stores.

20. In "Az alternatív kultúra vége, a párhuzamos kultúra születése" [The end of alternative culture and the rise of parallel culture], *Magyar Narancs*, July 13, 1995, pp. 32–33.

21. However, the oft-repeated assumption that this scene now lacks any political leanings (see, for example, Kürti 1994) is not well founded. The alternative music scene, which initially was closely allied with the two liberal parties, the Alliance of Free Democrats (SZDSZ) and the Federation of Young Democrats (FIDESZ), is increasingly an integral aspect of alternative politics, and thus increasingly distant from parliamentary politicking.

creativity and offered a sense of autonomy, choices of lifestyle and career that earlier were unthinkable. Now they can tour abroad, form bands with foreign musicians, run alternative boutiques and clubs, direct pop music programs on cable television.

Others have been grappling with the ambiguities inherent in the current situation. Previously idolized by their audiences, they face sharper competition and considerable indifference even at the local level (for other national contexts, see Leitner 1994, Klíma 1994).[22] Since problems of material and artistic survival are intertwined, these musicians are compelled to re-create their cultural identities by interrogating the continuities and disruptions between past and present and between socialist and capitalist cultural politics. Likewise, they explore the connections and contradictions between local and global cultural spaces, between the uses of technology and the production of aesthetic value, between creative integrity and commercial success, artistic and political commitments, and so forth. These issues are addressed in detail in Chapters 2–5.

Of particular importance are the entirely altered relations between local and global musical processes with regard to musicians' ability or inability to readjust their careers and rethink their membership in subcultures that change with bewildering speed. More intense interactions between sectors of the local and global music industry, between independent and major companies, between alternative music communities on an international plane; a greater exposure of local musicians to a larger variety of transnational and indigenous or, in Mark Slobin's (1993) phrase, micromusics; and musicians' increased physical and geographical mobility have released new creative energies, but also set new constraints on both the innovative and the commercial aspects of music production.

Through its embrace of ethnic musics and the organization of musical events around alternative political themes, it articulates values such as racial and ethnic solidarity, multiculturalism, and environmentalism.

22. The pop artist András Wahorn of the Committee recalled being angered by a party bureaucrat's comment to him sometime in the mid-1980s: "You should be grateful to us. We made you guys hot shots. If we hadn't canceled some of your shows, your music would be far less popular now." Pondering the reasons for his emigration to the United States in 1995, Wahorn figured that, cynical as it sounded, the statement had more than a grain of truth to it. In postsocialist Hungary, mavericks such as the Committee no longer provoke so much excitement. (Personal communication, San Diego, April 1997.)

Politics and the Cultural Study of Popular Music

What makes a certain kind of music political? Where can the political be located in popular music? What theoretical tools can capture the often elusive politics of pop and rock?

While the main thrust of research on popular music in the communist world emphasized its pervasively political nature, few studies addressed the peculiarities of pop and rock music as a unique form of political expression. With a few exceptions (Jones 1992, Brace and Friedlander 1992,[23] Kloet 1999, Mitchell 1992), analysts did not discern the political meanings and effects of rock in the complex interplay of sound, lyrics, and performance style. They failed to place rock in a set of discursive, institutional, and cultural contexts in which the music was played and listened to, talked and written about. According to such accounts, the politics of a piece or a musical group amounted to barely more than its verbal message, which in turn was read off of the lyrics, as if the same message could have been expressed equally effectively in a political speech or samizdat. Even as the symbolic extravaganza—the high volume of the sound, the extravagant hairdos, clothing, and street behavior—was registered as somehow tied up with youth politics, it rarely became incorporated in a semiotically sensitive framework of interpretation. These approaches rendered the sounding medium of rock a mere container of verbal messages. In deliberating on the ultra-right-wing sympathies of heavy metal rockers in present-day Russia, for instance, Ramet observed: "Indeed, there is nothing automatic about the social content of rock music. It is a medium open to diverse uses, and—Marshall McLuhan notwithstanding—the message conveyed by any particular rock artist stands quite apart from the rock medium as such" (1994: 208). While indeed the musical sign, rock musical or any other, can be invested with a variety of meanings, perhaps even controversial ideological meanings, to state that the message of any one musician or band is not internally related to the

23. Jones (1992), Brace and Friedlander (1992), and Kloet 2000 have made valuable contributions on the predicament of popular music in the People's Republic of China. Although Chinese popular culture has its own distinctive characteristics, the ideological and political processes and institutions that impinge on popular music there display many similarities to those in the former Soviet bloc.

medium chosen to articulate it is to reinstate logocentrism in the sociology of music. This position evades altogether the difficult question of how a musical form and sound become the site of meaning production; why musicians draw on and (re-)create such forms and sounds to forge collective and individual identities. Implicit in Ramet's stance is the idea that what matters in music is the manifest ideological content of the words sung to it. The political is thus sought in the lyrics, which, however, are treated reductively as if they were words on a poster. The lyrics' poetic attributes and their conveyance through the medium of singing are overlooked. The "grain" of the voice, as Roland Barthes (1977) called its inherently sensuous character, carries far more (or maybe far less!) than explicit ideological messages; it is the expressive vehicle of the performer persona. As Simon Frith (1987: 145–46) noted, the words constitute an essential source of rock's effectiveness, not only because of their obvious capacity to articulate ideas and sentiments but because they provide a "pretext" for the voice to sound. The sound in turn signifies the performer's individual personality, a privileged source of pleasure and power as well as meaning in music. In Iain Chambers's eloquent phrasing: "Romanticism in pop music and popular culture is quite clearly the site of the imaginary, the site of an excess of sound and bodies and desires. . . . Accounts that intend to 'reveal' the so-called real relations of cultural production often avoid altogether the tissues and textures of their real relationships and how their meanings are actually embodied in everyday life" (1992: 183).

Criticisms of popular music research that dismisses the sonic aspect of this form of cultural expression are not new. To a significant extent, the rise of the cross-disciplinary study of popular music is a result of dissatisfaction with earlier sociological interpretations of pop and rock that had muted the music in their concern with the songs' words. Developed within the larger arena of cultural studies, popular music research, however, focuses predominantly on the English-speaking world: its theoretical and analytical framework, despite drawing on European critical theory and semiotics, is distilled from the pop music culture and social life of Britain, the United States, and, to a lesser extent, Canada and Australia. While researchers want to account for and respond to global cultural and political processes, their analytical apparatus cannot be applied to the historical and cultural realities of Central and Eastern Europe without significant rethinking. As I have suggested, however, much of the research on the politics of popular music in Central and Eastern Europe is heir to a tradition that is one-dimensional and lacking in cultural sensitivity (Slobin 1993: 62, Downing 1996).

The academic study of popular music has thrived on the post-1960s redefinition of the concepts of music and politics. Unlike researchers of classical music or ordinary consumers and critics of any musical style, most popular music scholars appear to be "tasteless" when it comes to selecting the music they study (for a seminal piece, see Brooks 1982). No musical style or practice is considered aesthetically too poor for close attention. In fact, the aesthetic has largely been displaced in favor of the political (Born 1993). Analysts of such varied musical practices as Tin Pan Alley songs, rock'n'roll, jazz, and acid house, by looking at these musical forms in the contexts of their production, transmission, and uses, have challenged the value judgments and essentialism inherent in traditional classifications of music as art versus popular, serious versus light, urban pop versus rural folk.[24] Such cross-disciplinary studies also have thrown into relief the reciprocal limitations inherent in both the social sciences and musicology: the former dealing almost exclusively with the conditions of the production, consumption, and verbal "content" of the music, the latter attributing too much autonomy to intramusical factors (Wolff 1992).

In parallel with the deconstruction of music as a concept, politics has been redefined from a limited set of government and party institutional practices and structures to relations pervading all aspects of everyday life. While conventional social science approaches address musical practice and politics as separate categories in conjunction, cultural studies view politics as intrinsic to a musical practice: the politics of heavy metal, for example, is not outside the music but is carried by this specific style of rock as it is played, listened to, or talked about in diverse social and subcultural settings.

While the abandonment of the narrow and elitist understanding

24. The "new musicologists" have challenged essentialized categories in the realm of classical music (see the work of Susan McClary, Philip Brett, Ruth Solie, and Jann Pasler, among others). Frith (1996), however, has argued for the importance of a value-based aesthetic theory in the study of the popular.

of music has been beneficial for its social and political analysis, the broadening of the concept of politics seems ambiguous in its theoretical implications. The politics of popular forms, with an emphasis on the creative aspect of consumption by different audiences, has often been interpreted in a vague or romanticizing manner. Some of this critique originates from within cultural studies. As Grossberg (1992: 90–96) contended, the empowerment some people experience by reading romance novels or engaging in rock becomes easily misconstrued as political resistance or even opposition. The value of activism in and through popular culture, according to David Harris (1992), is taken for granted rather than assessed as contingent on the entire web of political forces in play. Cultural studies unquestioningly value antistate politics, even though, as George Lipsitz warns, "the mere fact of opposition to the state does not guarantee progressive, democratic or egalitarian politics; the mere fusion of popular culture and politics does not automatically mean better culture or better politics" (1994: 151–52).

Such clarifications are necessary for two reasons: first, in celebrating popular culture, many academics tend to overlook the existing nexus between populist or extreme right-wing politics and its effective use of rock and other popular forms (Mukerji and Schudson 1991, Grossberg 1992, Ryback 1990, Kürti 1994). Second, central to the theoretical coherence of cultural studies is the neo-Gramscian notion of hegemony (Harris 1992).[25] Gramsci's theory as appropriated by Stuart Hall, James C. Scott, and others operates with a fundamentally bipolar system of (state) power and opposition, potential or real, and it assumes a relatively stable noncoercive state that makes culture the main site of ideological struggle. But John Downing perceptively notes that "the unexamined common presumption is that

25. Hegemony allows for the reading and appreciation of cultural texts and their reception as potentially or actually subversive, even as they remain confined to the realm of pleasure and leisure, unconcerned with or replacing political movements or ideologies. In "culturalizing" Marxism, Gramsci (1972) constructed this theory in an attempt to explain why in certain historical circumstances the working classes fail to organize politically in opposition to the state. This approach to power relations and culture was suited to the theoretical and political needs of the British left from the 1960s through the 1980s, when the terrain of culture, not unlike that in Gramsci's fascist Italy, seemed crucial in maintaining a system of social inequality and oppression: a system in which dissenting cultural forms arose from time to time and faded out without leaving a lasting impact on the larger society.

where there is oppression, there is resistance of some kind. This postulate contains a fatal flaw. That flaw is the failure to take into account the divisibility of oppression. Therefore, moreover, it discounts the corresponding fragmentation of resistance and additionally discounts the often easy mobilization of members of one extruded group against another" (1996: 231). The hostility of the predominantly working-class skinhead movement toward other working-class subcultures, such as punks, and its homophobic rejection of gay disco culture are cases in point. The bipolar perspective is often bound up with the Marxist idea of class struggle (class complemented or displaced by gender, race, and sexuality) and is coupled in cultural studies with a vision of social change pointing beyond the given capitalist system.

By the late 1980s, especially with the crisis of Marxism (Cohen and Arato 1992: 70) and the end of communist systems in Europe, as well as with the persistent clout of the right in Europe and in the United States, a few of cultural studies' central assumptions have become theoretically nebulous. In most so-called Western societies, as well as in the postcommunist region of Europe, the system of political relations between the state and the major political forces could hardly be captured adequately with the conceptual pair of hegemony and counterhegemony. Also, visions of social change have become blurred and multivalent, and thus have lost their guiding force in social theorizing.

In their preface to the series Culture: Politics and Policies, Tony Bennett and his colleagues (1993) define a new pragmatic turn in cultural studies. Extending its scope to the so far neglected area of cultural policy, the authors admit to having given up the prophetic and rebellious political voice traditionally associated with this intellectual movement. As they explain, "The private and civic environments in which cultural activities are funded and regulated are far too various—their ethical, legal, and economic orientations far too mundanely complex—to permit a single exemplary oppositional relation to them" (xi). For students of Central and Eastern Europe or the communist world in general, this move in cultural studies is especially pertinent, in view of the tension between the theoretical sophistication and richness of this tradition and its narrow geographical-societal focus. Several attempts have been made to apply the insights of neo-Gramscianism to accounts of culture, including pop music, outside the liberal capitalist world (Cushman 1991, Jones 1992). The theoretically more productive ones (e.g., Verdery 1991), however, had to face the limitations of this perspective regarding societies in which state power has been weak historically and therefore apt to rely on coercive rather than hegemonic rule, and in which dramatic breaks with the past have become the collective historical experience of successive generations. These societal characteristics imply that cultural production is always already politicized. In her book on intellectual production in Nicolae Ceauşescu's Romania, Katherine Verdery explains that one factor that played into the politicization of the cultural field was the lack of hegemony or a "weak" state. "Hegemony," she argues, "suggests a society-wide regularization of discursive productions and practices that elicit minimal contestation from the subjugated. It is provisional, a matter of degree, and is not present at all times in all societies. Among those from which it was wholly absent are those of East-European socialism" (1991: 10). Another important factor was the communist state's ambition to use the arts and sciences as educational tools to alter people's consciousness. This appropriation of what is largely free from state intervention in Western societies gave the arts a privileged position. Verdery states that language and the symbolic world in general were constitutive of social life in communist systems "because a new order of society-generating practices [had] not been regularized, [did] not function reliably" (91). Discourse and intellectual production represented the kind of state power and unity that was unattainable in the society at large.

What might be called the state's colonization of cultural life has multiple implications. In an effort to subjugate language as the maidservant of its own politics, the socialist state attempted to make public discourse transparent, expressive of singular intentions and free from ambiguities (Verdery 1991: 90). Only the most totalitarian (Stalinist) systems, however, were successful in achieving this goal, and their achievement was short-lived. They created a realm of public discourse that had no meaningful relation to either private discourse or social praxis in general (Szemere 1992a). Paradoxically, the state's push for a transparent and "cleansed" public discourse inadvertently played into the hands of those who sought to create and read texts with semantic ambiguity and multiple meanings. This trend grew more pronounced with the political thaw initiated by Nikita Khrushchev. Precisely because culture was defined as the privileged site of political education, intellectual and artistic producers, too, used it as a terrain of contestation and "reeducation."

The location of culture, especially pop and rock music, in this force field of politics ensured that subversive messages would be sought and found, no matter what (see also Wicke 1992). This feature of cultural production and reception is not contradicted but rather elucidated by Miklós Haraszti's point about self-censorship: that "the state represents not a monolithic body of rules but rather a live network of lobbies. We play with it, we know how to use it, and we have allies and enemies at the controls" (1987: 78–79). Thus the otherness of pop music's cultural politics in Central and Eastern Europe has two main aspects: one deriving from the colonization of the cultural sphere by state power in Sovietized society, another from the experience of social transition. I suggest that by exploring these aspects and their interrelations, one may arrive at a more complex and accurate understanding of the politics of popular music, one pointing beyond the rather static dichotomy of (state) hegemony versus counterhegemony.

Structure of the Book and Methodology

In Chapter 1 I depict the sociocultural and institutional environment in which underground rock music began to flourish, as well as the social organization and politics of the movement. The main theme of Chapter 2 is the subsequent decline of the subculture as its members struggled in a variety of ways to sustain a meaningful character and identity amidst the opening up of the political arena for organized political forces. I am also interested in the divergent uses of the music by individual musicians at this point in the cultural devaluation of rock, and how these various uses and respective discourses around the music promoted cultural autonomy and the re-creation of individual identities. Chapter 3 follows the disruption of underground music production into the change in regime and the specific extramusical strategies with which the pop community responded to and creatively adjusted itself to the new structural conditions of subcultural existence. Chapter 4 focuses on the development and stratification of rock entrepreneurship and the competition among independent record producers to define the values around which a new alternative culture was to be forged. Chapter 5 investigates the meaning and importance of the countercultural legacy as a form of symbolic capital in the cultural scene of the 1990s. It analyzes musicians' ability to use and reappropriate this legacy as a source of prestige and status. It thus became a site of aesthetic and political conflict reflecting and furthering the social fragmentation of the former underground community. In the conclusion I recapitulate my main ideas and their theoretical implications for the interrelations of pop culture, politics, social transition, and social reproduction.

In this work I have relied on personal interviews, participant observation, and archival material. The backbone of my research consists of forty-one in-depth interviews during two field trips to Budapest—one from October to December 1993, the second from April to July 1995—with musicians, rock critics, media personnel, and music fans. I have selected my subjects with an eye to representing the most intriguing aspects of the changing face of pop culture in Hungary. I inquired into their biographies, their aesthetic and political views, and the conditions and daily practice of their music making. Although "lived experience" has become an overused slogan in ethnographically oriented cultural sociology, its significance for the study of the sociopolitical transition in Central and Eastern Europe is difficult to overstate. I emphasized in my interviews the ways in which musicians and media personnel reflected on, interpreted, responded to, and acted upon external social and political processes in their career moves and in their artistic and entrepreneurial strategies.

The ethnographic data that I derived from attending musical events—concerts, club performances, festivals, rock bands' press conferences and rehearsals—were extremely helpful. At festivals and concerts I randomly interviewed audience members on the spot to gain their views of old and new alternative music life, their perception of the continuities and disruptions in the local rock scene, their tastes, and their patterns of using and consuming music.

The archival material used consists of numerous audio and a few video recordings of music programs, as well as a great variety of printed documents. I have glanced through the issues of the popular alternative cultural and political weekly magazine *Magyar Narancs* (Hungarian Orange) from its inception in 1989 through 1995, and paid special attention to the music section of each issue. This magazine is widely considered to have represented the only truly new voice in postsocialist journalism. It originated as the magazine of the Federation of Young Democrats (FYD), a liberal party in parliamentary opposition between 1990 and 1998. Then, having undergone a series of metamorphoses, the FYD won the 1998 elections on a platform accentuating national and family values. With the professionalization of political life and the FYD's shift from center to right liberalism, then to centrist conservatism, the trajectories of the party and the magazine diverged. *Magyar Narancs* became a forum of left-leaning alternative culture with a fresh, innovative style and language of its own. The publication stands for a particular cultural formation and reflects the shifting meaning of alternativity and marginal perspectives in the political and cultural arena of postsocialist Hungary.

Additionally, I used miscellaneous documents such as recording industry sales statistics, musicians' self-made promotional material, fanzines, art catalogs, posters, grant applications for sponsored art projects, unpublished local studies on alternative music, and magazine and newspaper clippings.

Unless I indicate otherwise, all translations from the Hungarian are my own. Discographic information may be found at:

http://www.psupress.org/szemere/

1
The Making of the Rock Underground and the Politics of Marginality

Social and existential marginality was the shared condition around which a rambunctious and innovative brand of rock music, experimental film and video art, poetry, drama, and dissident political thought were organized in Budapest at the beginning of the 1980s. The term "marginal" was loosely applied to a mixed group of mostly young intellectuals. They included writers whose work was occasionally or systematically banned; academics whose gestures of political protest against the party-state deprived them of a regular salary; and visual artists without academic credentials who took to electric guitars, drums, and saxophones to make their exhibition openings more exciting and socially inclusive. Many members of this close-knit art world were ridiculed or ignored by their established colleagues. The audience consisted of unemployed or freelance young adults and college students, who regularly hung out in clubs where their music was to be heard, alternating with poetry readings or discussions with writers and thinkers in the same marginal boat. This was a genuinely underground cultural and social space where the moral and political crisis of late socialist society was explored and dramatized. Rock music, which came to the forefront of this movement because of its perceived spontaneity, immediacy, and accessibility, ensured, according to "Doktor" Máriás, an avant-garde rocker and painter, what the high avant-garde could no longer achieve: the ability to communicate in open and fresh ways with a relatively large and increasingly varied public.

While the musicians enjoyed a significant amount of freedom in the creative process,[1] the price they paid for it was exclusion from the mass media and confinement to a semilegal existence. This condition raises the intriguing question of the relationships among popular art, politics, and cultural autonomy. George Lipsitz writes that "culture can seem like a substitute for politics, a way of posing only imaginary solutions to real problems, but under other circumstances, culture can become a rehearsal for politics, trying out values and beliefs permissible in art but forbidden in social life. Most often, however, culture exists as a form of politics, as a means of reshaping individual and collective practice for specified interests" (1990: 16–17). The conception of culture as a form of politics seems highly relevant to the predicament of the underground rock subculture, even though the musicians' attitude toward politics and issue-centered social movements was equivocal and contradictory. Robert Wuthnow (1989) argues for a strong relationship between the rise of social movements as producers of ideologies and the instability of social environments. The simultaneous production of numerous ideologies in a particular social setting, he claims, may be a response to uncertainty or disruption in the moral order. In the 1980s, Hungary witnessed the emergence of an increasing number and variety of cultural, religious, and strictly political movements and associations, a phenomenon detailed in Chapter 2. Wuthnow also asserts, rightly, that "the presence of uncertainty in the moral order cannot be assumed to lead automatically to the production of new ideologies. . . . An authoritarian state may prevent ideas from being discussed, economic conditions may force actors to concentrate on short-term survival rather than giving attention to longer-range problems" (158). This was precisely the situation of the popular music and youth cultures in late socialist Hungary. Before the punk/new wave move-

1. This statement needs qualification. In the composition of lyrics, underground rockers had more freedom than those musicians who enjoyed full publicity but were closely screened; but mainstream musicians had the advantage of access to studios, sound mixers, and other facilities essential to creation and performance.

ment could create a niche for itself, the state had to loosen its control over popular music and a new generation of self-consciously amateur musicians, too young or too ambitious or anarchistic to be corrupted by commercial motives, had to emerge.

The socially marginal position of this movement and the musicians' experience and representation of it were central to the politics and the pleasures associated with the music. A variety of spatial and temporal cleavages crisscrossed the contemporary sociomusical map. One important divide separated the pop/rock music styles that the domestic mass media favored from those they suppressed. Yet the subculture was not defined merely by its outlaw status or the musicians' indifference to commercial success; it was also identified by a clearly articulated ideological and aesthetic difference from other prevailing popular music styles, including the then fledgling nationalistic megarock, heavy metal, folk rock, country, and skinhead punk rock.

The so-called underground music community delineated itself primarily by reference to two traditions: the post-1960s local avant-garde art movements, encompassing experimental film and contemporary music, theater, and performance arts; and a particular strand of Western rock'n'roll, stemming from the pop art of the Velvet Underground through the glam rock of the likes of David Bowie to the avant-gardism of Captain Beefheart, Frank Zappa, and the like. A vital and immediate impetus to the flourishing of indigenous rock was provided by the philosophy, sounds, and images of British, American, and German punk and its diverse stylistic offshoots—postpunk, new wave, no wave, industrial and noise music—all of which came to be referred to collectively as "alternative music."

In appropriating these musical and artistic influences, the Hungarian musicians blended distinctly Eastern European flavors with the existential exasperation expressed in the punks' famous slogan, "No future!" Policed far more systematically than their Western counterparts, these musicians and artists lived, performed, and represented marginality not merely as a specific sociomusical space. Outside official or legitimate culture and with no professional status, they found their plight exacerbated by a sense of being on the margins of modern Western history, off the map as far as the broader cultural and historical conditions of their existence were concerned. The music drew attention to gaps between societies in the politically defined East and West, between past and present, present and future. It represented a perspective from which the surrounding social world appeared historically marginal—that is, anachronistic and ephemeral. It also defined a lifestyle and, although less explicitly, a dissident political stance that was rehearsed in imaginative musical and lyrical texts, performance practices, even direct confrontations with officialdom. The rock critic Tamás Szõnyei's eyewitness account of a show by the Ultra Rock Agency in 1981 and its exhilarating impact on the audience captures some crucial aspects of this marginality:

> [These musicians] did not try to adjust themselves to the inconsistent and incalculable twists of prevailing cultural policies or the presupposed tolerance level of functionaries and the audience. This was exactly what rendered their music so credible, call it rock'n'roll or art. At their concerts I just gaped and . . . occasionally looked over my shoulder to check if the others heard the same words I did! No, such words on a Hungarian stage, it can't be possible! But it was. (1992: 353)

What were some of the words that Szőnyei and many others, including me, had difficulty believing were coming off the stage? What kind of public realm was being formed through the music? Let Szőnyei be our guide. He was startled by the absurdity of the words of the URA song "Vote for Me":

> "I don't know if you've ever tried to picture me on the top of the pop charts," Péter Iván Müller opened the song. . . . "I'm rolling down [*gördülök*] the airport ramp in a Mercedes convertible. I'm being escorted by handsome motorcyclists on both sides. I'm waving amiably as my car's taking me to the plane. The plane's door opens, a man steps out and kisses me on the mouth. One'd consider him a diplomat from the East but he's Alice Cooper. I recognize him by the boa rolled around his neck."[2] (1992: 353)

2. Alice Cooper, originally the name of his band, is a U.S. rocker famous for his high-energy music and his stage antics.

Szőnyei then provides us with a moment-to-moment report on how the event unfolded:

> The hands of the guitarist Jenő Menyhárt, the bassist László Kiss, and the drummer András Salamon begin to move and a staccato rhythm, raw force, and distorted noise erupt from the amplifiers. The singer continues: "Vote for me. I'll fulfill all your hopes. You have no voice? Then use mine. I set out for the elections. If it's a fight, let's fight. Vote for me! You've wanted me for so long. I'm awfully [*pokoli*] popular. I'm extremely trustworthy. I'll sing beautifully if I get one more vote. Even when I'm at the top, I'll love you. You'll be my folk and I'll be your folk musician [A népem leszel és én a népzenészed]. Please vote for me! I'm enjoying your trust so much. I'm beautiful in just the way you need it and your word is final. Vote for me. . . ." Mesmerizing moments. The phantom of liberty visits a concert in Budapest. Election lists and pop charts are inscribed on each other at a time . . . when, in line with the Brezhnev doctrine, the Soviet army is already in Afghanistan and everyone's trying to figure out if Solidarity's Poland will be its next destination. Meanwhile in our country, there's only one candidate to vote for. (1992: 353–54)

The Politics of Pop and Rock in a Socialist Society

Under Hungarian state socialism, with its restrictions on civic freedoms, its limited market economy, and its relative geopolitical isolation, rock was stifled: its technology lacked sophistication, its meanings were impoverished in the absence of professional rock criticism, and it never maintained a web of other expressive practices, what Dick Hebdige (1979) called subcultural "style." Musicians exercised very limited control over the creative process, and that control was curtailed by the absence of their own proper institutions: rock had no infrastructure. The predominance of a centralized state-run music industry, which provided no space for small-scale, independent music making, weighed particularly heavily on musicians outside the established mainstream world of pop.[3]

In his book on British pop culture, Iain Chambers (1985) defines pop music's essence as a fast-paced succession of sounds and images. Challenging Adorno's (1990) mass culture argument, Chambers claims that despite the hype that the music business looses at the emergence of every subcultural fad, real creative breakthroughs do happen. "In some cases these [novelties] may merely involve the latest twist in marketing strategy, the quick business eye for a possible trend. More frequently, fresh proposals represent a real intrusion upon an earlier organization of the music and its surrounding culture. Whenever a sound powerful enough to threaten existing arrangements emerges, previous interpretations, choices and tastes are put in question" (xi–xii). The dynamic of the popular music field looked entirely different in the socialist countries. Here the intricate and collaborative relationship between fresh musical proposals and imaginative business strategies never evolved. The centralized record industry, in many ways typifying the whole system of managed cultural production, failed or refused to notice emergent trends, since they jeopardized established arrangements on which the material existence of the entire noncompetitive network of old-timers depended: performers, composers, lyricists, studio personnel, producing managers, television and radio programmers, and all the rest. Hungaroton, the national record company, did not even have the equivalent of the Western A&R (artists and repertoire) person. Its popular music managers (*márka menedzser*) lacked the monetary incentives to seek out, sign up, and develop promising talent. On the contrary, new and exciting music styles that drew crowds of enthusiastic followers induced anxiety rather than thrill in the music business. After all, the top management consisted of business bureaucrats, accountable to the various representatives of the Communist Party and the Ministry of Culture for the political correctness of the products they put out.

When members of a musical subculture on the rise grew too strident in their demands for recording or broadcasting their bands'

3. For a comparative discussion of the music industries of socialist Eastern Europe and Western and Third World countries, see Robinson et al. 1991.

music, media personnel used one of two strategies: they either screened and selectively recorded the group's music or attempted to divert the audience's interest in the band toward some little-known group that played in the same style and was considered "safe" (Hadas 1983). These strategies seldom worked well, and the most popular bands ended up in the industry's recording studio—but after such a long delay that the resulting albums simply registered rather than contributed to the more memorable moments of Hungarian pop/rock history. As one musician, Jenő Menyhárt, put it, "By the time six committees and nervous officials come to decide whether this or that music should exist or not [on vinyl or tape], the music will simply no longer be around."

Any public discourse about the meaning and politics of a new music style, a provocative song, or a charismatic rock personality made the pop music industry nervous. As in any authoritarian system, officials treated the polysemy inherent in any cultural text as a potential threat to the status quo, although the actual content and limits of political propriety were vaguely defined. The mid-level managers of cultural institutions pointed their fingers at their bosses and supervisors to justify requests for changes in a song's lyrics. Art and cultural policies in the 1980s were unpredictable. The 1983 performance of the rock opera *István, a király* (Stephen the king), for example, which its creators expected to provoke a major backlash from the party-state apparatus, received official recognition. Nonetheless, radio broadcasters, record company managers, and directors of music venues and houses of culture (*művelődési házak*) acted as gatekeepers of the public arena. The co-optation of some musicians and the suppression of others were charged with heavy moral and political implications.

Hungary's monopolized but market-conscious culture industry rendered pop musicians vulnerable and corruptible, politically as well as commercially. This circumstance imbued the predicament of the recalcitrant ones with an aura of heroism. Histories of the local rock scene abound in accounts of the disjointed careers of formidable talents, icons of a particular generation or subculture, who broke in with a sound and an image "powerful enough to threaten the existing arrangements." Yet rather than shaking up the whole scene, they either disappeared without ever being recorded or misused their talents for the sake of survival. Many of them chose the lucrative but draining and deprecated job of bar or night club entertainer, while others stopped playing, became alcoholics, or defected to the West, where the reputation earned in their home country could rarely be regained. Bitterness and frustration pervaded the narratives of even successful musicians who managed, by a rare combination of circumstance, temperament, and talent, to strike a balance between mass popularity and official acceptance. Like their less fortunate colleagues, they saw their creative talents and career chances curtailed by an arbitrarily operated, overbearing, and incompetent system of music production (Sebők 1983–84, Dám 1987).

Virtually no pop musicians had escaped censorship in their careers.[4] Paradoxically, this form of coercive rather than hegemonic control over the production and distribution of music resulted in musical texts layered with meaning. Not only marginal musicians but many mainstream musicians too resorted to coded language as a poetic and political strategy to avoid confrontations with media personnel. Song lyrics that on the surface dealt with the vicissitudes of love and desire often addressed on another level the vicissitudes of an unfree public life. "Yellow Rose" (Sárga rózsa), a song by the rock group Illés, expressed through metaphors of blooming and withering many people's disappointment in the government when it participated, with other Warsaw Pact countries, in the occupation of Alexander Dubček's Czechoslovakia in August 1968:

> Do you believe the yellow rose is still in bloom?
> Do you believe we still heed mendacious words?
> Do you believe we'll always forgive everything?
> Do you believe we'll forget all our dreams?
>
> It'd be so fine, my love, to lie among flowers
> But the flowers are gone, just as you are.
> Why did we let this happen?[5]

4. For a comparative study of the impact of the transnational music industry on the production of peripheral popular music for the International Communication and Youth Culture Consortium, Csaba Hajnóczy, Gabi Kenderesi, and I prepared a survey of local musicians under the auspices of the Institute for Musicology of the Hungarian Academy of Sciences, Budapest. Its results may be found in Robinson et al. 1991.

5. The music was composed by Levente Szörényi and the lyrics by János Bródy.

Musicians' use of allusions and wordplay grew beyond a political or creative strategy to deal with censorship. It became a mark of seriousness and a source of status enhancement until the rise of homegrown punk and new wave, when lyrics became outspoken and belligerent.

The long tradition of writing allegorical and allusive texts with multiple meanings had taught audiences a particular mode of reading, or rather a mode of hearing. Thus the politicization of rock had a self-perpetuating logic of its own. The musicians' strategic use of music to articulate their political positions or messages played a relatively limited role in this phenomenon. The politicization of the space inhabited by underground rock was to a large extent precipitated by the system of controlling and regulating youth cultures. Peter Wicke observes that in East Germany the "[state-socialist] authorities tended to read into the most innocuous songs a potential for serious political statement," and as a consequence audiences were led "to read into such songs a more serious political content than was ever intended by the musicians" (1990: 10). Tibor Bornai of the group KFT (Korlátolt Felelősségű Társaság, or Limited Liability Company) told me of the following episode:

> We played the number called "Africa" with a bit of uneasiness onstage 'cause it had no hidden meanings to it whatsoever. The whole idea was to convince the record company [Hungaroton] that there's one hit on our album that will persuade people to buy it. This was a good bet. But we were most amused when we had people coming up to us from the audience and starting to analyze the words of "Africa." They found a variety of hidden messages that were simply not there. To some of them I said, "Look, nothing like that is in the song." But I just nodded at other times 'cause that's how people's minds worked at the time . . . and from that very moment of putting out "Africa" our audience grew large.

As we can see, the political meanings and effects of rock music can be determined no more directly in Eastern European social contexts than in the West. The socialist institutional framework in which rock music had to find its niche did produce creative strategies that appealed to people's heightened political sensibilities, because musicians and audiences alike were embedded in the same repressive network. Yet these circumstances do not render the relationship between politics and music transparent.

Ragged Rock and the Rise of the Pop Avant-Garde

By the end of the 1970s, popular music in Hungary was fraught with social tensions. It was a time of economic recession, and a sense of insecurity spread through the society. As László Kürti (1991a) notes, growing inflation, trade deficits, international debt, and external economic shocks were among the most serious elements of the situation. Export earnings slumped. Yet the economy was being liberalized by the establishment and legitimization of new forms of enterprise in the second economy, which produced an apparently thriving consumer and leisure sector. Young people did not enjoy the benefits of these economic reforms. Indeed, numerous sociological studies, surveys, and essays prepared at the time suggest that masses of young people were losing faith in the future and resented the older generation's failure to provide stable, credible, and consistent values to adhere to (Csengey 1983, Csörsz 1986).

While the international rockabilly revival reached Hungary with the alluring sounds and images of 1950s America, a subculture of young people preoccupied with the harsher realities of working-class and lumpen existence was forming. Its most militant core was recruited from homeless and jobless teenagers, mostly male, some recently released from state orphanages when they turned eighteen. Others were runaways from predominantly but not exclusively broken lower-income families.[6] They sought relief in drugs, alcohol, and heavy rock (Kőbányai 1979). Music provided them with an effective medium through which to articulate nihilist despair and frustration.

6. This is not to equate dysfunctional family life with the working class. Although some ragged rockers did come from middle-class families, the ethos of ragged rock was shaped by the street culture of working-class youth. I do not have sufficient ethnographic and statistical data to explain this phenomenon. It seems reasonable to surmise that the causes and effects of divorce and alcoholism, which are most often associated with the erosion of the traditional family, may vary with position in the social structure.

Official discourse labeled them "problem youth," and the establishment attempted to restore communication with them by favoring some of their "sincere and hard-as-stone" (*őszinte kőkemény*) bands while disfavoring others. The musicians who took it upon themselves to speak for these youth groups inevitably clashed with the pop business. In fact, a dominant strand of the early punk movement gained a nationwide reputation less by virtue of their music than because of their stark refusal to comply with the media in their attempts to domesticate them.

The group Beatrice voiced social dissent in a crude and straightforward manner. They presented themselves as socially responsible musicians. A British journalist called them "social(ist) realists" because of their graphic description of lower-class life, of the bleak world of dirty subways, pubs, and the gray blocks of high-rises that ringed the city (Bohn 1981). They were the band of the "ragged crowd" (*csövesek*).[7] For them to admit publicly to being punks would have been to subscribe to a musical ideology that the guards of law and order in Hungary proclaimed to be right-wing and fascist.[8] Still, Beatrice could not escape the label attached to it after an oft-cited concert whose main attraction was, allegedly, the grinding up of a live chicken.

In the meantime, a notable revival of an amateur music movement was shaping up, mobilizing a broad age range (from twelve to thirty) and cutting across several social strata. As in so many other countries in Europe and in North America, punk brought a remarkable surge of new voices.[9] Some of these bands did not survive even

7. The word *csöves* refers both to the cut of their pants, which resembled drainpipes, and their hobo lifestyle.

8. Because punk performers everywhere displayed Nazi symbols, punk came to be associated with neo-fascists. But since the main thrust of the movement was more closely allied with the left, it's not surprising that the right suspected communist influence. Greil Marcus notes that the famed British punk group Sex Pistols was "denounced in Parliament as a threat to the British way of life, by socialists as fascist, by fascists as communist" (1989: 10).

9. Punk's power and conspicuousness are to a large extent inherent in the musical style itself, irrespective of its wider sociopolitical or national context. The acclaimed BBC disc jockey John Peel speaks for many who witnessed the movement's rise in Budapest: "It was so wonderful to have rediscovered at what was already an advanced age the sort of feelings I first had when I heard Little Richard and Elvis Presley as a kid. It was exciting, but there was an element of fear as well—you thought: 'Can this be real?' You went to the gigs and there was a feeling that you were participating in something that had come from another planet, it seemed so remarkable that it was happening at all" (quoted in Greil Marcus 1989: 41).

a second rehearsal. A self-conscious subculture with all the sartorial extravagance and garishness of punk was nurtured in centers such as the Young Artists' Club (YAC, Fiatal Művészek Klubja), art galleries, and college venues. Unlike Beatrice, they were well informed about their British and North American prototypes. Better educated and older than the ragged punks, they possessed the intellectual and political resources to challenge the official representations of Western punk as fascist.

Of the venues where the bohemian punks gathered, the YAC was perhaps the most important, as it hosted a mixed constituency called the "marginal intelligentsia." It was a place for connections and exchanges between the democratic opposition[10]—writers, artists, popular musicians, academics, recent college graduates, and other people drifting in and out of jobs, on and off various blacklists. They enacted various versions of marginality, negotiating its meanings, politics, and style. With its hard-edged punk concerts the club attracted members of the "ragged" working-class subcultures too. The YAC was notorious for political brouhahas triggered by raucous shows and such officially disapproved events as discussions with a dissident celebrity in the arts or social sciences. These nose-thumbings then prompted various punitive measures—temporary shutdowns, restrictions on membership eligibility, the wholesale removal of the club's management.

The YAC, located just a few blocks from the Soviet embassy, had a bohemian, casual, at times dismal atmosphere related to excessive alcohol consumption. Since membership was limited to art college

10. The democratic opposition, formed in the late 1970s, comprised an active group of people with diverse political orientations. The core consisted of hard-core liberals and social democrats who engaged in extensive underground political activities. They circulated samizdat (self-published) writings and later, after they acquired a printing machine, published their own underground journals (*Beszélo, Hírmondó*) and a variety of Hungarian and foreign books, classic and contemporary, banned by the state. They drafted petitions and manifestos to the government to protest against human rights violations in Hungary and other Warsaw Pact countries. The democratic opposition cooperated with organizations of similar purpose in Czechoslovakia (Charta '77), Poland (Solidarity, KOR), the GDR (the evangelical churches), and the Soviet Union (samizdat writers), as well as in the West (Amnesty International, Helsinki Watch). The idea and practice of the "moving universities" consisted of illegal gatherings at private apartments where social scientists and other thinkers voiced unorthodox political/ideological opinions. In 1989 members of the democratic opposition established the Alliance of Free Democrats (AFD), which became the largest opposition party in 1990, then a member of the coalition government with the Socialist Party (MSZP) in 1994. The 1998 elections demoted the party to a minor position, its representation in Parliament comparable to that of the ultraright Hungarian Party of Life and Truth (MIÉP).

students and hundreds of nonmembers were eager to attend the club's more popular events, tumultuous confrontations with burly guards at the door formed an integral part of the overall defiant and unruly atmosphere. All this made the YAC emblematic of the underground culture.

Although the club nurtured contacts between the various groups of middle-class and working-class marginals, it could not overcome the social fragmentation among its constituency. Some young writers' attempts to forge a meaningful alliance with the ragged crowd failed, primarily because the intellectuals themselves were split into factions and were vulnerable to the party and state officials' political maneuvers.[11]

The beginnings of the art punk subculture date back to 1978, when a band called the Spions held three unannounced and brutally provocative punk concerts for a selected audience. The events drew on conceptualist performance art and Antonin Artaud's "theater of cruelty."[12] The Spions gave out manifestos written in a neo-avant-garde/anarchist vein in which they represented themselves as the "soldiers" of rock'n'roll, redefined as the synthesis of history and art, simultaneously a subculture and mass culture (Szőnyei 1992: 337).[13]

11. A memorable incident of political maneuvering took place around the journal *Mozgó Világ*, dedicated to publishing the work of young avant-garde writers, poets, and essayists and radical social scientists. Since the paper was sponsored by the Communist Youth League, the Communist Party and the Ministry of Culture deployed an array of measures to smooth off its oppositional edges. Eventually, when the editor in chief was removed, the whole staff resigned in protest. The ministry appointed a new editor to run the journal under the same name, but most of the earlier contributors and readers had nothing further to do with *Mozgó*.

12. This is how Péter I. Müller, a musician who was inspired by the Spions, described a fantasy played out at one of their performances:

> An intellectual conception infiltrated rock music and found its audience. . . . One of the numbers was about the relationship between Anne Frank and her murderer. It was a game where erotica and war became associated. . . . The concert started with an identification game. Two girls were standing in underwear. To the sounds of an old Zarah Leander recording one cut off the underwear from the other with a razor, then put on a World War II-era women's suit and froze into a mannequin pose. The undressed girl then symbolically cut the face of the mannequin, by now senseless, with lipstick and razor. This was an unmistakable punk reference. I think, in a telepathic manner, they put their finger on punk. (Quoted in Szőnyei 1992: 336)

13. The Spions' overall artistic approach, along with their harsh but still oblique political rhetoric and their obsession with symbols of totalitarianism, curiously parallels that of a widely known Slovenian art rock group called Laibach (see Barber-Keršovan 1989).

Their domestic career was short-lived. Faithful to the tradition of the Hungarian avant-garde, two of the Spions' members defected to the West and continued their musical activities there. This is how one of the group, Péter Hegedüs, explains their emigration:

> We decided to leave. We weren't driven away but the situation was tough. Of course it was tough abroad too, we'd had no illusions about that. The point is that our space here was very limited. . . . It was an intelligent form of surveillance but it did exist. Even though half of the audience was taken in [to police headquarters] after a concert, everyone got released right away. We were summoned to the Ministry of the Interior, where they showed us taped conversations to make us aware that we were being watched. They talked to us. They tried to corner me by questioning me about my future, what jobs I'd get once I'd completed my studies at the Music Academy if I continued to act like this. They trusted that I'm a smart guy and would get the message: I'll keep quiet and make no trouble. (Szőnyei 1992: 339)

The Spions' myth grew in underground fanzine-style publications. They became celebrated as founders of a whole new style and attitude in local rock music. These two musically and socially diverse wings of punk corresponded to Simon Frith and Howard Horne's distinction between punk as a youth subculture and punk as a pop style (1987: 124).

The avant-garde rock music scene began to appeal to a broader public when bands adopted outlandish names such as Petting, Orgasm, and Galloping Coroners (Vágtázó Halottkémek). Others masqueraded in the names of such respectable institutions as Europe Publishing House (Európa Kiadó) and the Committee (Bizottság), which the audience read as alluding to the Central Committee of the Communist Party.[14] The initials URH, for Ultra Rövid Hullám (Ultra Short Wave), offered a straightforward association with a police patrol known by the same initials, but the band's members insisted that they stood for Ultra Rock Hírügynökség (Ultra Rock Agency). This

14. Rumor had it that originally the band members called themselves the Central Committee, but some official pressured them to drop the adjective. In another Dadaist move, the Committee eventually adopted the initials of Albert Einstein: A. E. Committee.

doubling technique in the choice of stage name served to assert an alternative social space with mirror images that challenged and mocked the existing social world.

Dave Laing (1985: 44) argued that the bizarre names chosen by British and American bands (Buzzcocks, Joy Division, Police, Dead Kennedys) were anything but revolutionary, in view of their hippie/underground predecessors. In Hungary, where there had been no Grateful Deads or Electric Prunes, such cacophonous names proved useful in both recruiting followers and bewildering the public. But Laing was also right in observing that shock tactics in themselves lose their value quickly. Punk, having built its whole paraphernalia of expressive strategies around shock effects, soon gave way, internationally and locally, to new wave, a loose conglomerate of styles that were subtler and more individuated than punk (for Anglo-American examples, see Grossberg 1984a, Rimmer 1985). The underground new wave as a subcultural style in Hungary was held together by a shared set of experiences derived from its members' similar social situation, age, and educational background; by a common perspective and sensibility arising from a particular historical awareness; and by a dauntless innovative impulse that, quite without precedent in local rock culture, freely absorbed the techniques and media of other contemporary art forms.

Music Making: The Underground Network

Although the members of the punk/new wave subculture had a high school or college education, many of them were drifters without a goal. They made a living primarily from unskilled free-lance jobs. In age they ranged between twenty and thirty. Staying on the margins was usually their own choice and allowed them a materially more secure existence than the ragged punks enjoyed. The art punks were of middle-class background and many of them had ties to artistic and academic networks, which occasionally provided them with well-paying or otherwise rewarding work (composition of film scores or acting, for example). Amateurs in music, quite a few of them were or had been engaged in the visual arts, design, film, or drama. Péter Iván Müller of the Control Group (Kontroll Csoport) had been trained as a circus clown. Others had a musical past in jazz or folk rock. They discovered and used punk rock as yet another means to experiment with new ideas and forms of expression.

In the beginning the punk/new wave set revived the early informality of the beat club scene of the 1960s. Again the boundaries between performers and listeners were blurry. The latter were not fans in the sense of pledging their loyalty to one band or performer. The most popular groups attracted the same crowd to their live performances. Accordingly, there was virtually no rivalry among the bands. Line-ups were fluid and the players of one band frequently showed up as guest performers at another's concert. Music making was interwoven with other creative activities, all embedded in webs of friendships and romantic relationships. The prevalence of joint shows also reflected a proclivity for cooperation and intergroup solidarity rare among professional musicians. The bands certainly were not impervious to controversies, however, and their quarrels caused many regroupings and suspensions of musical activities over the years.

The subculture's public remained relatively undivided even as its composition changed. As the original bohemian and intellectual constituency left the scene or merged into a younger and more socioeconomically diverse audience, the concerts increasingly resembled ordinary rock events. The underground scene also expanded geographically as the provinces broke Budapest's monopoly as the exclusive site of concert life.

This brand of highly outspoken yet not always directly accessible rock'n'roll was never integrated into the machinery of the national recording industry. Although pop music was considerably more commodified in Hungary than in most other socialist countries, the combination of political caution and a kind of pedestrian mentality prevented the music industry from exploiting the market potential of these bands. No quick business eye wanted to recognize that the shows were attracting crowds of about a thousand people to venues designed for just a few hundred. It made more sense for the officials and managers of the music business to limit the size of the audience, with the help of the police if necessary, rather than give in to its demand. (Of course, one cannot overlook the forbidden-fruit effect in accounting for the ebullient interest in this music.) Of the seven or eight most popular and solid underground groups, only two had an opportunity to issue albums with Hungaroton. Altogether three albums and a couple of singles came out to represent a large and varied set of repertoires, which had their effect not only on later generations of amateurs but on mainstream rockers as well. Even these records were sadly belated.

The way the political and cultural apparatus treated these bands suggested a great deal of ambivalence. Negotiations over record contracts were often abruptly terminated. Apparently the lower-ranking staff were unable to win their superiors' consent to their projects. Similarly, the state-run radio recorded concerts that it never broadcast. The people who made the recordings were balked when they wanted to play them on the air. This split in the pop music establishment can be seen in other media as well. The pop journalists were all but unanimous in their admiration for the underground bands. In the annual official appraisals of rock bands, the EPH and the Committee were repeatedly listed among the critics' favorites, and the lists were widely published. Yet the bands themselves were denied access to the music industry's technologically sophisticated recording and marketing facilities, without which their music could not reach a large public.

The musicians also displayed mixed feelings about mass popularity. Although they rarely turned down an opportunity for wide public exposure, few of them actively sought the favor of the media and the recording industry. Playing for fun, staying a "leisure band," and enjoying the loyalty of an audience they saw as desperately needing them were recurring themes in the musicians' statements on their music making. Keeping their distance from the institutionalized pop world was more important to them than their appeal to a broader public.

The ethos of marginality was forged within what Elemér Hankiss called a second public, a network of alternative communication channels.[15] This public depended on the dedicated work of the "enthusiasts"; that is, the active small-scale business people who operate at the periphery of the music market to protect spaces for "en-

15. Cushman provides an interesting analysis of the political and social significance of friendship in the counterculture of the Soviet Union (1995: 169–72).

dangered" local music as the sounds and images of international pop expand their territory (Wallis and Malm, 1984). In Hungary the enthusiast as a type of culture broker emerged with the liberalization of the private sector and the gradual decentralization of the music business. His (rarely, if ever, her) presence was instrumental in expanding the infrastructural spaces for rock music in the early 1980s. Stage equipment and studios made available by private renters gave some freedom and mobility in organizing small-scale events and preparing good-quality demo tapes. The enthusiasts were determined to promote and preserve underground music against incursions by the transnational music industry and the neglect of the slow-moving state-run monopolies. Most enthusiasts were student organizers for a college music club; many played in bands of their own. Their systematic taping of the club's live events and extensive circulating of duplicates created a second music public. Unlike the wider and better organized *magnitizdat* system in Russia (Troitsky 1987: 83–86, Cushman 1995: 40), this practice involved no monetary transactions at all: a tape of a 1981 URA concert, for example, could be traded for a home-taped album of a Western alternative band.[16] Thanks to this network, the most prominent musicians became known to foreign promoters and record labels. Despite the difficulties of travel, finances, and management, they become part of a broader European cultural scene.

Young Hungarian moviemakers were particularly responsive to the punk/new wave scene, partly because of their personal involvement in it. Film studios were the first to issue audio tapes with these musicians and commissioned them to compose original scores and to

16. The idea of a second public was theorized by Hankiss as an aspect of the second society in socialist Hungary. According to his structuralist model, the official or first society, which represented Marxist/Leninist/Stalinist ideals, can be contrasted with the second society, a spontaneously arising , entirely unplanned social realm, by means of binary oppositions such as homogeneity vs. differentiation and integration, hierarchical vs. horizontal organization, downward vs. upward flow of information, and presence vs. absence of the dominant ideology, visibility, and legitimacy. The second society is assumed to embrace a very tangible but chaotic second economy, a more or less organized political grouping, a second cultural sphere (subcultures and countercultures), a second consciousness (identified by Hankiss, somewhat imprecisely, with a set of political philosophies and belief systems), and a second, mostly hidden domain of political and social interactions (1989: 117–44).

participate in other ways in the making of their films. The Committee and the Galloping Coroners appeared in the late Gábor Bódy's *A kutya éji dala* [The dog's night song]; János Xantus's film *Eszkimó asszony fázik* [The Eskimo woman is cold] featured the group Trabant.

Nonetheless, live shows continued to be the chief mode of communication between the performers and their public. Constraints of media access played about as important a role here as the music's inherent dependence on a live audience for its power and effect.[17] Since the Hungarian musicians were amateurs and never gave a thought to obtaining a license, they had to contend with poor technical conditions and unresponsive crews hired by the particular venue. The concerts were often canceled at the last moment for political or technical reasons, usually for both. The crowd, determined to get in with or without a ticket, was typically larger than the auditorium's capacity and thus posed a threat to physical and political safety. Many club directors did not want to risk clashes between their guards and the frustrated fans at the entrance. The atmosphere was always pregnant with violence. Police wielding nightsticks to restore order at the gates were not an uncommon sight.

Despite the risk and anxiety involved, the shows were lucrative, owing to the full house that such concerts ensured. Musicians complained to me of the exploitive payment practices of most venues. Because they were amateurs, they received very low fees or none at all, while the ticket prices were in the same range as those for performances of licensed musicians. Thus by adhering to the old restrictive bureaucratic requirement of a license, the cultural establishment stifled underground music even as it capitalized on the demand for it.

Marginality as Style and Ideology

The politics of marginality not only was marked by disruptions and cleavages; it also created alliances. The alliance most consequential for

17. An increasing range of Western cassette tapes and LPs were imported by private retail stores as well as state-run outlets, but the choice to be found at any store seemed random and unpredictable.

the ideology and practice of the underground music scene was formed between the practitioners of visual arts, amateur drama, and music.

The arts and rock music had been connected, most conspicuously since the late 1960s, when rock critics appraised both the music and lyrics of songs as art (Frith 1981). Exploring this connection in Britain, Frith and Horne (1987) proposed that the superpower status of British pop was an effect of the heavy involvement of the domestic art school set in music making. Art students found in rock a commercially viable outlet for their talents. Former art school graduates such as John Lennon and Peter Townshend added style, image, and self-consciousness to the sounds imported from North America.

In Hungary visual art had no connection with pop and rock until the emergence of bohemian punk. As I mentioned earlier, rock music in Hungary was less a complex cultural practice than a musical idiom. As Gordy (1997) remarked with regard to Eastern European pop, in a political-economic environment that downplayed consumer and fashion-related industries, the negotiation of subcultural difference through the careful construction of looks was certainly constrained.

With the enlargement of the second economy and the mushrooming of private businesses in the early 1980s, the overall conditions of popular music were affected as well. Now that young people could purchase the latest tapes and music magazines from private retail stores, they were able to see and respond to the visual antics of European and American pop artists. They could piece their outfits together from an increasing number of fashion boutiques. Hungarian pop became not only more in synch with contemporary global music trends but also more observant of the nonmusical stylistic aspects of pop culture. This trend was reinforced by other circumstances, notably by the rise of the pop video and Hungary's increasingly frequent inclusion in Western performers' touring schedules.

As elsewhere in the world, the first punk events were initiated by schools of visual arts, and the boldest and most cacophonous outfits were designed and worn by art students. The alliance between rock and the avant-garde art world encouraged a more self-reflective and analytical discourse, exuberance, innovation, and style. Remarkable was the adoption of the term "rock'n'roll" with a new meaning. Previously, as well as in contemporary mainstream language, "rock-'n'roll" referred to the dance music of the 1950s. The underground took over the term to denote a self-constructed tradition of rock music connoting relevance and substance as well as subversion and threat.[18] Consider these excerpts:

> When the sun sets I rise
> I ring up my partner
> And shout in the street
> That rock'n'roll ain't no dance[19]
> (Neurotic)

> Rock'n'roll's a beast
> More dangerous than you
> You feed it from your palm
> Rock'n'roll's a human
> You can't keep an eye on him
> You ain't got no free time for that
> (Control Group)

Performers and commentators highlighted the music's darker and more transgressive fringes, its preoccupation with sex and drugs, and its unsettling flirtation with the forbidden, all of which had been carefully bracketed in its Eastern European incarnations. Visual images, stage setting, and choreography gained a whole new significance when it conveyed such sentiments and ideas.

The group called Kex had a brief existence on the periphery of the 1960s local music scene, but its surrealistic, cabaret-style pop eclecticism drew a remarkably devoted following, mainly middle-class high school students. To most members of the 1980s audience and even to the musicians themselves, Kex evoked no personal memories, and the group made no commercial recordings, yet its legend survived for decades. Digging out a few poor-quality amateur concert tapes, older fans resuscitated the music and with it the

18. Even in Britain the official space of pop was off limits to most punk groups because of the music's brutality or obscenity (Greil Marcus 1989: 75–76).

19. Quoted in Szőnyei 1992: 396.

cult in popular memory. Kex became the starting point of a freshly invented tradition of Hungarian rock'n'roll.

In many other respects the movement echoed the artistic ideology and practice of its Western counterpart. In response to its cultural and political milieu, however, it accentuated different themes and dramatized different problems. The avant-garde/punk tie, for example, loosened or erased the conventional boundaries between diverse artistic forms and practices, such as performance art, video and film art, installations, slides, and, of course, music. It also blurred the boundaries between art and everyday life, and between performers and audience—concerns that had recurrently been on the agenda of twentieth-century isms.

The avant-garde discourse of rock confounded the expressive vocabulary and analytic concepts of high ("autonomous") and popular (commercial) arts. In British punk, this conventional dichotomy was complicated by the disputed notions of political credibility (authenticity) and sellout. In discussing the way the Sex Pistols' manager, Malcolm McLaren, played on these manifold tensions, Frith and Horn observe that

> previous pop art musicians had been recuperated either as "stars" (like Pete Townshend) or as "artists" (Brian Eno) or as both (Bowie and Ferry); either way, they lost control of themselves. McLaren's aim was to stay sharp by burrowing into the money-making core of the pop machine, to be both blatantly commercial (and thus resist the traditional labels of art and Bohemia) and deliberately troublesome (so that the usually smooth, hidden gears of commerce were always on noisy display). (1987: 132)

This game could not be played in Hungary, where the gears of commerce operated far less smoothly and were much more visible. Pop music was not a site of subtle hegemonic absorption. In the Hungarian cultural caste system, high art was often synonymous with the politically compromised forms of artistic respectability. This system marginalized not only the oppositional rock culture but also certain types of "serious" avant-garde expression that in the West had long been commodified and thus co-opted. Therefore the conflation of high and popular art at the juncture of punk and the avant-garde in Hungary highlighted a conflict between "legitimate," official, and respectable arts, on the one hand, and rejected, forbidden, and outcast arts, on the other. These cultural conditions provided the programmatic ideas that gave the underground publication *Jó világ* (Good world) a sharp political edge:

> We cannot assume that this narrow terrain [of marginal culture] is at the forefront of nationwide interest. Nonetheless, it seems remarkable that thousands of people gather at the rock concerts of the bands covered by our journal; that in the fine arts world nothing evokes as much debate as the emerging processes herein represented; and that there always appears an established film director who arouses public interest through the portrayal of the "types" we have picked out to contribute or to be appreciated. . . . At the present moment we are more intrigued by a high school student's ideas as to why she or he is bored with the Kossuth Prize-winning poet than by the ideas of the Kossuth Prize-winning poet himself. (Beke and Szőke 1984: 7)

Music: A Textual Approach

The most common underlying theme of punk and new wave songs was existential angst and frustration arising from a particular historical and geopolitical awareness. This awareness can most easily be captured in negative terms: a lost or blurred sense of the spatial and temporal framework of existence. The despair encoded in the songs had to do with a perception that the times were out of joint and was rooted in a characteristically postmodern life-feeling. Exploring its nature and sociohistorical context, Grossberg writes: "We have been thrown into the maelstrom of constant change, apparently under no-one's control and without direction. Both the past and the future have collapsed into the present, and our lives are organized without any appeal to the place of the present within an historical continuum. We have neither a sense of indebtedness to the past nor of our obligation to the future" (1984b: 7). The song lyrics frequently employed metaphors of travel to express a similar idea. But such travels seemed curiously directionless, decentered, and lacking what travels are normally valued for, the excitement of the novel and the unfamiliar:

> You arrive here as a traveler who lost his way
> History is a rusty city
> (EPH)

If the metaphor of travel is used to capture an aimless and bleak economy of boredom in everyday life, one cannot help feeling a stranger, a tourist at home too:

> I raise my head and look around
> What can a tourist do?
> He's happy just to be here
> (EPH)

The meaningless duality of "here" and "elsewhere" is relocated in the individual self in the form of an internal split: "I'm somewhere else / Yet I'll be here" (EPH); "Existence is a background / There's no suffering / Our desires tramped into the ground" (Trabant); "He's not gone / but somehow remained here" (Trabant). The apparent randomness of the outer world sometimes provokes the most desperate and self-destructive attempts to regain control over one's life: "No one called you and you'll live here / But will vanish from here too / 'Cause you're fed up" (Control Group); "No time! / No space! / A triple salto high up!" (Galloping Coroners). According to Dénes Csengey (1983: 9), postwar Hungarian youth generations grew into adulthood with an increasing awareness of their disenfranchisement. Immediately after World War II, many young people were drunk with optimism and they promised in their songs to "shake up the whole wide world by tomorrow."[20] The beat generation of the 1960s still nourished the illusion of being able to con-

20. Miklós Jancsó's film *Fényes szelek* [Shiny Breeze] (1969) is a poignant representation of the controversial politics of these young communists and their hopes that the new system would bring social justice and moral renovation. Many of them had come from lower-class families and ended up in the ranks of the professional and political elite. The spontaneous activism associated with the *Shiny Breeze* generation, however, was soon repressed by the regime of Mátyás Rákosi (1949–56).

tribute to a society that was being transformed: "I don't wanna stand when the minutes run fast, I don't wanna stand when the earth moves" was the message the group Illés addressed to hard-line or narrow-minded bureaucrats at the onset of the cultural and political thaw. The children of the 1970s and 1980s, however, felt deprived even of disenchantment with the regime. They had been outsiders and apathetic survivors from the start:

We're nobody's children
Just happened to be born here
And still are alive
(Control Group)

The messenger is comin' and wavin'
There's been no news for a long time[21]
(EPH)

Many songs employed images associated with war zones and refugee camps:

Oversized souls go to hide in cellars
(EPH)

You're sittin' in the grave of the Unknown Soldier
A familiar situation but the smell's so distressing
(URA)

The anarchic separation from square society opens up possibilities of in-group solidarity:

I am you and you are me
We are in the same army[22]
(Control Group)

21. Nina Bachkatov and Andrew Wilson made a similar point about the malaise among different generations in Gorbachev's Soviet Union: "The parents lost their faith, but the children never had it" (quoted in Downing 1996: 92).

22. This verse was composed and sung in English with the apparent intention of reinforcing alterity. It is also an interesting example of rock intertextuality. It clearly rhymes with the Beatles' line: "I am he as you are he as you are me and we are all together" ("I Am the Walrus," in the album *Magical Mystery Tour*, EMI Records Ltd., 1967).

A sense of disempowerment also found an outlet in a scathing parody of the mainstream society's rhetoric of ideological crisis and moral decay:

Value, value, without value,
without value-free value
You can hardly react!
You can't raise your voice!
You can hardly resist!
(Committee)

The Committee (Bizottság)

The Committee was founded by visual artists, who incorporated contemporary multimedia styles in their performances and their posters (Fig. 2). The stage setting, the costumes, the movements and gestures were harsh, obscene, and caricature-like, creating an ambience more common in a cabaret or a circus than at a rock show.[23] At center stage stood three singers: a woman and two men, one of whom also played the saxophone and keyboards. At their first public appearance one musician drew attention to himself with a beard long enough to cover his guitar; another produced a genuine visual shock effect with his blood-soaked butcher's apron (Szőnyei 1992: 376). The comments and jokes that poured forth over and between the songs were always essential elements of the performance. Many of these spoken and sung texts were, as Walter Benjamin said about Dadaist poems, "'word salad' containing obscenities and every imaginable waste product of language" (1968: 239). In the song "Konyhagyeplő" (Kitchenrein) a male and a female singer chant over and over, in a shrilly hysterical tone typical of punk vocals, the following badly accentuated words over a highly dissonant, mechanically repeated instrumental figure at a quick tempo:

23. Punk and postpunk styles reached back to Dadaist uses of the cabaret. The British group Cabaret Voltaire paid homage to the night club of the same name, where "the artists' promise to reveal the meaning of life was turned into a vaudeville show" (Greil Marcus 1989: 192).

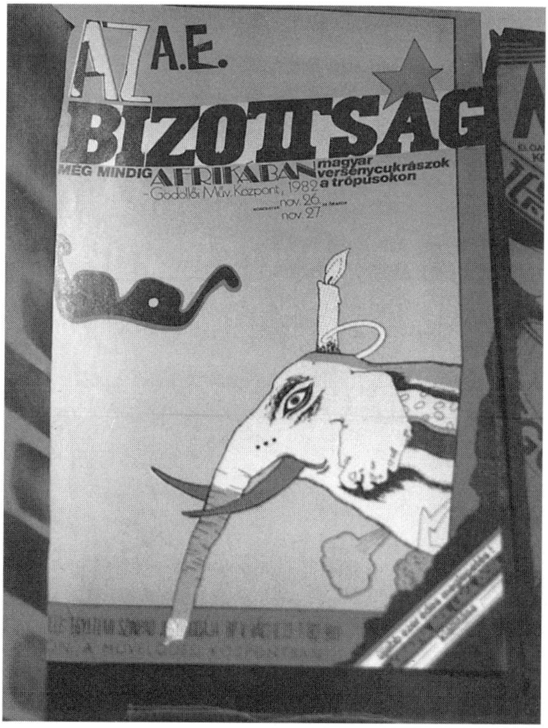

2
Poster advertising an A. E. Committee concert: "The A. E. Committee still in Africa: Top-Notch Hungarian Confectioners in the Tropics." Photo by Nora Gruber; courtesy of Tamás Szőnyei. (Rock poster collection exhibited in Budapest, 1995.)

> Small pans and small pots
> Small plates and small glasses
> Dessert forks and dessert spoons

The listing, delivered with great urgency, is abruptly suspended by the sinister refrain:

> Knives, knives, huge knives
> Knives, knives, popular knives!
> Super Swiss Army knives and ultrabayonets! . . .
> Super Swiss Army knives and ultrabayonets!

At this point, the music suddenly changes character again, then stops altogether to give special emphasis to the male singer's nonsensical spoken words: "The secret of my beauty's beauty is the metaphysical crank beautician, O mother!" The last word is washed away by the subsequent instrumental part, a cacophonous parody of rock guitar solos performed with great intensity. Few other bands on the local scene were more aptly portrayed by the slogan originated by the Sex Pistols' Johnny Rotten: "We're into chaos, not music." And, as Greil Marcus has pointed out, this punk chaos drew heavily on its Dada antecedents of the 1920s: "Dada became a game; powered by a loathing so strong at times it was all but undifferentiated, dada became fun. Throwing off all vestiges of aesthetics, philosophy, ethics, dada became what perhaps it had always wanted to be: merely a voice, a sound. The voice battered itself against the walls of honor and decency, looking for limits, finding none" (1989: 231).

Another strand in the Committee's repertoire was more directly political, although the hyperbolic, the hilarious, and a self-effacing irony were rarely absent from the pieces. Many people heard the following song as a reference to the "intelligent yet existing" apparatus of repression. The implication that the person addressed, the beast (*bestia*), was a woman somewhat obscured this reading:

I know you have axes too
I know you have knives too
I know what the bottom line is
Beast, beast, I see you!
You're on the floor but still after me
You're following me, I fear you
You're a monster
I know this is the bottom line
A serious state! an awkward state!
a tormenting state! a state of emergency [*szükségállapot*]![24]

The Committee also liked to pop out whatever remained of the utopia of the workers' state by the 1980s. The song that included the

24. The last word alluded to the Polish political situation, which in the album was covered by sound effects added later in the studio, to avoid censorship (Szőnyei 1992: 378–79). Other groups, such as the Control Group and Trabant, also dedicated songs to the recently defeated Solidarity movement. This was at a time when public demonstrations of loyalty, even the wearing of a Solidarity badge, provoked brutal harassment by the local police.

following excerpt was sung in the pompous manner of postwar official labor marches. The song was performed only at concerts; it was off limits for a Hungaroton album.

> Rise, rise, work awaits you, the factory awaits you
> Rise, rise, the office awaits you. . . .
> I quickly get out of bed
> Stagger into the bathroom
> I shave and I brush my teeth
> I don't think
> 'Cause I'm today's typical labor force
> I live in the slave estate of Békásmegyer[25]

The Committee's performances depended on a live audience for their distinctive spontaneity, visual effects, and interactive humor. The album *Up to Adventure!* was pieced together from several recorded live events. The music the group composed for their films was even more disjointed than the songs they performed in concert. They joked even with the label they chose to depict their output: "catastrophe music" signified an improbable and unique collage of free jazz, minimalism, reggae, and Central European pop.

Control Group (Kontroll Csoport)

The Control Group's performance concept, like the Committee's, exploited the dramatic potential in the contrast and collaboration of a female and two male singers (Hajnóczy 1983a). Whereas the Committee thrived on spontaneity and improvisation, however, the CG's success hinged on meticulously prearranged scenarios complete with complex multimedia effects. The succession of songs, interspersed with dialogues and projected slides, elaborated a particular theme or conception. The show called *Hystereo Polaroid Experiments,* for example, voiced the performers' "phantoms of desire and

25. Quoted in Szőnyei 1992: 380. In the Hungarian original the rhyming line endings and the incorrect grammar (*gondolkodok, lakok*) enhanced the effect of parody. Békásmegyer is a working-class/lower-middle-class suburb of Budapest known for its huge blocks of gray concrete high-rises.

horror." On another occasion the audience's phantoms were put on display: immediately before the concert, designated interviewers taped the audience members' responses, which the musicians conveyed in the course of the program.

If the Committee's image was modeled on a circus act, the Control Group combined cabaret with the features of an anarchist commando. (Let us remember their line "I am you and you are me / We are in the same army.") In contrast to the Committee's flamboyant visual imagery, the Control Group's color was black. (The female singer, Ági Bárdos Deák, posturing as a chanteuse, was clad in black fetishist clothing.) Their disciplined though energetic and emotionally charged music was not all that gave an impression of desperation and militancy; so did their preoccupation with death, war, and global annihilation. These visions were embedded in an indeterminate historical context: Orwellian images of totalitarianism translated into the everyday were blended with post-apocalyptic fantasies of a destroyed civilization. The ballad "The Unknown Soldier's Grave" evoked these themes with particular power:

> You don't understand anything but feel as if the earth
>   is opening beneath your feet
> You're innocent who's never even killed anyone
> No one talks crime here, don't try to make trouble
> Your reward will be if someone punishes you.
> Everything will be all right, my love
> Don't enjoy and don't defend yourself
> This ain't a life worth living
> Don't ask anything and don't defend yourself
> Destroy what destroys you! . . .
> You're an alien who's somehow got stranded here
> You don't quite comprehend the news
> Your mind is what your brain has left
> You don't think, therefore you don't exist[26]
> Your mind is torn in two
> Civilization surpasses life. . . .

26. A paraphrase of Descartes's axiom: Cogito ergo sum.

Other songs addressed the immediate present and the politics of music. The Control Group's poetics came closest to what George Lipsitz (1990) termed a cultural form's rehearsal for politics. The song "Music Is for Everyone" represents underground rock as a menace to the status quo, almost a rallying cry for something momentous to follow. The politically charged lyrics are sung to a light, jazzy, danceable rhythm:

> Every show is crowded
> Everybody's singing
> Music is for everyone
> It only takes a step
> Crowded place,
> It only takes a step to crash into something
> What is it that's only a step away from you?
> Your head is buzzing [*A fejed tömve van*]
> Everyone's quiet
> Every gun's loaded
> It only takes a step, it only takes a step
> A step away from you
> Music is for everyone.

The refrain "Music is for everyone" was borrowed from Zoltán Kodály, the composer who instituted an educational program aimed at making music a possession of the masses. Certainly his idea of music did not include rock'n'roll, only classical and folk music. The slogan was taken up by Hungaroton as a commercial logo for classical music releases. The song's message, then, was addressed not just to the power elite in general but, as Szőnyei suggests, specifically to the record company that refused to make this group's and other groups' music accessible to everyone (1992: 362).

The Europe Publishing House (Európa Kiadó)

With its all-male lineup and exclusive concern with the musical aspects of their performance, the Europe Publishing House fell closest to mainstream rock'n'roll. Still, their proclivity for experimentation with musical forms and sounds, as well as their subject matter and lyrical sensibilities, placed them right at the heart of the alternative music scene. (Both the Control Group and EPH were descendants of the pioneering URA and played the latter's repertoire.)

The group acknowledged the dominance of the lead singer and guitarist, Jenő Menyhárt, whose identity was inextricably fused with the lyrical subjects of his songs.[27] One aspect of EPH's popularity may have been precisely the powerful and intense ways in which his "personal history," as he put it, unfolded in the sequence of overtly subjective songs. Paradoxically, Menyhárt's almost masochistic sense of self-inquiry and his desperate attempts to mark a purely individual difference produced songs that were appropriated by the audience as a kind of collective property, their sing-along hymns. One of them, "Deliver Me from Evil," the audience almost always demanded to be the concluding piece of the event. The verses, set to a simple, declining, open-ended melody, spoke poignantly to a generation's alienation, anger, and self-hatred. The gloom of the song had an unmistakably Central European Kafkaesque feel to it:

> A bald censor's sittin' in my brain
> Eager to hear each of my words
> Someone's thinkin' instead of me
> Someone's leavin' instead of me
> I can't win and can't lose
> I don't care if I die
> We've bought into all the blahblah
> We now wear the dog tag
> We've messed up our language
> We've used up our reserves
>
> Death is not here yet
> Death is not here yet
> It visits us every day
> Faces and fears everywhere
> I dunno how I am

EPH reworked the punk slogan "No future!" Deconstructing history as a meaningful continuum of past, present, and future, punk

27. For a perceptive discussion of the relationship between lyrical subjects and performers in various pop styles, see Laing 1985: 63–68.

musicians popularized the ideas spelled out by postmodern philosophers ("Ghosts in the depths of time / Missing links," EPH sang). Therefore, the future, on one level, appeared unreal, a nonentity, as unreal as the subjects for whom this absence translated into a lost sense of identity. The future signified a void by merging with the present: "The future is here and will never end"; "The future has become the present." It became dated and anachronistic before it had actually arrived. Such a problematization of temporality on a global scale intersected with a special Eastern European sense of crisis: a daunting sense of backwardness in a society that had taken a dead-end route through history:

> We'll disappear like the last metro
> Everything's for sale
> but we've run out of everything;
>
> What's today has long been past;
>
> My watch says it's been tomorrow for a long time.

On another level, however, which became increasingly dominant in the group's later songs, the future appears challenging and exciting. This perspective was inspired by science fiction representations of the awesome, even bizarre potential of late twentieth-century developments in technology: "The machines wander away beyond the boundaries of imagination." This fascination with the future did not turn it into a site of genuine escape. Out of the tension between the fantasies constructed around it and the depressingly anachronistic and morally bankrupt day-to-day life, a playful but profoundly melancholic voice was born:

> It's gonna be good for us
> It's gonna be good for us
> We'll be making love in weightlessness
> We'll be traveling in the dust of alien stars
> And if it's better there, we'll be staying there.
> It's gonna be good for us
> It's gonna be good for us

If we turn into intelligent machines
History will end
Eternity will be a long moment
It's gonna be good for us
It's gonna be good for us
We'll lock our spirit into a bottle
I'm glad to be here
Since this is the place where gods are designed
It's gonna be good for us
It's gonna be good for us
Except that we'll have gently decayed by then
Neither can I protect you
Nor can you protect me
Not even sin can protect us anymore. . . .

Trabant and Balaton

"If the Ultra Rock Agency transformed my life, gave direction to it, thrust me to the ground, and opened my eyes, Trabant allowed me to hover above the ground with eyes shut, never letting me forget that they're of the same country, the same city, and the same historical era," confessed Szőnyei, the best local analyst of the underground music scene (1992: 382) Originally two separate groups, Trabant[28] (Fig. 3) and Balaton[29] worked and performed in symbiosis. A unique feature of the two groups' repertoire was that many of the individual songs were sung sometimes by a woman, Marietta Méhes, at other times by Mihály Víg, the male singer, guitarist, and composer of many of the songs. The songs' ability to articulate both the female and the male subjectivity challenged prevailing stereotypes of feminine and masculine. The unisex character of the songs underscored the common experience of women and men in this social group.

Trabant never gave concerts but produced homemade, rather

28. The name Trabant expresses the same ironic self-deprecation as the many jokes about the cheap little East German car ("I don't have a car, I have a Trabant"). Trabant appeared as a metaphor for the rough surfaces of everyday life in Eastern Europe in the song "Blu Trabant" by a Yugoslav band called Atheist Rap (thanks to Eric Gordy for showing it to me). In the reunited Germany, Trabant, like cigarettes "with the old taste" and "bread without air," became a revalorized marker of East German identity (Merkel 1994).

29. Named after Hungary's largest lake, a popular place to go for recreation.

3
Poster advertising Trabant. Photo by Nora Gruber; courtesy of Tamás Szőnyei. (Rock poster collection exhibited in Budapest, 1995.)

rudimentary recordings and circulated them among their friends. Balaton's concerts had the air of intimacy and introversion of a group of friends playing at home. Their overall musical/artistic stance owed a debt to the Velvet Underground, Andy Warhol's New York art rock band of the late 1960s. The shows took advantage of visual media in a way that obscured the boundaries between performance and real life. The lyrics, like the projected slides, chronicled the musicians' own lives, whereas their everyday lives seemed to have been self-consciously fashioned and stylized in accordance with preexisting ideas and images.[30] Trabant's politics of with-

30. Victor Bockris and Gerard Malanga's account of Andy Warhol's subtle use of images and portraits of the Velvet Underground could describe the essence of Balaton's live shows: "The movies were portraits of the people on stage. The people on stage were portraits of themselves. The songs the Velvets were singing were portraits of people" (quoted in Frith and Horn 1987: 112).

drawal from public appearance thus corresponded to the secluded world created and sustained by their expressive forms and media.

The individual numbers in their repertoire were strung together like pearls, each distinct yet similar to the others in character. They constituted a flow of loosely related, poetic narratives and minidramas. They spoke about the minutiae of daily life—thus suggesting that life consisted only of minutiae, not genuine events:

> He's here, though no one called him
> I feel his gaze but don't see his eyes
> And I don't know but remember I didn't
> understand what he was sayin.' . . .
> I move from the chair to the sofa
> I'd better leave early tonight
> No doubt everything's been thoroughly screwed up
> I don't know what may follow after this
> He's not attending to me
> I'm looking straight into his face
> Which always stirs me
> He says something but I don't get it
> It's too late and it's too soon.

The songs highlighted the precariousness of the boundary between the real and the unreal, the plastic and the authentic, the ordinary and the special. The music was unsettling: the predominantly soft, full, sonorous, and pastel-toned sound mixtures and the descending melodic lines were counteracted by screeching and faltering guitar riffs. Banal poetic and musical clichés were freely used but they became suffused with fresh significance as the songs explored the uncharted territory of everyday life and the fine texture of feelings, desires, and dreams. An unexpected twist in a poetic stock phrase, the insertion of an inappropriate word or the use of paradox abruptly destabilized the meaning of conventional pop rhetoric. The obfuscation of distinctions between the real and the unreal produced a special ambience, rife with ambiguity; a sensation of lonely floating in a self-enclosed space suspended in time. Isolation and estrangement were ubiquitous themes of the songs, even as the characters of the narratives were entangled in webs of intimate relationships:

No one helps, though I'm never alone
There's always someone with me
Who knows what's good for me;

This house may crumble for all I care,
it stole my time
The corner of my eye quivers,
it makes no difference
Still there's a moment
that mutes you
A tremendous feeling
but from here there's no looking back
She's draggin' me across the city
by private taxi or by bus
You can't fail to recognize
From where to where you're traveling
It seems far from a distance
and even farther as you go near
Pull your curtains together
There ain't nobody you belong to.

You must regret everything you do
Can't share anything without remorse
They get all your words wrong
And there's no one out there to help.

Despite the songs' preoccupation with private acts, feelings, and moods, one could find numerous subtle allusions to the geographical and temporal coordinates of these characters' lives. A most enigmatic Trabant song, for example, expressed a fear of global nuclear war in a minimalist text consisting of one line repeated over and over again:

The first is four,
the second is six,
the third is just a moment long. . . .[31]

31. "Four" and "six" refer to the number of years' duration of the two world wars.

The Galloping Coroners (Vágtázó Halottkémek)

In interviews the Galloping Coroners—the only one of the groups mentioned here that survived into the mid-1990s—like to claim that their hefty punklike music dates back to the mid-1970s—that is, before punk as a musical style had been invented. Ever since that time they have sustained a remarkably consistent profile and a relatively stable group membership. They also take pride in being the best known outside Hungary—and, let me add, the Hungarian rock band most subjected to academic research (see, for example, Milun 1992, 1993). This interest can be attributed not only to the uniqueness of the music but to the passionate theorization of this music by the band's leader, Attila Grandpierre. If the Committee's character was defined by the musicians' background in visual art, the Galloping Coroners' distinctive image was shaped by the professional involvement in the sciences of Grandpierre and two other members. Grandpierre makes his living as an astronomer and works also as an amateur ethnologist. He has studied and written profusely on the relationship between shamanistic folk music, poetry, and punk rock.

When I interviewed him in 1993 he denied that "punk" was an apt characterization of their music, but in the early 1980s—admittedly, to express solidarity with the emergent movement—he defined and legitimized punk as the revival of shamanistic practices. Punk, he claimed, returned to "forgotten underground layers of ancient culture" that had such "cultural impact and consistent radicalism" that they are worth "the attention of people in different fields of art. . . . Totem music, the music of shamanistic ceremonies, was truly a working, effective magic force for its creators, which led to ecstasy, and, through its force, elevated the participant's relation to himself and the world into a symbolic order," and thus enabled "the first step toward practical action."[32] Grandpierre gives no clue as to what kind of practical action this postmodern version of shamanistic music may prepare its listeners to take. His construal of a nexus between shamanism and punk—the pre- and the postmodern—hinges on an instinctual critique of modernity and its fragmented culture. Ecstasy, according to Kathryn Milun, is the central category in

32. Grandpierre 1984: 1.

4
Ecstasy at an underground concert: Tamás Pajor. Photo by Tamás Ligeti Nagy.

Grandpierre's shaman-punk ideology. She likens it to George Bataille's idea of ecstasy "as an individual experience of the transgression of limits. This exorbitant experience produces, for Grandpierre too, something like the sovereign subject" (1992: 14) (Fig. 4). Let me quote Grandpierre again: "The self moves from the real of subordination . . . to that of independence. . . . Thus ecstasy makes possible the experience of intimate unity with an embodiment of the forces of nature. In experiencing the harmony of a boundless sensate world, we find companions for our most personal feelings" (quoted ibid.). The discursive and the musical elaboration of punk-shamanism, however, raises another interesting issue: punk's obsession with charismatic figures—with superstars, heroes,

33. David Bowie has several songs dealing with heroism; his own as well as punk musicians' interest in the style and symbols of Weimar Germany and the Hitler era are other ex-

and leaders.[33] Grandpierre inscribes naturalness and authenticity onto punk radicalism: "All is artificial but we won't be artificial."

The Galloping Coroners' live shows aim to perform cult rituals that provoke the audience's active physical response with agitated body movements, shouts, and screams. Occasionally the band simulates pagan rituals with props (ropes, leaves, reed mats), makeup, hairdos, and bizarre costumes. (I saw them once with feathers attached to their naked upper bodies; Szőnyei remembers a concert when fish were hanging from them [1992: 436].)

The typical concert features merely a few lengthy sets bearing no title, the pieces following one after another without pause, verbal introduction, comments, or talk of any kind. The music creates a completely self-contained acoustic space. An apparently chaotic but carefully constructed soundscape is produced by the howling and screaming vocals, guitars, and an array of drums, timpani, and a host of unconventional percussion instruments. The group employs excessive amplification, fuzz, and echo to make a thick noise that obliterates the lyrics. All the same, it is worth sampling an early piece titled ". . . XX . . ." (read: twentieth century), which, along with its celebration of prehistoric barbarism, conjures up images of the apocalypse:

> I've been waiting too long, the snow's too deep
> I'm too happy, I'm too wimpy
> Now here's the time
> No more lost future
> There's nothin' more shameful than to wait in vain
> Nothin's more urgent than to rush
> To run into the walls with one's head
> If everyone's rushing, they'll crumble
> The silence is too deep, the mud's gonna swallow you
> Only the ravishing house of delirium awaits you
> Human corpses pile up to the sky
> As our century's towers

amples of hero worship. Besides the tasteless, though not serious, play with the swastika, some punk bands chose stage names evoking fascist rhetoric (Joy Division, New Order), and the Sex Pistols wrote a number called "Belsen Was a Gas" (Greil Marcus 1989: 59).

So let the new fire flood come
My goal of a fire flood becomes fulfilled
And lo! I'm here again
And the lumps of the earth will move
And the bells of heavens will toll
And everything, everything will come up to the surface . . .

Conclusion

The Hungarian avant-garde rock scene both rehearsed for politics—in trying out anarchistic values and beliefs encoded in a particular ideology and practice of art—and existed as politics by virtue of its marginal professional, social, and political position. The rehearsal neither constituted a consistent political agenda of social change nor served any strictly political movement. Even though these pop artists formed part of the wider network of the marginal intelligentsia, which included the active core of political opposition, the politics of marginality itself signified a shared condition of living on the edge rather than any kind of organized activity.

But then, this music did not exist solely as politics; it was also entertainment and leisure activity. The jokes, the allusions, and the whole discourse of punk/new wave would not have worked for a larger set of marginals had there not been a shared set of assumptions about the nature of the existing power structure, the meanings and possibilities of subversion, and the profound social and political crisis of Hungary and Eastern Europe. This commonality of values and beliefs constituted a "structure of feeling" (Williams 1977) that rested on collective experiences and interpretations of what it meant to come of age in post-Stalinist Hungary.

The musicians gave highly individual voices to the collective traumas, anxieties, and fantasies of their generation. In doing so, they became ghettoized, and they turned that condition into cultural politics and practices. On the most fundamental level, politics meant producing and performing texts that were directly or indirectly subversive. The musicians stepped not merely beyond the current limits of political decency but also beyond the conventions defining the range of themes, characters, and performance of popular music. The sustenance of creative autonomy called for attempts to establish an infrastructure, an institutionalized space to minimize the surveillance and control exercised by state bureaucracies. Embryonic as this alternative infrastructure was, it proved vital in enhancing the social and political pull of the movement.

Being political, however, had ambiguous connotations for most popular musicians and other artists in socialist Hungary, where, for historical reasons, the arts, both high and low, had always been colonized by the political realm. The state apparatuses viewed the arts either as potential promoters of the ruling ideology or as its enemy. The social organization of culture thus rendered the arts the site of political meanings, whether or not such meanings were intentionally encoded in the texts. The centralized monolithic control over the various art worlds—to which popular culture was considerably more exposed than the high arts—added a systemic component to the political perception and interpretation of cultural texts. The colonization and instrumentalization of culture thus led to another, more subtle form of constraint imposed on the artists by their audience, often precisely by their most devoted fans, who were eager to read and hear texts in an exclusively political mode. This audience was unique in its heightened sensibilities and special skill at deciphering coded texts—anything from pop song lyrics through film and literary narratives to political speeches.

Certainly the political framing of cultural texts by diverse social actors encouraged the producers themselves to use the art form to convey covertly political messages. Most of the time, such communicative strategies and skills between artist and audience formed the basis of subcultural cohesion and identities defined in opposition to the official culture. The artists, however, while thoroughly immersed in politics, tended to resist any political framing of their work. They felt it jeopardized their freedom and control over the creative process. The more a musician or an artist subscribed to the ideologies of high art, the more likely they were to define their work in terms of individual expression. A concern for individuality, in turn, entailed ambivalence toward the politicization of their work.

When I interviewed Jenő Menyhárt of EPH, he asserted his distance from politics by distinguishing what he called "cultural matters" from realpolitik. With a bent for paradox, he said:

> Everybody is more oppositional than me . . . including the functionary at the record company. To be oppositional, you have to be a realpolitiker. . . . The level of realpolitik means that you go out to the street to demonstrate, saying, "Down with censorship!" or write a song against censorship. Cultural matters such as this [i.e., the punk/new wave] are of no strategic importance in that they merely embrace and register an all-encompassing mood. These matters, I guess, speak to the ways we feel ourselves and the way we live in this place.

Indeed, the punk/new wave movement was not political in any straightforward manner. While the censors and the audience heard the music in a narrowly political mode, the musicians sought autonomy by pursuing the politics of obscurity. The ideology of independence from politics, paradoxically, promoted an intensely transgressive position because it enabled the musicians to survive and thrive at the margins of the pop music scene and at the boundary between tolerated and forbidden subcultures. (This paradox will be explored in greater detail in the next chapter.)

To sum up, marginality as a social force operated, first, on the level of textual production; second, on the political economic level through the creation of an infrastructural space; and third, on an ideological level that, based on the idea of art's autonomy, both ensured a sense of creative control for the musicians and shielded the community from more repressive measures of state surveillance.

2

"We've Kicked the Habit"

Marginal Identities in Transition

Rock musicians dramatized society's moral and political plight years before it surfaced in public political speech. Theirs was the first and clearest voice to articulate the insight that the Hungarian social world as they knew it was doomed to end. The role of this music corroborates Jacques Attali's observation about the intuitive and prefiguring, rather than reflective, nature of music; that "it is not the image of things, but the transcending of the everyday, the herald of the future" (1985: 11). As the problems of social life became more extensively felt and exposed, however, underground art lost much of its unique visionary and transgressive power. While its popularity and infrastructure were on the rise, it showed signs of creative exhaustion. Amid the expanding and increasingly multivocal public realm, rock music struggled to retain its own distinctive voice. The limelight was turning toward the revitalized and vibrant realm of party politics, where activists were preparing the ground for societal transformation, and away from artists and rock musicians.[1]

Most discussions of the shifting character of rock music and youth subcultures in Central and Eastern Europe treat the year 1989

1. Chapter 3 discusses the most relevant events in the political transformation of Hungary.

as symbolic of a well-definable set of political events that suddenly transformed the social and political conditions of cultural production. Consequently, the music is also portrayed as having made a 180-degree turn (Ramet 1994, Mitchell 1992). Few studies have analyzed the intricacies of the situation in which oppositional musicians found themselves in those societies. Too, most authors overlook the progressive steps in the reorganization taking place in the production and politics of culture, and so assume that social change actually occurred in 1989.[2] Thomas Cushman's study of Russian underground rock is an important exception. His depiction of what he succinctly terms cultural obsolescence and the banalization of dissent during the glasnost era is particularly relevant to rock's struggle in Hungary to remain unique and meaningful amid the shifting social and political circumstances of the time. Underground rock became obsolete because it was unable to remain relevant in the buoyant marketplace of ideas and ideologies as late socialism was nearing its collapse. In the Soviet Union glasnost brought not only ideological thaw but also cultural and political renewal. Previously a privileged site of oppositional consciousness, rock found itself merely one among many critical voices that made themselves heard (Cushman 1995: 231–36).

Hungary had no glasnost era comparable to that of Soviet society, since political repression had been softer throughout the previous years. But glasnost in the Soviet Union eventually went beyond the limits of Hungary's freedoms and thus triggered a set of political decisions and legislative measures in Hungary that led to the formation of a similarly vibrant public sphere in 1988–89.

"We're Gettin' Out of It All": The End of an Era

As early as 1983 the underground movement was past its peak. Its social world grew less exciting and more embattled. Most groups struggled with internal conflicts and experienced difficulty in put-

2. It is important to recognize that the pace of change varied from country to country. Hungary experienced a more gradual and peaceful change than the bloody revolution that toppled Ceauşescu's dictatorship in Romania or the peaceful but dramatic "velvet revolution" in Czechoslovakia.

ting out new work. They sought to resolve their creative and relationship crises by reshuffling themselves in new but often unstable configurations.

The innovations in outlook, sound, and style introduced by the underground infiltrated mainstream rock while serving as models for the younger musicians on the fringes. The emergent new styles, such as industrial and instinct music, however, rarely managed to empower their audiences, and the audiences, in turn, no longer inspired the music. The scene started to lose its subcultural cohesion, character, and popularity among the marginal intelligentsia.[3] Paradoxically, its influence became more broadly felt among the less educated, underprivileged, and younger groups and in the provinces. While part of the art and intellectual crowd dropped out as the shows lost their novelty and exclusive character, newcomers to the scene were lured precisely by the bohemian aura of the events.

In 1987 an unusual film, *Moziklip* (Movie clip), played in local theaters.[4] A sequence of short musical pieces, it prompted Hungarian pop musicians to try their hands at a recent arrival from the West, the pop video. Among their efforts was the song "We've Kicked the Habit," performed by the rock group Sziámi (Siamese), whose members included some of the old Control Group. This video stood out for its ability to capture the spirit of its times, the Hungarian zeitgeist of the late 1980s. Let me quote from the words written and sung by Péter Iván Müller:

> We've kicked the habit
> We're using nothing
> This is the last hour
> We'll be sober now.
>
> We're watching the time
> It's different from what it used to be
> It cares about neither saints nor humans
> except for a few men and a woman.

3. See, e.g., Feuer 1984: 106; "Club MM," *Magyar Narancs*, Nov. 8, 1989, p. 12.
4. Hungarian, directed by Péter Tímár (1987).

We're heading out
That was the last straw
We're watching the last watch [*óra*][5]
that's still going.

We're watching the time
It's shrunk! It's grown!
Everything happens
at a different pace than before

. . .

We're getting out of it all
So you'd better not count on us.

. . .

We're not afraid of anything
that might come and destroy us
Oi, oi, oi, oi . . .

The visuals accompanying the music were simple but telling: we get a bird's-eye view of the group members in a small enclosed space resembling a prison yard. The music and lyrics, in contrast, convey a whole new and different temporal sensation, a radical change of pace formulated in the paradoxical perception of time as simultaneously accelerated and slowed: "We're watching the time / It's shrunk! It's grown!"

Integral to the revolutionary experience is the actors' sense of accelerated time produced by charismatic events such as mass rallies and rituals (Arato 1994: 184–85). In 1987 only a foretaste of the revolution could be discerned, yet cultural and political ferment was evident. "We've Kicked the Habit" may be regarded as an apprehensive farewell to a whole era and to the underground music scene, which, as the lyrics suggest, was about to sink along with the decade it memorialized, the 1980s. How was this farewell expressed and what did it involve? Back in the early 1980s, underground rock songs were uniquely concerned with a postmodern theme: the temporal and spatial disjointedness of social existence in late socialist Hungary. While musicians articulated the malady of a whole civilization—

5. *Óra* can mean either "hour" or "timepiece" (watch or clock). The verse in which it appears plays on this double meaning.

anxiety about nuclear threat, global totalitarianization of social life, and so forth—this theme intersected with the motif of social and moral bankruptcy in Central and Eastern Europe. Many songs represented the experience of living in the here and now as anachronistic, and the future as an absence devoured or stolen away by the present. The Galloping Coroners' performances critiqued modernity by constructing "authentic" experience by simulating ancient shamanist rituals. What all these groups of diverse perspectives, sounds, and styles had in common was the need to address young people's existential anxiety and interpret their feelings and experiences in a wider historical context of schisms and absences. This broad commonality of philosophical outlook coupled with appreciation of a bold creative impulse was arguably the cement of the rock underground's collective identity (Kürti 1991a, Szőnyei 1992, Szemere 1992b).

The Siamese's song addresses the imminent social transformation of the late 1980s on two levels. First, it gives a twist to the theme of "the times are out of joint": what previously had seemed a stationary and familiar condition of disorder was now set in motion; it turned out to be shifting reality itself. Yet despite hints at peril and insecurity ("We're not afraid of anything / that might come and destroy us"), the song is not without a tint of self-satire and tongue-in-cheek humor. Kicking the habit—a barely hidden reference to the drug use that earlier songs openly exalted—for the sake of celebrating the last hour (of the year? of socialism? of peace? of a relatively orderly social world? of the underground rock era? of modern civilization?) sounds simultaneously somber and ludicrous. The rhyming clichés ("we're heading out" [*nekünk már kifele áll*]; "this was the last straw" [*betelt a pohár*])[6] and the puns also counterpoint fear and insecurity caused by the perception of a disintegrating social world and the unknown lurking behind it. The music sustains a similar tension between anxiety and relieved self-mockery: a saxophone's interjections of descending melodic riffs are comically exaggerated gestures of melancholy and hangover; a female vocal ensemble's reiteration of a single syllable (ha-ha-ha-ha) on the same pitch resembles the ticking of a strange and undependable clock.

6. "The glass is full now." The imagery plays with the theme of drunkenness and sobriety as it ironically counterpoints the suggestion of "kicking the habit." I thank Martha Lampland for making this point.

Second, the song makes clear that the coming of a new era inevitably undermines the foundations of an underground rock community ("We're getting out of it all / So you'd better not count on us"). The sense of rupture and finality prevalent in the songs of the countercultural era now becomes extended to "us," to the rock/art community itself. How can this swan song be related to the existential situation of the community?

Previously, songs represented travel or going away to faraway lands as a metaphor for troubled self-identity and a loss of meaning. Except for the two artists who initiated the art punk movement in the late 1970s and defected to France soon afterward, the music scene was stable in the sense that nobody left the country up to the mid-1980s. In an essay on cultural pessimism in the early twentieth century, György Lukács (1982) remarked that the Austro-Hungarian writer Robert Musil created a self-enclosed intellectual world, which Lukács sarcastically called "Grand Hotel Abyss" (Grand Hotel "Abgrund"). This metaphorical hotel provided comfort and a livelihood for its residents, despite or precisely because of its precarious foundations.[7] As an interesting parallel, Jenő Menyhárt referred in one of his songs to his underground art world as "a five-star mental ward." The music scene was vibrant and stable enough to deter musicians from leaving this "ward." A few years later, however, the motif of quitting the country or the dilemma of leaving or staying becomes a commonplace in underground songs and films. The metaphorical language and the philosophical treatment of the theme give way to transparent realism, as in another song of the Siamese from 1987:

> I can't make up my mind, honey,
> If I want hamburger or hot dog
> I can't make up my mind, honey,
> If it's worse to be here or better over there.

But leaving the country in 1987 was no longer a heroic venture, since the laws regulating travel had been significantly liberalized by then.

7. Lukács used this metaphor in his sarcastic comments on several other Central European intellectuals of his time, including Theodor Adorno.

Within a predominantly privileged social stratum many people received permits to stay abroad for extended periods to take advantage of scholarships or research appointments.[8] The legalization of multiple-year employment in Western countries signaled the shredding of the Iron Curtain. The immense political significance of the liberalization of travel was not limited to the ability to leave the country; more important, now one could return home without retaliation. This was a crucial aspect of people's altered perception of time, aptly expressed by "We've Kicked the Habit."

Yet another meaning may be attached to the sobriety that the Siamese celebrated: the opening up of the country to the West foreshadowed the end of another addiction: to the imaginary monster known as the West.[9] By lifting the barriers to travel and information exchange, Hungary took, so people felt, an initial step toward synchronizing its own history with that of the Western world, or at least with the rest of Europe.[10] Traveling back and forth without having to abandon one's home country forever gave a whole new meaning to the East-West dichotomy. The legal vocabulary of leaving Hungary changed as well: no longer did one "defect"; now one "emigrated," or simply left for a certain period of time. Inevitably, emigration lost the ethical and political connotation carried by the act of defection, especially in the avant-garde art world, where fame and reputation were tied up with either defection or premature death.[11]

8. Éva Forgács (1994: 9) argues for the immense importance of the billionaire philanthropist György Soros's appearance on the local cultural scene. Soros issued scholarships for researchers, teachers, artists; purchased technical facilities for schools, museums, scientific centers, and libraries; and enlivened intellectual life in countless other ways. Especially noteworthy was his support of dissidents and artists marginalized for political reasons. By breaking the monopoly of the state's cultural policy, Forgács stresses, he contributed to people's growing awareness that the ideology underlying that policy was collapsing.

9. I thank Martha Lampland for this pertinent observation.

10. The writer György Dalos (1991) set up a connection between the shifting spatial coordinates of Europe after 1989 and the respective histories of Eastern and Western Europe. With the elimination of communist systems, he believed, Europe would have not only a shared geographic space but a synchronized history as well. He wrote: "Eastern Europe has always lived in a time that was out of joint. Now this out-of-joint time got out of joint again. Through the system changes we are thrown into European simultaneity."

11. Among the emigrant idols of the avant-garde, mention should be made of the filmmaker Tamás Szentjóby (later spelled St. Auby), the rock musician János Baksa Sós, the theatrical director and actor Péter Halász (later founder of the Squat Theater in New York), and Gergely Molnár and Péter Hegedüs (later Peter Ogi), punk rockers and performance artists

The Spions' defection in 1978 thus marked the beginning of art rock, a new, transgressive local tradition of rock'n'roll. This tradition drew not only on the two artists' creative efforts but also on the brevity of their career at home, which lent itself to mythmaking. In contrast, the leaving of Marietta Méhes[12] and Gábor Lukin of Trabant for the United States some eight years later marked the disintegration of the scene. In my discussion of Balaton and Trabant I suggested that the boundary between the musicians' real lives and their musical narratives was intentionally blurry. Faithful to this artistic approach, Méhes's emigration was prefigured in the film *Eskimo Woman Is Cold,* which ended with the image of the heroine leaving for the New World on a cruise ship. Méhes played the role of this character, which had been modeled on the persona of her songs.

The Crisis of Marginal Identities

The search for spiritual renewal in utopian or archaic cultural forms became removed from the immediate realities of late socialist Hungary as mainstream society began to adopt the rhetoric of crisis. Pessimism and frustration set the tone of public disputes on social, cultural, and political issues, even of the traditionally optimistic editorials of the Communist Party's daily paper, *Népszabadság*. A journalist retrospectively put it in this way: "The political quasi-thaw . . . undermined the reputation of many bands that had based their careers merely on the politics of their lyrics. The critical attitude toward the state lost its charm. Some of the most scandalous lyrics seemed a communist manifesto in comparison with what one could hear in the mass media."[13] As a result, underground artists' and musicians' attempts to abandon their pervasive nihilism became more pronounced. Part of the problem was that this community had been

---

of the group Spions. Some of these artists resettled in Hungary after 1989. St. Auby, for example, became a professor in the Budapest Art Institute [Kšpzőművészeti Főiskola]. Those who died a premature, quasi-suicidal death included the performance artist Tibor Hajas and the renowned filmmaker Gábor Bódy.

12. I must note for the sake of precision that Marietta Méhes settled in the United States when she married a U.S. citizen, a means of emigration that was always open to women in socialist Hungary. Although no law formally denied the privilege to men, they could acquire this kind of exit visa only in exceptional circumstances because of their military obligation.

13. "Alternatív rock," *Magyar Narancs*, Nov. 8, 1989, p. 12.

glued together primarily by culturally and politically shocking representations and enactments of despair.

To pursue oppositional politics through popular culture was a vocation—in the Weberian sense of the term—a lifestyle, and a powerful source of collective and individual identity. The rock avant-garde's position and politics of marginality were jeopardized not only by the co-optation of decadent rhetoric by the official culture but also by the sprouting of political and cultural movements—some of them the forerunners of conventional parties—that challenged the existing power structure. The boundaries of the political hegemony were growing blurry. Along with other Soviet bloc countries, Hungary witnessed the formation of an increasing number of new or resuscitated cultural, religious, and political movements, clubs and associations, journals and magazines. Elemér Hankiss (1989) characterized the process as the self-organization of society. Merely by looking at the rich variety of the issues and sites of young people's activities gives an idea of the scope and intensity of Hungary's ferment in the latter half of the 1980s. Outstanding among them were the peace and environmental groups; those championing alternative lifestyles; university-based literary and social science clubs; religious groups within and outside established churches; political clubs with a whole range of political colors: nationalist, conservative, liberal democratic, and liberal socialist orientations; and more besides (Hankiss 1989: 126–27, citing Miklós Sükösd).

The erosion of the political system had two important consequences for the rock community. First, the boundary between what was approved and what was forbidden evaporated. The onset of the transition also called into question the meaning of and forms of defiance and difference in and through music and art in general. The margins that both separated the subculture from square society and connected it with other fringe groups ceased to define a collective identity. The most highly valued qualities of avant-garde culture—provocation, shock, novelty—erupted from the political arena, from the written and spoken word, rather than from anything as socially and demographically segregated as rock and the arts.[14]

The marginal intelligentsia dissolved. While rock remained on

14. As the previously suppressed movements and organizations metamorphosed into political parties in 1988 (Hungarian Democratic Forum, Alliance of Free Democrats, Federation of Young Democrats, Smallholders' Party, Christian Democrats, etc.) and began to nego-

the periphery of the unfolding social change, the transition placed many members of this coalition of subcultures and movements in the highest ranks of the cultural and political elite. Fellow artists in the previously suppressed high avant-garde began to occupy important academic positions as the socialist cultural establishment lost ground. The former democratic opposition entered what was to become multiparty politics. Its activists soon found themselves in local governments and parliamentary factions.

Several strategies emerged to reinvent opposition and handle the banality that dissent had become.[15] Among those strategies were redefining dissent and turning to religion.

Brave Good World: The Redefinition of Dissent

An enigmatically titled publication, *Jó Vilàg* (Good World), emerged in 1984 from the Liberal Arts Faculty of Eötvös Loránd, Hungary's largest university. The editors characterized it as a compilation by and for a subcultural group. But how marginal was this volume? The involvement of two high-level academics in the publication indicated the underground's reach beyond any subculture. The volume comprised essays, manifestos, descriptions of performance art events, criticisms, interviews with artists and rock musicians, rock lyrics, and the like. The inclusion of the best-known lyrics by the Committee, Galloping Coroners, and EPH demonstrated the music's rising cultural status, which opened up avenues for its political legitimization.

But where did the notion of "good world" come from and what did it mean? Was it just the perennial avant-garde gesture of baffling the audience by coming up with an entirely unexpected tune? Or did it mark a more profound change in the political situation and outlook of the avant-garde art world? Did it subtly foreshadow the fall of socialism and the coming of a "good world"?

---

tiate with the party-state, organized politics received an unprecedented degree of public interest. The semantics of the term "politics" changed drastically as well. Politics, which had had entirely negative connotations in the eyes of professional and working-class people alike, acquired a whole new significance when members of the marginal or established intelligentsia entered the political arena. As a most telling example, sociologists who commented on current affairs began to call themselves political scientists. For the populace at large, however, the popularity of politics wore away quickly.

15. For Slovenia, see Barber-Keršovan 1996.

The opening piece of the volume, headed "Let Us Face Realities!" lays out some central ideas and dilemmas suffusing—and perhaps confusing—the underground community at this conjuncture of social and cultural change. The writing is also interesting for its simultaneous use of irony, parody, and thoughtfulness. A mock-manifesto, its author's identity cloaked by the Russian-sounding pseudonym P. Lekov, it offers an astonishing motto: "Communism now!" The motto, invoking the slogans trumpeted by the early socialist state, is attributed to, of all people, János Vető, a painter and Trabant's songwriter, who wrote some of the most alienated and melancholy lyrics produced in this time of ideological uncertainty.

P. Lekov, however, has more ambitious things in mind than merely ridiculing a decaying political establishment. Speculation on the historical roots of what he perceives to be a worldwide millennial crisis leads him to criticize the goal-oriented, instrumental thought associated with Machiavelli. The world of isms—"ismism"—is dominated by this logic and must end, he argues. Now is the time to envision a good and peaceful world by rehabilitating noble ideals at the expense of "realities": freedom (even) at the expense of happiness, utopia at the expense of pragmatism and skepticism. He lays the foundations of a "postismist" movement, complete with a set of fourteen commandments[16] accentuating humanist and Enlightenment values with a postmodern emphasis on particularities, difference, play, and hedonism. Surprisingly, the concept of communism loses much of its parodistic overtones: "God is dead. Let's revive him! Not even amid the increasingly bitter struggle between the two world systems should we forget about communism! Let's voice our ideas and describe what we'd like it to be like!" (11). Underlying the usual fare of double entendre and exhilarating irony, one may detect here a naive openness to the future and genuine yearning for a renewal of values and a distinctive and worthwhile place for the individual in a "good world."

In the concluding essay, the editor, László Beke, expands the meaning and scope of optimism and a good world as an ongoing so-

16. In Hungary the standard number of bets at a soccer game is thirteen plus one; the style in which the commandments are formulated invokes the ten commandments of the Pioneers, the socialist equivalent of the Girl and Boy Scouts.

cial process derived from artists' daily activities: "*Good World*, as a matter of fact, has no ideology. It does not dream about a 'good world'—and in this sense it is not a utopia—but produces a 'good world' day by day, at times with strenuous effort . . . constantly reiterating values such as beauty, goodness, friendship, love, dynamic yet intimate human community" (136). Such statements have an air of the esoteric. Some Western critics misheard them as stale and banal (cited in Beke 1982: 134). Among the wider audience they had little resonance—all the less since the contents of *Good World* deviated only slightly from the macabre world of the old underground. Despite the title, most contributions exuded desperation, insecurity, dystopia, or Dadaist chaos. In other words, the codes—the signifiers—were too minimally altered to modify the signified in a way that changed their meaning.

Admittedly, even if the codes of a cultural text remain fundamentally unaltered, the meanings audiences derive from them may shift if new and compelling readings are offered to replace the entrenched ones. Beke attempted to offer such readings by taking advantage of the intentional polysemy and irony inherent in the rock underground's music, performances, and verbal comments. His innovation was to take at face value what audiences, so skilled in reading "hidden transcripts" (Scott 1990), interpreted as vicious irony. Debating with actual and potential skeptics, he maintains:

> What is the most important and so dear to us is that the Committee indeed express in their music their most sincere and heartfelt emotions, and these emotions indeed are directed at establishing a happy, creative, and productive community. Yet this is what seems so suspicious to all outside spectators. The same "new" mentality is the one sustaining *Good World*. János Vető and Lóránt Méhes were perhaps the first to recognize the possibility of this new spirit. At least, with their exquisite paintings and craft works they've been indeed working tirelessly for the good of the society; Jenő Menyhárt truly believes that we are again in need of handsome, noble, and strong youths, genuine heroes, "like the ones you see in the movies." P. Lekov, even while declaring himself to be a utopianist, suggests that happiness may be immediately achieved, right here and now. Ágnes

> Háy insists that it is exclusively up to us to make a "good world" happen. (1982: 135–36)

Art construed as dissent or difference needed to be recoded, or decoded in creative and meaningful ways. Beke attempted to steer the movement away from the narrow confines of resistant politics: "It is not our goal [to] criticize, attack, or 'expose social flaws'" (135), he asserts in response to a Western critic who called underground rock a protest movement. In doing so, according to Beke, the critic had reduced musicians and artists to singing, painting, rapping politicians. He argued for the aesthetic autonomy of this brand of art. Also, if resistance politics consisted in producing negative and estranged subjects, it no longer appeared viable from the mid-1980s on. Menyhárt put it this way: "We're faced with an incredibly decadent official culture. . . . To be optimistic and high-spirited today seems very deviant and suspicious. If you take a glance into any newspaper, you will read about 'the horrors of living in public housing,' 'the threat of a nuclear war,' 'worldwide famine'—that is, you may expect to learn about all kinds of misery" (quoted by Feuer 1984: 108). To be pessimistic amid the ever-present discourse of gloom, however, requires no ingenuity, he adds. Having attempted to silence the underground with no success, the official culture simply took over and reworked its perspectives and rhetoric. Menyhárt's version of a hegemony theory is of special interest. It indicates that by the mid-1980s the socialist state looked almost as subtle as its Western counterpart in defusing dissent by co-optation rather than by force. Later events, however, made clear that, rather than signaling a move toward hegemonic rule, as some observers believed (see, for instance, Cushman 1991), the state's increasingly elastic dominant discourse reflected the shaking foundations of the system, which no longer invested in the culture of control.

"Where Shall I Go Tonight—to the Disco or to Church?": The Religious Turn

The choice between disco and church appeared to be a real dilemma for many underground musicians in the mid-1980s, as a boisterous rap song played by the EPH testified. Two years after Jenő Menyhárt wrote the song, he claimed, half of the rock underground—the inner core consisted of about fifty people—chose the church instead of the disco. Several musicians joined the recently formed American-based evangelical Fellowship of Faith.

Jacques Attali (1985) assumes that music has the ability to illuminate rather than merely reflect the dynamic of social life. The EPH's song anticipated not only a community's qualms but those of individuals striving to fill an existential void in their lives. As the "disco," a self-effacing reference to the underground music scene, ceased to be a countercultural site, rock'n'roll lost its attraction for many of its former adherents. Meanwhile, public life was visited by a virtual explosion of ideologies and beliefs that stimulated serious introspection and a destabilization of identities. Several musicians' careers came to a halt. As Cushman (1995: 142–48) observed, countercultural rock'n'roll is serious play. With rock's slumping personal and social significance musicians explored ways to re-create their identities.

The powerful appeal of the Fellowship of Faith was evident not only in the underground art community but in the broader circle of young and middle-aged intellectuals, including politicians, historians, and psychologists. The cult's membership grew from 7 in 1979 to over 10,000 in 1990. The most widely read alternative cultural and political journal, *Magyar Narancs*, devoted an unusual amount of space to a bitter debate between the community's current and former adherents, between those who joined the Fellowship and those former friends and colleagues who found succumbing to religious authority and strict community life incomprehensible. While the editors of *Magyar Narancs* did not conceal their bewilderment, they aimed at a balanced and inquisitive approach to the phenomenon, which was so powerful as to crush friendships, romantic relationships, and even marriages.[17]

The sudden eruption of religious fervor was a salient issue in the alternative cultural and political community because it was so divisive. People who were once in the same boat found themselves

17. At the same time, some members claimed that belonging to the community had saved many marriages and lives. See, for example, Edit Szula's letter to the editor, *Magyar Narancs*, Mar. 21, 1991, p. 10.

inhabiting entirely different worlds. The debate about the Fellowship brought to the surface previously unquestioned assumptions about the meaning and role of group life, authority, transcendence, personal autonomy, and alternative lifestyles.[18]

The most widely discussed incidence of conversion was associated with Tamás Pajor, the popular lead singer of the punk/rap group Neurotic (see Fig. 4). In his documentary film *Rocktérítő*,[19] János Xantus, who belonged to the underground art world, set out to examine what it meant for Pajor to quit rock'n'roll and become a cult member. The opening scenes portray him as an unrestrained, emotionally disturbed young man on the roller-coaster of drug- and alcohol-induced ecstasies and outbursts of rage. We see him before a concert, smashing and kicking the amplifying equipment because it fails to meet his expectations. His life seems so asocial and destructive that he literally needs to be saved—spiritually and physically. Later he appears cleaned up, neatly shaved, and dressed in a business suit. He now sings with a group called Ámen, which performs at such venues as the recently renamed Christian Rock Café. Tamás now says that rock'n'roll is a satanic invention—echoing the most orthodox evangelist views—yet the music he plays is charged with the same untamed energy as before. He employs the same rock idiom, instrumentation, vocal technique, and body movements, but now he deploys them to celebrate the new focus of his life: the Holy Spirit, he explains, has become his drug. The film narrative exposes both the compatibilities and the contrasts between his old and new personas.[20]

For another charismatic musician, Mihály Víg of the group Balaton (Fig. 5), the encounter with the cult was motivated by a quest to make philosophical and moral sense of his life as he grew older. He

18. See the following contributions to *Magyar Narancs*, all in 1991: Róbert Zsebrák, "Egy volt gyülekezeti tag naplója" [Diary of a former Fellowship member], Mar. 7, p. 10; "Válaszol a Hit Gyülekezete" [Response by the Fellowship of Faith], Mar. 7, p. 11; Árpád Kulcsár, "Tisztelt Szerkesztőség!" (Letters to the editor), Sept. 11, p. 10; O. Varga, "Legfontosabb a hűség: Beszélgetés Pajor Tamással" (Fidelity is the most important: A conversation with Tamás Pajor"), Mar. 7, p. 12.

19. This title is an untranslatable pun associating Henry Miller's novel *Tropic of Cancer* (*Raktérítő* in Hungarian) with conversion and rock music.

20. Pajor's persistent use of the rock idiom while condemning rock'n'roll corresponds to what Jay Howard and John Streck (1996) discuss in the U.S. context as the separational strain in contemporary Christian music, which views music as a medium of proselytization and communication of "basic truths."

5
Mihály Víg. Photo by Dávid Lukács.

began to study the Bible and found "Jesus' texts were quite good." Tamás's conversion served as the immediate inspiration. With his wife, Mihály joined the Fellowship of Faith. For a few years he stopped playing music, but his infatuation with the Fellowship ended after about four months. A critical-minded person, Mihály figured before long that this Bible-preaching community did not live up to its professed ideals of caring for one another and for the poor. His antimaterialist sentiments were particularly hurt when he saw Tamás's car alarm system. The group encouraged members to grow rich and attracted many prosperous young business people.[21] Mi-

21. The Fellowship has strong personal ties to the Alliance of Free Democrats. One of the party's representatives in Parliament is known to be a member of the cult. Rumor has it that the party enjoys financial backing from the Fellowship. In view of the fact that the Free

hály did not want to belong to what he called the "Pharisees." The authoritarian style of leadership also alienated him. He groped his way back to the art community: "From time to time, once a year or so, I played at a concert, but it was far from regular. Meanwhile, I composed a lot of film music. . . . I wanted to return to the theater, something I'd always had in mind." His participation in Béla Tarr's idiosyncratic seven-hour film *Sátántangő* (Satan's Tango) not only marked his return to the art world but offered him a way to comprehend and represent aspects of his own lived experience. Yet while Mihály's life became absorbed in the making of the film, he could not break away from the Fellowship because of his wife's continuing devotion to it. He could not foresee the consequences for him and his family.[22]

Attali's theorization of music is equally applicable to film art: it is "a play of mirrors in which every activity is reflected, defined, recorded, and distorted. If we look at one mirror, we see only an image of another. But at times a complex mirror game yields a vision that is rich, because unexpected and prophetic" (1977: 5). *Satan's Tango* is a postsocialist cultural product: premiered in 1994, it had taken three years to make. The extended shooting of the film, its large foreign funding, and the eventual international critical acclaim rendered it a momentous cultural event.[23] Several members of the rock underground took some role in its production. Mihály played the chief character, co-authored the script, and composed the score. His filmic character and the story replicated his experience with the Fellowship and, more broadly, portrayed religious and pseudo-religious movements as a symptom of anomie in contemporary Hungary.

Satan's Tango is a black comedy of a people falling apart, the "death dance of the (still) living."[24] It portrays the life of a village

Democrats are the most consistent advocates of economic liberalism, one might assume, along the theoretical lines of Max Weber, a persistent "elective affinity" between the Protestant ethic and the spirit of evolving capitalism even in postsocialist society.

22. My discussion can do justice to neither the artistic and philosophical complexities of *Satan's Tango*, the intricacies of the mediations between lived experience and artistic representation, nor their interpretations. I will focus only on points that highlight the nature of Mihály's encounter with the Fellowship and his ensuing disenchantment with it.

23. *Sátántangó* 1994.

24. Rheinhold Zwick, quoted ibid., p. 7.

community in the most economically backward corner of Hungary. This village seems to be tucked into a corner of a land that time forgot. The German critic Rheinhold Zwick provides a fine summary of the basic situation from which the story departs:

> From the opening scenes it appears that something has fallen apart. Time, apparently, has come to a halt, and all of this foreshadows decay and disintegration. Just as life itself has slowed down, the contours of this godforsaken settlement are becoming visible. . . . With the breakdown of the economy, the inhabitants gradually moved out—months or years ago? . . . an invisible web of profound lethargy expands over the settlement. Everybody curses his or her life. Most of them still nurture grand dreams about some kind of new start; plans that usually amount to nothing more than gain at the expense of others. . . . Yet no one so far has had the courage to break out of this senseless waiting, of this state of being buried alive. (*Sátántangő* n.d.: 3)

Unexpectedly, however, a former inhabitant of the village returns, arousing hopes for a better life. He talks about a new prosperous model farm close by, which will ensure employment, peace, and security for the whole community. Having pocketed the private funds of some villagers, the man named Irimiás (the name evokes Jeremiás [Jeremiah], the Old Testament prophet) leads them to the new place, which, however, turns out to be more barren than the one they have left. And while Irimiás helps find them work and accommodations, before long he is revealed as a secret police agent. The exodus thus leads to the ultimate betrayal of the community's hopes and dreams.

The critics' discussions of *Satan's Tango* make it clear that the poverty, backwardness, and moral bankruptcy of this Hungarian village is only one layer of the film's complex message. The village stands for Hungarian society, even the art community itself—a society caught in a state of paralyzed waiting and yearning. Such situations bestow undue power on anyone with a bit of ingenuity. "This is the hour of figures like Irimiás," Zwick continues, "of con men, preachers who with false promises lead those who trust them into nothingness. They are followed even when they are not trusted because in the all-pervasive darkness they at least offer visions" (7).

Mihály brought to the role of Irimiás his own yearning, his commitment to and rapid disillusionment with the Fellowship of Faith. The Fellowship, he implied in one of our interviews, had a great deal in common with the villagers of the film. He depicted the Fellowship's leader as the real-life Irimiás, and he quoted Matthew 24:24–25: "For False Christs and false prophets will arise and show great signs and wonders, so as to lead astray, if possible, even the elect. Lo, I have told you beforehand." It is difficult to miss the autobiographical element in his ensuing comments: "Few people are capable of breaking out [*kitörni*] of their story. To digress [*kitérni*]. To convert [*megtérni*]. And even fewer can see beyond the story. It is only others' stories that they are able to contemplate with clarity and from a distance."[25] Years after his disenchantment, Mihály views the Fellowship as "others' stories": stories of people afraid to make their own decisions and choices and thus prone to succumb to a charismatic leader. Now he believes that human freedom is incompatible with a cult.

Engaging in art was once again a part of Mihály's daily life, as it had been when he wrote autobiographical songs for Balaton. His wife, still a devout believer, conveyed the community's resentment of Mihály's defection. The Fellowship was even more angered by his work in a film they considered sacrilegious and slanderous, and they subjected Mihály to constant harassment. His denunciation by the Fellowship led to his wife's psychic breakdown and the dissolution of their marriage.[26]

Tamás's and Mihály's stories evidence the profound disorientation that this highly creative group of young people experienced as participants in social change. Although people could opt out of the rock community in a variety of ways, religious conversion seems most crucial to the understanding and self-understanding of the musicians' community and its realignment. Conversions stirred a great deal of emotion among musicians and the alternative crowd in general. Elements of these stories came to be retold and debated not only in magazine articles and in the film *Rocktérítő* but in several of my interviewees' personal reflections. These narratives point to the dynamic of

25. "Szereplők a filmről" [Actors about the film], ibid., p. 18.

26. A curious parallel may be seen between Mihály's story—note the adjective "satanic" in the film's title—and Salman Rushdie's persecution for his *Satanic Verses* by Iran's fundamentalist Islamic community.

"identity work" propelled by the reorganization of cultural and political life and to the fault lines along which the rock community broke up.

Mihály's and Tamás's conversions have in common a desperate search for salvation from the underground, which for a time had sheltered them from a sense of meaninglessness in late socialist Hungary. But how might their disparate experiences with the Fellowship be understood? In some respects Tamás's encounter with evangelical Christianity disrupted his previous identity as a punk/rap rocker. But despite the wholesale change in his philosophical and moral outlook and lifestyle, the music he sang as a cult member remained fundamentally unaltered.[27] Both before and after his conversion he used music as a straightforward outlet for his passion, irrespective of the source and moral nature of that passion.

Mihály did not spend enough time with the Fellowship to accommodate his music to its exigencies. Seeking to regain his freedom, he resumed his ties with the avant-garde art world and used the film *Satan's Tango* as a medium of intellectual and emotional inquiry. For Tamás music became tied to a specific occasion and context. In semiotic terms, he managed to transpose his music as sound into a wholly different lifeworld without changing anything about it but its lyrics and performance context. For him making music served a purpose outside itself. Conversely, Mihály treated art as an autonomous cultural form, a self-sufficient activity and cultural entity; both a tool and a symbol of his liberation. For him the Fellowship's threats and persecution were in fact a repetition of the authoritarian control he had been socialized to defy as an underground musician in the culture of socialist Hungary.[28]

Alternative Subcultures and the Avant-Garde Art Tradition

How did a religious movement like the Fellowship of Faith come to occupy such an important place in the life of formerly underground

27. By "music" I mean music as sound. Certainly the music's overall meaning did not remain unchanged as a result of the radically different philosophical contents of the lyrics and the new purpose and context of performance.

28. Howard and Streck's account of a constantly differentiating Christian music scene in the United States includes the type of musician designated as "transformational." The

rock musicians? Why did religious faith and practices become the functional "other" of rock'n'roll at this conjuncture of micro and macro social change? Why was alternative religion a viable option for some individuals and not for others?

The youth movement of the 1960s in the United States, Steven Tipton (1982) contended, was a romantic successor to modernism and an expressive alternative to mainstream culture in that its ethical style emphasized self-expression, sensitivity, intuition, and emotional immediacy.[29] But it gave no moral rules to live by (232–34). This cultural contradiction was conspicuous also in the Hungarian rock underground, though it drew on the more nihilistic ideology of punk rather than on the love-and-peace collectivism of the hippies and was part of and a response to mainstream society's severely anomic processes.[30] Tamás's life before his conversion well exemplifies how the lack of rules in the counterculture could drive one to the brink of self-destruction. He was caught up in what the anthropologist Victor Turner (1990) has termed a "liminal antistructure," a breach of all structures of orderly life—the central theme of *Satan's Tango* as well.[31] The state of normlessness was both a condition of everyday life among artists and musicians and a theme they stylized in their art as the "human condition." This countercultural position, if translated into a lifestyle, may either lead to suicide[32] or function

transformational artist sees faith as a personal and permanent struggle, at times a failure. Art is used as a creative and autonomous medium to form questions and doubts and to criticize both the secular world and the church (1996: 46–49). Clearly, Mihály's assumptions about art's meaning and his creative choices accord with this position. In the Hungarian art scene of the 1980s, however, such a position—aesthetic autonomy within a Christian art world—was not available.

29. Drawing on Ralph Potter's analytical system, Tipton discerns four styles of ethical evaluation: authoritative, regular, consequential, and expressive. They are distinguished along axes such as orientation, mode of knowledge, discourse, right-making characteristics, and (ultimate) virtue (4).

30. Between 1960 and the early 1980s anomic processes were manifested in persistently rising divorce rates (especially in the younger age groups), declining life expectancy among middle-aged and older men, and a growing percentage of accidents and suicides within overall mortality rates. See Kamarás and Monigl 1984.

31. The history of Western rock music is studded with icons representing this type of existence: Jim Morrison, Janis Joplin, Jimi Hendrix, the Rolling Stones of the 1960s, Iggy Pop, Sid Vicious of the Sex Pistols, and perhaps Kurt Cobain of Nirvana.

32. The connection with suicide is nicely demonstrated in Paul Willis's (1978) ethnography on the hippie subculture and in Fred and Judy Vermorel's (1978) study of punks.

as a catapult into alternative ways of living. For Tamás and Mihály, the evangelical Christian cult embodied the latter option.

The somewhat forced optimism exemplified by *Good World*, the playful utopianism of P. Lekov, EPH's turn toward "posthistory," and Galloping Coroners' staging of the premodern are rooted in the same kind of anomie and insecurity that drove Tamás and Mihály to the evangelical Christian cult. Tipton claims that alternative religious movements as a class sustain essential continuities with both the counterculture and mainstream cultural traditions. Yet what these movements offer is more than the sum of their parts. A most crucial aspect of alternative religions is that they "lay out a relatively detailed picture of reality that is analytically complete in its own terms. So does every religion and in a more diffuse way every culture. But the typical alternative movement is remarkable for how well closed its reality picture is, how solidly it rests upon ritual experience, and in turn how solidly it supports an explicit, unified ethic" (233). In doing so, small gemeinschaft-type religious communities such as the Fellowship negate the structureless nihilism associated with the rock underground. Could this be, indeed, what musicians so desperately sought? Much as they yearned for an alternative vision and a set of ethical rules to live by, the total commitment the cult required proved as forbidding to some of them as it was attractive to others. Mihály's and Tamás's divergent experiences typify the polarizing and ambiguous impact of religious cults on the rock community. The powerful initial attraction of the Fellowship lay in its appearance of offering what the rock subculture lacked—a solid ethical and epistemological structure—while preserving its essential cohesive force, its expressiveness.

All over Central and Eastern Europe, the birth of an autonomous public sphere and the ensuing transition was accompanied by a marked rise in expressions of religious belief even as the prestige of dominant historical churches—Catholic, Reformed Protestant, and Lutheran—waned, especially in Hungary and Poland. As Iván Varga (1994) has shown, the conservative structure and outlook of the established churches and their various degrees of co-optation by the socialist party-state lost them credibility in the eyes of the large majority of believers. These churches proved unable to respond adequately to the pervasive anomie that systemic social change only exacerbated.[33]

New religious movements and sectlike communities, Varga found, were the only religious formations to increase their influence in postcommunist Hungary. They seemed to offer solutions to people's existential, moral, and social needs, particularly those of the young (116). These communities had been oppressed by the state; Jehovah's Witnesses had even been outlawed. In this effort the state often acted in concert with the large authoritarian Christian organizations.[34] As a result, the small sectlike communities had found political and moral support in the early 1980s within the highly secularized circles of dissidents, the democratic opposition (Broun 1988: 157). This may explain why in the ensuing multiparty system the umbrella organization for the smaller Christian churches, the Alliance of Free Churches, adhered to the Alliance of Free Democrats, the party founded by the democratic opposition, which had been concerned with the human rights of religious and ethnic minorities.

Despite the broad trend of growing spiritual interest, several musicians in the avant-garde rock community were surprised when some of its most charismatic figures embraced evangelical Christianity.[35] Taoism or Buddhism sporadically informed individual musicians' perspectives, without, however, interfering with their self-identity or creative outlook. In fact, as in the Western counterculture, these influences colored their art rather than subverted it. The militancy of fundamentalist Christians tended to thwart such a

33. See also Cipriani 1994 and Tomasi 1994.

34. Mention should be made of the so-called base groups, a movement of theological renewal and criticism in the Catholic Church. In the latter half of the 1980s this movement developed several branches that embraced from 60,000 to 100,000 persons in 4,000 to 6,000 groups, mostly in cities. They were particularly attractive to adolescents and young families. See Broun 1988: 148–53.

35. Music-based subcultures and religious interests intersected in numerous ways in those years. Some mainstream rock musicians too turned to small evangelical fellowships as well as to the established historical churches. Efforts to (re)construct national identity led to the revival of traditional Christianity and the rewriting of Hungarian history. A series of monumental, high-budget stage works such as rock operas and rock masses were produced in this spirit. Religious movements also conquered new urban spaces in the late 1980s: it was common to see foreign and domestic missionaries singing in the streets in an effort to convert teenage drug abusers.

seamless confluence of religion and art. They deemed rock'n'roll, as Tamás said, Satan's tango. Retreating from their intransigent position, most cults now reject not music as sound but the lifestyle and mentality associated with it.[36] This shift reflects a recent differentiation of fundamentalist Christianity, especially in the United States. The Fellowship stood out among alternative religious groups because of its authoritarian ethical style.[37] Unconditional faith and obedience to authority were acceptable for Tamás but not for Mihály. As the film *Rocktérítő* testifies, Tamás's conversion from a Neurotic to an Ámen musician was smooth because he experienced a structural similarity between the emotional effects of drugs and those of faith. Following Tipton's reasoning, we may say that the Fellowship translated psychedelic ecstasies into devotional ritual ecstasy (236). This function of evangelical Christianity helps explain why some former rebels such as Tamás willingly subjected themselves to the extremely restrictive ethic of the cult.[38]

Why did this transformation not occur in Mihály? Why were his art and identity as a person and a musician impervious to the doctrines and ritual practices of the Fellowship? Part of his resistance may be attributed to his family background. Mihály comes from an educated middle-class home. Defying authority—state authority, in this case—is a part of the family heritage of which he seemed quite conscious.[39] Consider how he introduced his life story:

36. Even the doctrinally most rigid separationists make use of the whole spectrum of contemporary pop and rock idioms (grunge, heavy metal, rave, etc.), tied together by lyrical homogeneity (Howard and Streck 1996: 43).

37. On evangelical Christianity see Tipton 1982: 3, 4, 282–86.

38. Tipton notes that a social class component may be identified in people's choice of an alternative religion. In the 1960s, young people with a lower-middle-class background were more likely to join evangelical Christian groups, whereas those of the educated upper middle classes were attracted to Zen Buddhism and therapeutic programs such as est. The explanation lies in the diverse outlooks of the social classes: the lower middle class's emphasis on authoritarian norms and values tied in with the authoritarian ethical style of Bible-based Christian sects, while the humanism that upper-middle-class homes tend to convey to their children is in congruence with the ethic of the other two teachings (232–45).

39. It is highly problematic to correlate musicians' and other avant-garde artists' family background with their membership in this subculture. Social class position does not in itself seem to be a predictor of a family's outlook, especially its political sympathies, its advocacy or rejection of authoritarianism. Some of the most prominent figures of the avant-garde were known to have police and even secret police workers in their families, whereas others came from nonpolitical professional or artistic environments.

M.V.: I was born in '57. Right after '56. My father was fired after the events of '56. He'd been a conductor at the State Folk Ensemble. . . .
A. S.: Did your father take part in the events?
M. V.: No. But instead of rehearsing with the ensemble, he tuned in to Radio Free Europe, saying, "Okay, let's ditch [*elblicceljük*] this rehearsal now because everyone's interested in what's going on." After this I. C. [a composer] . . . denounced him, and the next thing he knew, he was laid off.

Even more important is Mihály's long history of involvement with amateur avant-garde art movements. He dropped out of high school in the early 1970s. At sixteen he was sniffing glue and abusing alcohol and prescription drugs. Like Tamás, he was a "deviant youth," but his deviance followed the distinctive pattern of middle-class intellectuals. In the mid-1970s he joined a leftist commune. While he made a living doing menial jobs, he immersed himself in the politicized art world of young filmmakers, drama groups, and protest and folk musicians, whose oppositional character was forged in a climate of constant threats and persecution (see Forgács 1994). This art world originated in the Western countercultural and art movements. Some of Mihály's songs, such as "Tango," written in the 1980s, invoke this submerged legacy of the 1960s:

Peking Autumn[40]
Russian winter
Hungarian summer
Prague Spring[41]

Nobody remembers Paris, sweetheart
nobody knows what the matter is
nobody is interested because here
everybody is
everybody is a sportsman. . . .

40. This is a reference to a cult book of the 1970s, *L'Automne à Pékin*, by the French novelist Boris Vian.

41. The spring of 1968, when the Czechoslovak reform movement known as "Socialism with a Human Face" reached its peak in Prague.

Paris is over long long ago
because it ain't enough for anybody
nobody remembers the past, sweetheart
nobody knows why that was good. . . .

Mihály's life story thus gives us a clue to his later conflict with the Fellowship. Moreover, it illuminates why this conflict came to be crystallized in and through his art activities. Through his family background and his peers, I suggest, Mihály became socialized into a distinctly Central and Eastern European cultural tradition—the avant-garde art tradition—which construed art as an aesthetically complex code imbued with critical or subversive potential. In James Scott's terms, it operated as a "hidden transcript"; that is, "a critique of power spoken behind the back of the dominant [group]" (1990: xii). But art's critical function did not automatically drive it underground. And when it did, art constituted more than merely an oppositional code, the secret language of subordinates. It was a medium of interrogation and introspection as well, a realm removed from that of everyday life and politics. Despite its subversiveness—perceived as explicitly political in the suppressive culture of Eastern Europe—it always aimed at autonomy. It attempted to carve out a space of its own and determine its own traditions, conventions, and rules.

At a specific intersection of cultural and political change, rock music became incorporated into the high-art-oriented avant-garde tradition as a favored medium for the younger generation of bohemians—heirs to the movements of the 1960s and 1970s—who earlier or simultaneously pursued other art forms as creative outlets. Rock's shift into the center of the movement may be attributed to properties the high avant-garde lacked: immediacy, spontaneity, and wide social appeal. The predominance of these characteristics marked a transition from the ascetic modernism of the local art scene, as Forgács notes, to a more sensuous and subjective style of self-expression associated with postmodernity (24–27).

Despite this shift at the turn of the 1970s, the rock community continued to connect their music and art in general with a specific idea of freedom and autonomy, rooted in but not restricted to the discourse of high culture.[42] This leads us to several pivotal theoretical questions: What is the nature of art's autonomy? How is it related to the subversive politics of cultural movements? When and why is art regarded as needing insulation to be meaningful? And, finally, in what sociopolitical and historical contexts is the ideology of art's separation from politics mobilized as a source of empowerment?

THE (ANTI-)POLITICS OF AESTHETIC AUTONOMY

Aesthetic autonomy is a contested idea referring to the extent and nature of connections between a representational form called art and the social world at large. In new cultural sociology and cultural studies, aesthetic autonomy and related concepts such as cultural freedom, even the concept of art itself, have come to be treated as ideological constructs that serve to obfuscate, ignore, or even reject the embeddedness of all cultural forms in a web of social relations.[43] From this stance, the claim for art's autonomy is traceable to the Enlightenment ideals of the integrated individual self and individual freedom.

Marxist-leaning social sciences, feminism, constructivism, and postmodernism have dissected this discourse in Western social and political philosophy as the legitimizing myth of white middle-class heterosexual male social power. In the same way, the notion of autonomous art, along with the categories and institutional practices surrounding it, has been discredited as exclusionary along the axes of race, gender/sexuality, and social class. Assumptions of autonomy, so the argument goes, encourages hegemonic meanings and uses of art as either cultural capital or pure entertainment, since the concept, associated exclusively with Western high art, assumes and reiterates a value-based polarization between "serious" and popular culture.[44]

42. Frith and Horne (1987) offer a thorough analysis of the high art/avant-garde linkages of punk and new wave as postmodern cultural forms.

43. Some of the most eloquent critiques of aesthetic autonomy are offered by Terry Eagleton (1996), Janet Wolff (1987), and Stanley Aronowitz (1994).

44. See, e.g., Bourdieu 1980, Schiach 1989, Willis 1990.

A closer look at the debate about aesthetic autonomy, however, reveals interesting ambiguities and tensions. Deconstructionists often choose to debate with the most theoretically sterile and narrow versions of artistic autonomy. Furthermore, they tend to decontextualize the concept by ignoring the variety of social and historical conditions and settings in which the arts' aspiration for autonomy and its philosophical representation evolved. Therefore they fail to recognize instances when that aspiration constitutes a progressive response or a challenge to oppressive social forces. In state-socialist societies, the aesthetic ideology of autonomy and related practices served as tools to resist the colonizing attempts of the state and its crude politicization of culture.

Lydia Goehr (1994) remedies both failings in proposing "a delicate middle position" between the rejection of music's—and, by extension, art's—autonomy and an absolutist stance. She distinguishes between crude and critical approaches to this issue. Crude approaches mirror one another according to a Cold War logic. On the Western side, such theorists professed the purity of art music and its insulation from the ordinary world, encompassing all social and cultural domains.[45] On the Eastern side were social determinists who denied the possibility of free art in a bourgeois—and therefore presumably unfree—society. This brand of Marxism held that only in communist society could art be free. Artists, then, "choose in freedom to serve the society" (103), although, I should add, in the actual practice of socialism, society was conveniently replaced by the party-state.

The critical position states that music's autonomy, far from connoting apoliticism, is indeed the precondition of music's truly political character and effects. Goehr aims to reconcile "the demand that we be true to the political in music while also remaining true to the musical in music" (102). While this dual commitment is not missing from the best work in cultural studies, Goehr shows us how and why it should be harmonized with the precept, if not the actual conditions, of autonomy. She reaches back to German philosophical and political thought—to Romantic aesthetics, Hegelianism, and critical theory—a tradition largely ignored on both sides of recent debates

45. Although Goehr does not make this point, this crude position seems to inform most critical cultural studies in their challenge of art's autonomy.

on autonomy. This tradition evolved within and in defiance of the authoritarian political culture of Central Europe, under the threat of intervention by or surveillance of a weak and therefore overbearing state.[46] She construes autonomy not as a condition whereby music is separated from social and political forces but one that grants music freedom within those forces.

> When the critical solution separates out the aesthetic from the political, it does so only as the first step. The second is to demonstrate that this separation is necessary for art to fulfill its function, to serve in its aesthetic freedom the cause also of political freedom. In its original articulations around 1800, the doctrine of art for art's sake . . . rested on two claims: 1) that the fine arts had at last been released from their hitherto servile and ritualistic, courtly and religious, roles; and 2) that, now in their freedom and newly emancipated state, the fine arts could help bring about political freedom in the world. (105)

The initial historical conditions of art's emerging autonomy in modern society is thus not altogether different from the conditions in which the arts, especially the hard-edged avant-garde, existed in twentieth-century autocratic systems. Goehr also notes this parallel:

> When Sartre reminded us . . . that it would be impossible to write a great novel in support of fascism, he was reiterating a view held a century earlier. Though beauty is an end in itself, it nonetheless still serves as a "symbol," or "analogue" of morality and of the political good. Contrary to crude interpretations, there is no contradiction in holding both claims. The claim to autonomy thus has a history separating aesthetics from politics and morality, but also a history that reconnects aesthetics back to politics and morality once separated. (105)

The distinction between crude and critical notions of autonomy leads Goehr to duplicate the concept of the political in art. On one

46. Despite its excessive appropriation of French theory, cultural studies' approach to the relations of politics, culture, and issues of autonomy is predicated largely on the liberal hegemonic state culture of the Anglo-Saxon world.

level, she identifies it with manifest political messages; on another, she sees it achieved in and through art's own formal material, through the ways in which art creatively manipulates, subverts, and recombines existing traditions and techniques. The "truly political" can be captured on this second level. Replicating an Adorno-style argument without its high cultural elitism, she construes the freedom of art as the most effective form of resistance.

Goehr's claims are compelling and go a long way to account for the apparent contradiction between the political effects of underground rock and its valorization of artistic freedom and insulation from politics. Cultural studies have relegated art's divorce from politics to elitist and conservative aesthetics. While Goehr departs from this position, she too overstretches the category of the political. The (abstractly) political represents to her the ultimate value of art and is theorized as if it were located outside or beyond what Weber and Habermas construed as cultural rationalization. This is a process, integral to the emergence of modernity, whereby different realms of culture (religion, ethics, the arts and sciences, and so forth) become differentiated from a previously unified belief system (Habermas 1984: 237–42).

This aspect of modernity lies at the center of Jeffrey Goldfarb's sophisticated theory of cultural autonomy (1998, 2000). In contrast to Goehr's reification of the political, he is anxious to define culture at a considerable remove from politics. He borrows Milan Kundera's provocative statement: "The novelist needs to answer to no one but Cervantes" (2000). The political and economic pressure under which artists and other creative intellectuals work should be acknowledged and analyzed. But such analysis should not obliterate the distinctive histories, institutions, and practices of culture. Cultural autonomy, in Goldfarb's view, is neither the ideology of the elite nor a tool to permit the oppressed to be heard. It is a socially constituted and contingent space that enables intellectuals to exert an influence on the powers that be; it enables dialogues. Goldfarb's argument, like Goehr's, rejects any association of culture's independence with the ivory tower.

What remains unaccounted for in both discussions is the paradox of the intellectuals' role in totalitarian or authoritarian societies. If the dialogues of these intellectuals—whether apologists or dissidents, as Goldfarb makes clear—are more politically consequential than those engendered in the West, why do many of them avoid the language and rhetoric of *all* politics? In other words, what is the relationship between the actually existing autonomy of culture—its social space—and the discourse of autonomy cultural actors adopt?

György Konrád's (1989) idea of "antipolitics" is certainly pertinent here as a form of personal and artistic self-assertion in the face of institutions, collectivities, and, most important, the state. In a society entirely colonized by state power, he suggests, individuals who seek autonomy withdraw their language and philosophy from politicians. Artists' participation in antipolitics translated into a refusal to commit themselves to politics in what Goehr defined as its first (direct, overt) meaning. Antipolitics in art reiterated such apparently high cultural ideals as the complexity and autonomy of art's language, meanings, and effects.

The problematics of cultural freedom, politics, and resistance is highlighted in Cushman's (1995) investigation of the Russian rock community's discourse and experience of cultural freedom in the context of the transition to capitalism. Intrigued by what he viewed as the paradox of a resistant cultural movement shying away from the idea of being political, he scrutinizes the musicians' own language of self-understanding. Even more pointedly than its Hungarian counterpart, the Leningrad/St. Petersburg rock'n'roll community upheld the aesthetic paradigm of art's independence and transcendence of the everyday, and especially of the political: "the very ideas of politics and politicized music took on decidedly negative connotations" (93). Cushman asks why the taboo of engaging in politics was so powerful in the musicians' symbolic critique of their society and its institutions. A respondent who condemned the politicized rock of his fellow musicians answered: "They think that they are fighting against this but adapting such methods of struggle, they become the same. You see? This is interesting . . . when you begin fighting against somebody with his own means, you somehow grow like him" (106). Here is a powerful reiteration of Konrad's antipolitics. Politics in Soviet society was too corrupt and banal to encourage the musicians to adopt its language, symbols, and categories, Cushman concludes. Yet their search for an autonomous space was anything but escapist: musicians saw their distance from politics as potentially revolutionary. Only by establishing such distance could they envision profound social change.

This idea ties in with Goehr's view as to how autonomous art must first sever its ties with the political and social realities of its times in order to reconnect with them on another level. Her understanding of the "truly political" corresponds to what the Russian rockers referred to as the "truly revolutionary."

The Russian and the Hungarian underground envisioned art's social role and cultural freedom in stunningly similar terms. Freedom is a property of good art, Laca FeLugossy explained to me. Even in foreign songs whose lyrics he cannot understand it is palpable to him: "Language is an extra communicational channel that helps you comprehend the lyrics. But if it's not there for you, the performer's personality, the freedom in the music, or the secret, the oddity—these are the characteristics that give you a clue as to what the songs are about. Those who have such freedom will offer this clue. You kind of sense how the conventions are being screwed." Freedom lies in the ways an artist spurns the conventions of his or her medium. Freedom in art embodies the artist's freedom: the ability to be different from convention-bound society. Péter Magyar highlighted the sensuous and expressive aspects of this idea by reference to flying: Freedom, he said, "is a life feeling in which you fly and fully experience existence." Laca associated freedom in art with oddity and secrecy. This view rhymed with Csaba Hajnóczy's, that art's final meanings and effects are always murky. It is interesting to note that Hajnóczy, like many other local popular musicians, referred to high art to authenticate his ideas. Citing Debussy, he argued for the indeterminacy, ineffability, and openness of textual meaning in art. Ágnes Kamondy saw art as a complex form of human expression in which the conceptual and the sensuous, will and spontaneity, must be kept in balance. But she believed—and her reference is the Polish dramatist Witold Gombrowicz—that freedom should not be willed too much: "There must be a bit of Buddha and a bit of Tao [in art]" and "a bit less of the West." This is an important point, implying that art as an expressive medium has its own distinct rules, styles, and logics, which resist the excesses of human will. Ágnes's aesthetic concept also included art's ability to pose difficult and complex existential questions. She took part in some of the same countercultural movements as Mihály, but even at her most overtly political, she sought in her creative activities not merely defiance but a "complex mode of living."

In presenting these ideas I do not intend to suggest that people involved in this tradition have had identical views about the nature of art, cultural freedom, autonomy, and their relations to everyday life and politics. László Kistamás, for example, contended that the face of countercultural rock had been shaped primarily by its opposition to the party-state and its culture. In contrast, István ef Zámbó believed that his creative activity—both his music and his visual art—was countercultural no matter what kind of political system he pursued it in. His Dadaist provocations targeted certain human values and forms of behavior that he regarded as constants despite and beyond social and political change.

It would be a mistake to assume that the way individuals handled issues of art and politics remained consistent over the years. In accordance with internationally shifting political and cultural trends and climates, the avant-gardism of the 1960s and early 1970s in Hungary was far more suffused with revolutionary zeal than the postmodern and often obscure politics of the fringe movements in the 1980s. To nostalgically evoke the youth movements of Paris and Prague of the 1960s, as Mihály did in the song "Tango," did not imply an unbroken commitment to those values and ideals. Yet underlying the postwar avant-garde of which the rock movement was an outgrowth one can trace a few persistent concepts and assumptions.

One such assumption is that art, whether conventionally classified as high or popular, is a complex cultural form in its own right. Its meanings are neither transparent nor fixed. Second, art is a terrain separate from pragmatic everyday existence. Despite his cultural relativism, Péter Iván Müller articulated this stance clearly:

> I think it's very important that some rather sharp line is drawn between pragmatic everyday life and poetic life, which is a little elevated. I classify pragmatic culture as part of pragmatic life, which means that I regard certain enormous cultural achievements as no different from buying half a pound of bologna at the supermarket. And, conversely, sometimes the most primary acts of everyday life I consider art. What makes a difference is who does them, out of what, and how.

Even in dismissing the distinction between high and popular, Péter did not dissolve the category of art as a cultural entity capable of transcending ordinary existence. Art being a "primary act of everyday life," its meaning is not clear-cut or banal. In a conjectural aesthetic realm—which may or may not involve a complex aesthetic vocabulary—transcendence and autonomy are essential to musicians' artistic endeavor. To take the argument one step further, I suggest that this aesthetic ideology was integral to the avant-garde subculture's resistance and identity in state-socialist Hungary. The precept of autonomy served to shield their art from being either wholly suppressed or co-opted by the political, represented, as I have shown, by both the state and the consumers of the avant-garde.

This lengthy theoretical parenthesis should illuminate why Mihály, whose identity as a musician owed more than Tamás's to the local avant-garde tradition and its persistent demand for autonomy, resisted and eventually defied the totalizing claims of the evangelical Christian community. The community reproduced an authoritarian society, albeit based on principles that differed from those of state socialism. Mihály's entrenched ideal of cultural freedom forbade him to use art for ideological persuasion, whether the ideology was oppositional or hegemonic, religious or secular, emergent or residual.

Conclusion

In the latter half of the 1980s underground rock lost its capacity to serve as a breeding ground of subversive identities and a site of creative articulations of difference from the mainstream. As its creativity showed signs of depletion, the community expressed concern about its future and developed interesting interpretive strategies to keep rock from becoming banal in a burgeoning public sphere.

Several musicians' encounters with evangelical Christianity severed them from the rock underground, whereas for others its attraction proved temporary. For Tamás Pajor, the Fellowship of Faith helped reestablish a sacred realm once occupied by rock'n'roll. For Mihály Víg, the tightly knit community threatened the individual autonomy he had exercised in countercultural art. Underlying this divergence I detected different assumptions about the nature of art and how art may be used so that it can still resonate with their existential concerns. The instrumental versus the autonomous concepts of art led me to recognize the differential impacts of the local avant-garde tradition on the rock music scene. They informed musicians' creative practices as well as their discourses. Along with a growing number of studies across disciplines, this finding suggests the distinctive political meaning and effects of the paradigm of cultural autonomy in Central and Eastern Europe, which goes back to the region's authoritarian politics and its exploitation of the arts.

3

Experiencing the Fall

In Search of Places and Spaces

During the years 1988–90, the discourse of autonomy was no longer relevant to the community's self-understanding. When the prohibited (pre-1989) issues of the democratic opposition's formerly samizdat journal *Beszélő* (Jail Talk) were legally published in one volume in 1991, its advertisers assigned rock musicians and fans a prominent role in the toppling of the regime. At that point no musician found the politicization of music offensive. One ad in particular (Fig. 6) illuminates how many former marginals perceived underground rock'n'roll, along with theater and other art forms, as symbolic of political struggle.[1]

> I remember you very well. We've met in the theater, at concerts including the one pictured above. We've met in Bercsényi, Közgáz, the University Theater, the Kassák Club, the Ikarusz, and the Ganz Mávag.[2] We've met at out-of-sight places and later on at festivals, too. You were there when we marched on

1. Beneath the photo of Péter Iván Müller and Jenő Menyhárt as they played together in the short-lived punk band Ultra Rock Agency (URA) appear the lyrics of one of Menyhárt's most popular songs, "Deliver Me from Evil."

2. These are the names of underground clubs.

6
Advertisement for *Beszélő*.

March 15.[3] And certainly you were with us in the theater of Kaposvár.[4]

These past ten years have fled. No need for you to say that you knew all along that just a few years after the banned gigs of the '80s, we'd have no uninvited guests at our gatherings, such as informers and the secret police. . . .

If you look into the old issues [of *Beszélő*] you'll find it incredible that we're no longer to be punished for our clandestine thoughts and we can express them freely. Unbelievable as it may seem, you'll realize that all those gatherings, marches, all the

3. On March 15 Hungarians commemorate the outbreak of the failed 1848 Bourgeois Revolution and War for Independence from Hapsburg rule. The honoring of this anniversary was suppressed by the People's Republic because of its alleged nationalist and anti-Soviet overtones.

4. Kaposvár—that is, the Kaposvári Csiky Gergely Színház—was celebrated for its artistically innovative and politically charged performances. Along with several other pro-

applause, all the words to those songs, and the secretly or semi-legally propagated texts helped to attain our freedoms today.

In fact, the association of dissident intellectuals and artists came to an end as the landslide began. Consumers of the marginal culture of the mid-1980s could enjoy a Committee concert in Budapest on a Saturday night, say, drive to Kaposvár for a theatrical premier on Sunday, and occasionally borrow or buy an issue of *Beszélő* from the regularly raided underground store of the democratic opposition. A few years later, however, this lifestyle dissipated. As we have seen, the underground art world came to be split between the bohemians and the emerging group of active politicians. Increasingly separate from politics per se, alternative cultural movements multiplied, broke up, branched off. Ideologies and beliefs were swiftly embraced and often just as abruptly discarded, producing conflicts and tumult within and across various elective communities.

Writing About Transition: Narratives, Voices, Perspectives

Even as I emphasize the gradualness of Hungary's socioeconomic and political transition from state socialism to a liberal market-based system, it must also be recognized that social change gained momentum between 1988 and 1990. A harbinger of political change could be heard in the Siamese's song "We've Kicked the Habit." Exciting and charismatic events took place all over Central and Eastern Europe, and they were lived less as a process than as a genuine revolution, however peaceful, "quiet," and "bloodless" (Garton Ash 1989, Arato 1994).[5] In fact, Hungarians most commonly speak of "regime change" (*rendszerváltás*) rather than "transition" (*átmenet, átalakulás*),

vincial theaters, Kaposvár revitalized contemporary Hungarian theater, dominated by the conventional performances and often corrupt leadership of major Budapest theaters. Kaposvár was also unique in forging a cohesive and loyal community devoted entirely to its artistic activity.

5. Timothy Garton Ash's panoramic report of the events of 1988 that gave him a sense of an impending revolution is worth quoting here:

> Eight years after the birth of Solidarity, occupation strikes once again spread across Poland. The workers' first demand is: Solidarity. On the twentieth anniversary of the

the word used by Western journalists and academics. While admittedly a change of systems is not necessarily a revolution (Arato 1994: 193–203), for my purposes the distinction is not relevant. Both terms refer to what I emphasize here—the relative radicalism, comprehensiveness, and short time frame of certain processes associated with the transformation. Most of these processes contributed to the dismantling of state socialism rather than to the building of a new system. Therefore, in a sense, they constitute the relatively less problematic and more easily graspable aspect of social transition.[6]

A most intriguing but daunting question about this short era concerns the connections between the political transition and the underground community.[7] What did the exchange of systems—the political, the economic, the legal—actually mean for cultural producers and their audience? What kind of narratives provide a context or a frame for understanding the reorganization of popular culture?

Soviet invasion, ten thousand Czechs march through the streets of Prague, chanting "Dubček"! and "Freedom!" With official permission some 40,000 people demonstrate in Budapest—against the policies of a neighboring socialist state. Without official permission, more than half a million Czechs and Slovaks sign a petition for religious freedom. The Protestant churches in East Germany try to praise the recent policies in the Soviet Union but are censored by the state. The Polish government spokesman invites himself to visit Radio Free Europe. A Hungarian politburo member says he has "no arguments in principle for the one-party system." (1989: 218–19)

6. Kennedy (1994) and Meštrovic; (1993) take issue with the teleological frame of discussion about the Central and Eastern European transition, which assumes a well-defined point of departure and destination for social change in the region: from plan to market, from dictatorship to democracy, from ideology to reason. From a narrower point of view, however, the process of social transition integral to the dismantling of the socialist system may be more transparent than the processes and structures relevant to postcommunist reorganization.

7. András Körösényi (1992) identifies six stages in the fall of the political system: (1) 1985–87: the "golden age of political reformism," characterized by reformist claims in both official and unofficial public spheres. (2) Fall 1987–Spring 1988: emergence of political opposition with organized mass meetings. (3) May 1988–January 1989: the fall of General Secretary János Kádár, proliferation of mass meetings, lifting of censorship, establishment of new political parties and revival of old ones. (4) January–June 1989: Reassessment of the events of 1956, "counterrevolution" becomes "national uprising." (5) June–October 1989: reburial and rehabilitation of Imre Nagy, prime minister of the 1956 revolution, executed in 1958; the Communist Party, after negotiations with the opposition to review criminal law, dissolve Workers' Militia (the party's private army), and amend the Constitution, splits up into reform and hard-line splinters. (6) October 1989–March 1990: power vacuum until parliamentary elections in April.

From which actors' perspectives can this complex story most appropriately be told? How can a narrative and an analytical approach be combined to the best effect when every domain of social life was in a state of flux?

"When actors describe their action as revolution," Andrew Arato argues, "they are generally referring to the coexistence of experience, event, and structural change" (1994: 185). Arato distinguishes between the cognitive-objective level of interpretation, which enables external observers to study both structures and events, and the phenomenological-experiential level, which recognizes the actors' point of view as they make sense of their actions.[8] Most chroniclers of transition have ignored the latter, since they tacitly assumed that insiders had very limited or epistemologically problematic access to the "story" to be told. Yet I would like to show that rock musicians and other artists were particularly insightful providers of experiential observations, first, because their public identity and significance as social actors subtly changed as the events unfolded, and second, because, in articulating their position, sentiments, and visions, they used the medium of art—music, visual and verbal images, and symbolic acts.

Rock Musicians and the Change in Regime

The scenarios of transition offered considerably more visibility to rock music and musicians in some countries of the former Soviet bloc than in Hungary. Let us see how rock musicians' plight intersected with the *Wende* (upheaval, the East Germans' term for social transition) in the German Democratic Republic and Czechoslovakia.[9] Over the summer and fall of 1989, the massive flight of young East Germans to West Germany through Hungary, which had opened its borders with

8. Arato adds two more levels to his theory: third is the hermeneutic level, on which discursive connections are made between a specific revolution and the tradition that it regards as its own; finally, the legal normative level deals with the extent and procedures through which one legal order is replaced by another.

9. My choice of Czechoslovakia and East Germany for this brief comparison is based on the facts that both countries are in many ways culturally similar to Hungary and each has a fairly well developed rock music life, yet state-socialist policies concerning youth culture differed among the three countries.

Austria that year, highlighted the hypocrisy and cynicism of the regime of Erich Honecker. The political leadership continued to be silent about these new developments in the face of daily reports by West German television, which was accessible to East Germans as well. (As in Romania, live broadcasts of clashes between oppositional and government forces actively influenced the outcome of the events.) The antigovernment protests that toppled the party-state in ten weeks mobilized many prominent rock musicians (Wicke 1992: 196–99, Leitner 1994: 19–21).[10] Their previous regimentation by a centralized entertainment industry, as Wicke argues, explains why at the moment of crisis they were able to act collectively and thus intervene in the course of events.

The so-called Velvet Revolution in Czechoslovakia treated rock music as a symbol of resistance and "an island of independent expression" (Mitchell 1992: 189), which was stifled during the twenty-one years of Gustav Husák's government. This government ousted many varieties of African-American music from the media. It repeatedly banned the Jazz Section of the Musicians' Association (Jazzova Sekce Svazu Hudebniku), comprising rock and jazz musicians, and harassed, even imprisoned several of its prominent members. Nostalgically reenacting the Prague Spring of 1968, the festive events of 1989—elections and antiracist festivals—created a rare and virtually seamless unity between the politics of art, popular culture, and the state's cultural policies. Václav Havel, long an advocate of avant-garde rock music, played a major role in this invigorating situation. In 1990 he appointed the famed American maverick musician Frank Zappa[11] as a special adviser on trade, culture, and tourism to the Czech government; pop musicians and disc jockeys took their places in the administration of the Civic Forum. It was no less extravagant of Havel to sponsor a free concert by the Rolling Stones in Prague's

10. Wicke (1992) provides the most detailed account of rock musicians' contribution to the collapse of the GDR, but its accuracy is questionable. Wicke is mistaken in suggesting that the New Forum (Neue Forum), the association of dissident East German intellectuals, was founded by rock musicians. Olaf Leitner's version of the story acknowledges the rock musicians' political activism without any hint of a connection between them and the New Forum.

11. Several generations of music fans in Czechoslovakia celebrated Zappa as the symbol of freedom. Touring the country in 1990, he was received with a tumult of adulation that surprised even him (PBS-NPR radio program on Frank Zappa, May 30, 1996).

7
Poster: "Koncertre! Koncertre!" Photo by Nora Gruber; courtesy of Tamás Szőnyei. (Rock poster collection exhibited in Budapest, 1995.)

Spártákiadni Stadium and invite another icon of the counterculture, the New York musician Lou Reed (ibid.: 190). In the celebration of the end of communist rule, rock not only figured as a symbol of dissident art and politics but provided an acoustic background and a carnivalesque face to the political transformations in Czechoslovakia.[12]

Taking the City

Musicians were not so prominent in the events of 1988–90 in Hungary as they were in Czechoslovakia and East Germany, yet they articulated, celebrated, and in a sense performed what people talked about as "history in the making." Arguably, state socialism was not dismantled merely as a result of the Opposition Roundtable's negotiations or even of mass rallies. Even during these more tumultuous times, underground artists' creative practices played a part in the process.

One major contribution involved the visual media and the imaginative expropriation of urban spaces. Perhaps more than the songs themselves, posters advertising the rock and art events of 1989–90 give us a clue as to how musicians felt about the transition. A recurring pattern discernible in these posters is the humorous or iconoclastic use of what had been the sacred symbols of the old regime. One poster (Fig. 7) depicts a well-known statue of a male worker passionately bending forward, as if marching at a demonstration, waving a flag and shouting. The huge bronze figure enjoyed high visibility at Budapest's

12. For a detailed account, see Mitchell 1992.

8
Poster: "Ostblock Punk'n'Roll." Photo by Nora Gruber; courtesy of Tamás Szőnyei. (Rock poster collection exhibited in Budapest, 1995.)

Hősök tere (Heroes' Square), where state-organized mass festivities and May Day marches were held. Now the figure reappears on the poster passionately communicating a new slogan: "To the concert! To the concert!" written over the statue's head in red block letters.[13] A more solemn poster announces in German (commonly understood in Central Europe) a Budapest underground concert (Fig. 8). Above " Ostblock Punk'n'Roll" we see a torn white star on a red background. The message is transparent: the empire has been fatally wounded; the familiar red star of the socialist system has bled to death.

On another poster (Fig. 9) a happy clown invites viewers to a ball held by the Alliance of Free Democrats, where a popular under-

13. The statue was inspired by a poster designed in 1919 by the avant-garde artist Béla Uitz and bore the title "To Arms! To Arms!" (*Fegyverbe! Fegyverbe!*). The bronze figure became a target of jokes even during socialism. Since it bent in the direction of the nearest cross street, its name was said to be "To Damjanich Street!"

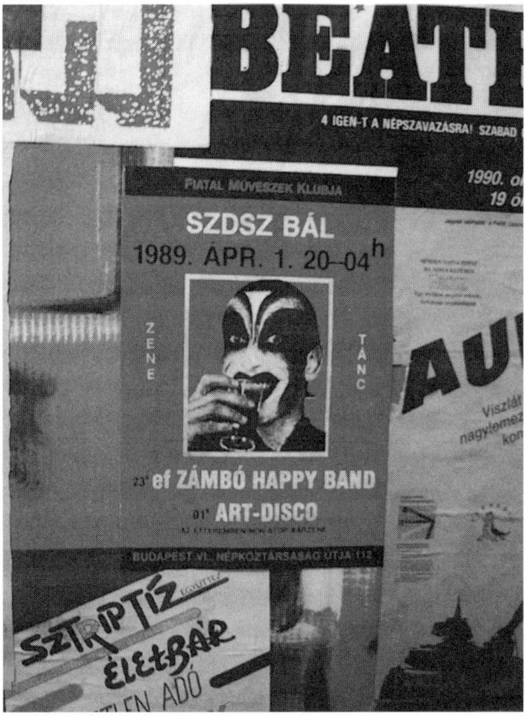

9
Poster: Alliance of Free Democrats ball. Photo by Nora Gruber; courtesy of Tamás Szőnyei. (Rock poster collection exhibited in Budapest, 1995.)

ground band (the ef Zámbó Happy Band) will provide music to dance to. Finally, EPH's poster (Fig. 10) bears the title "Vote for Me '89."[14] In the upper half of the picture, a smiling and waving Jenő Menyhárt masquerades as a politician. In the lower half, the other members of EPH loom above the "masses," who appear in the dual roles of concert audience and voters for the rock star. Jenő told me that when the picture was designed (originally as an album cover in 1988), no one yet anticipated the arrival of a multiparty system two years later. A rock star calling his audience to vote for him appeared subversively funny. These posters, which covered the city in 1989, turned out to be precursors of the posters put up for the first real

14. The album took its title from a song originally composed and performed by the Ultra Rock Agency as early as 1981. A hilarious satire operating on multiple levels, it ridicules the theatricality and manipulation inherent in Western parliamentary practices by collapsing this domain with the explicitly seductive star machinery of rock'n'roll and by reference to Soviet bloc politics. See the comments on this song in Chapter 1.

10
Poster: EPH's "Vote for Me." Photo by Nora Gruber; courtesy of Tamás Szőnyei. (Rock poster collection exhibited in Budapest, 1995.)

election campaign in 1990. Rock had jokingly intuited the major political events of the next few years.

The posters convey a characteristic and short-lived mood prevalent in the art community. László Kiss, another musician in EPH, remembers thus:

> These transformations were really grandiose! For the first time in my life I felt that, well, at last, something on a truly historical scale was happening to me. How cool and exciting! But at that very moment I sensed that the excitement would be momentary and the good side of this whole thing would last only a short while. . . . Our friend András Szirtes[15] had a rental apartment at

15. András Szirtes is an internationally acclaimed avant-garde filmmaker who has been working for the Balázs Béla Film Studio, where several rock-related experimental low-budget projects originated or came to be sponsored.

> the corner of Deák Square and Dohány Street,[16] up in the dome of the building. And Szirtes put out a huge sign up in the facade of the dome that read: SZIRTES FILM. When I first saw this, I felt exhilarated because at similar spots in other cities you see the neon sign of SONY or something like that. And here we have SZIRTES FILM! . . . But I was also aware that as soon as the sign got removed, everything here would become crappy again.

László's memory of the huge sign advertising a barely known experimental filmmaker is of symbolic significance. It speaks to the intense yet ambivalent feelings with which underground musicians invested the social transition.[17] First, discernible in this story is people's initial joy over having history come alive—a powerful reversal of the pervasive sense throughout the 1980s of a dead or lost history. This joy and excitement, even if temporarily, linked members of the former underground community to the larger collectivity of Hungarian—or even Central European—citizens. Before new boundaries and barriers of hostility had arisen between social and ethnic groups, political movements and parties, and nation-states, previous definitions had lost their validity. This suspension of existing institutional and group boundaries, László's story suggests, was immensely empowering.

Second, putting out the huge sign SZIRTES FILM was an act of taking the city; of using its thus far unavailable prominent spaces by the avant-garde art community to boldly assert itself and its claim for visibility in the new postcommunist society. The act reflected these artists' yearning for what P. Lekov had expressed a few years earlier in his "postismist" manifesto: a no longer marginal but distinct identity and presence in the larger community. Power vacuums such as the one resulting from this revolution particularly favored such symbolic self-assertions.

Third, the sign SZIRTES FILM, placed at this most prominent spot in the bustling city center, points beyond the plight of local artists

16. A vibrant area in the city center.

17. Of course, one should bear in mind that this memory is inevitably skewed, as all memories are. In the rest of the interview László disclosed considerable disillusionment with the long-term effects of the transition, so I assume the picture he projected of his perception of the events of 1989 was gloomier and more ambivalent than the way he had actually felt at the time.

freed from communist shackles. The sign enacts the ultimate, perhaps narcissistic utopia of the avant-garde artist: the aspiration to fame and prominence without sacrificing individuality at the altar of mass society's dictates. From this perspective, the distinction between the outgoing state-defined mass culture and the incoming one shaped by the global marketplace is erased. For the short time while the sign was up, László and his fellow artists could claim Budapest as their own in a way not possible for their counterparts in Tokyo, London, or New York.

One might ask why members of the underground asserted their presence in the larger community by competing with conventional neon signs in the city. To be sure, Szirtes as an artist could have used other signs of identity, such as the national flag or the Star of David, to greet the end of the one-party system. Can one legitimately attribute such complex meanings to a self-promoting gag? I argue that the unconventional use of urban spaces as a mode of self-expression followed integrally from the underground's close and intimate ties to the city of Budapest and to big-city culture in general.[18]

The City: A Metaphor of Belonging and Estrangement

A rapidly growing literature has addressed the connections between space, place, national, ethnic, and subcultural communities and their cultural identities (Clifford 1992, Stokes 1994, Lipsitz 1994, Slobin 1993, Chamber 1994, Boym 1994). More conventional analyses emphasize a homology or correspondence between a physical space or structure and the sense of identity within a subcultural, national, or ethnic community (for music, see, for example, Robinson et al. 1991, Wallis and Malm 1984, Survilla 1994, Bahry 1994). Analyses written in a more postmodern vein, especially those concerned with issues of globalization, urban culture, and national and ethnic movements, problematize the strict correspondence between places, communities, and cultural identities. The dislocations resulting from massive

18. Cushman's discussion of the Leningrad/St. Petersburg rock counterculture also underscores the importance of the city as a major source of the musicians' identity. He offers a fine analysis of an extraordinary art event—the use of one of the bridges over the river Neva for an exhibition—to illustrate how the counterculture subverted the ordinary organization of space and time in that city (1995: 172–80).

migrations, a globalized economy and culture industry, and multicultural populations within the boundaries of modern nation-states have made increasingly visible the socioculturally constructed nature of what might appear to be biologically, geographically, or demographically given entities: ethnicity, nation, generation, and so forth. And since communities can be imagined rather than confined to territorial spaces (Anderson 1991), cultural identities should be construed as composite and contingent, often translocal (Slobin 1993, Stokes 1994, Cohen 1994, Straw 1991, Lipsitz 1994).

An increasing amount of work in cultural geography deals with the city and views it as the penultimate site and symbol of modernity. Here, too, the sociological or more conventional approach tends to view cities as physical-geographical structures, whereas postmodern cultural criticism treats the city as a text or a work of art to be deciphered through the detached, aestheticizing gaze of the *flâneur*, the walking and contemplating subject as construed by Walter Benjamin. As Janet Wolff (1995) has argued, the structural-sociological and the discursive-literary perspectives should complement rather than exclude each other. Cities may be seen in a multitude of ways by their residents as well as by their detached *flâneurs*. But these visions are overdetermined by the physical and social organization of a city's spaces and structures, its history, as well as by the social characteristics—gender, class, age—of the subjects who inhabit and represent it. Cities may appear as richly and diversely meaningful places and sites of experience and identity; yet the variety and range of their meanings do not render them purely imaginary spaces, mere projections of ephemeral identities. Péter Esterházy noted that "a city, a place is worthy of mention because there one can gaze at oneself in a manner not possible anywhere else" (1994: 176). Cities embody not only individual but collective subjectivities, identities, and histories. The astounding complexity of the underground's way of viewing and making sense of Budapest is worth studying for precisely this reason.

It was in the capital that the movement started, and up to the 1990s it remained the center of alternative music.[19] The city's special importance to the subculture derived to a large extent from the lat-

19. This statement needs some qualification. First, the Committee lived, worked, and often performed in Szentendre, a medieval artists' town not far from Budapest. Szentendre has a character of its own, but its nearness to the capital prevented both the musicians and

ter's political ghettoization. As I claimed earlier, the rock underground's semilegal existence had implied that these performers were absent from the broadcast media and had quite limited access to record production, and their live events were surveilled. For this reason, the concerts were seen as outstanding, politically and affectively charged events, instrumental in the existence of the community. Many of the noncommercially circulated audio tapes were live recordings rather than studio pieces. Collectors as well as the musicians identified these tapes by reference to the venue and the year in which a given concert was recorded. Therefore names of places such as Ikarusz, Közgáz, and Bercsényi signified not only memorable musical events but collective events in and of the city. Also serving as album titles, these names reinforced in public memory the embeddedness of concerts and other music-related art shows in the daily life of the city. This is striking in the manner in which the ad for *Beszélő* quoted at the beginning of this chapter enlisted places to appeal to a subculture's shared framework of time and space, which is tantamount to a shared identity.

Throughout the 1980s, the city appears as a principal trope in underground song lyrics. It was hardly the first time that Budapest had stood as a metaphor for cultural identity and historical experience for a specific social group. Like all big cities, Budapest has been a favored theme of a wide variety of popular musical genres. Usually it is evoked by name, as in operetta numbers and chansons ("Budapest, Budapest, you're wonderful"; "This is the city, we're her residents / . . . It even has a name: Budapest").[20] Conversely, in the underground rock'n'roll songs Budapest is addressed abstractly and metaphorically, as "the city" (*a város*), the locus of daily life and a regulator of its rhythms. With its unspecified bars, pubs, and means of transportation, the city is the sign of a lifestyle and a life-feeling:

their audience from viewing it as the small-town "other" of Budapest. Second, the underground's cultural and ideological face was not entirely unified. Its hard core, the innermost circle of friends, was thoroughly urban/cosmopolitan, whereas other musicians (e.g., GC), irrespective of their residence, construed their music in a nativist or nationalist cultural framework.

20. The first quote is from a local operetta composed in the early 1950s; the second is from an urban chanson composed by János Másik and Géza Bereményi and performed by the semi-underground cult singer Tamás Cseh in the album *Levél nõvéremnek* (A letter to my sister), Hungaroton, 1976.

At night when you go to the bar
In the morning when you slip into your bed
At noon when the mailman rings the doorbell
(Balaton)

He's draggin' me across the city
by private taxi or by bus
You can't fail to recognize
From where to where you're traveling
(Trabant)

For many artists, underground and professional alike, Budapest represented the contradictory experience of involuntary membership in late socialist Hungarian society. On the positive side was the appreciation of Budapest's ability to sustain a relatively rich and varied cosmopolitan culture. In accord with the country's privileged status among the more blatantly oppressed and economically deprived Soviet bloc societies, Budapest compared favorably with the provinces. It offered a considerable variety and freedom of lifestyles that the provinces—even the larger provincial cities—failed to do. The somewhat tarnished but still visible grandeur of Budapest, its attractive physical and architectural qualities, its not particularly glitzy but relatively numerous clubs, pubs, theaters, and galleries, its relaxed cultural policies, and its big-city anonymity allowed for a bohemian existence and cultural creativity to flourish.

This bohemian existence was fashioned to some extent by fantasies of Budapest's similarity to New York. In an essay on the changing character of Budapest over the transition of 1989, Esterházy sarcastically but lovingly calls the city "the New York of the Plains" (*a puszta New York-ja*) and "Manhattan behind the Iron Curtain" (*vasfüggönyös Manhattan*) (1994: 176). Indeed, the rock underground as part of a broader art world was especially preoccupied with a mythic idea of New York based at least as much on cultural representations as on personal familiarity with it. Being as it was the center of post-World War II avant-garde, minimalism, and pop art, the instigator of crossovers between high and low culture—including the art punk scene itself (Frith and Horne 1987, Walker 1987)—New York signified for many young Hungarian artists the essence of metropolitan culture and living. Even a song was dedicated to the city: "New York, New York," by the group Ági és fiúk (Ági and the Guys). Several members of the avant-garde/underground community emigrated to or spent extended periods of time in the Big Apple in search of artistic stimulation, career opportunities, and personal growth.

Like the New York represented by the Velvet Underground's songs of low life or by Martin Scorsese's violent and dark films, the Budapest envisioned in the songs by EPH, Balaton, and Trabant also conveyed—besides a sense of identity, intimacy, and belonging—images of oppression, emptiness, and alienation. Bound up as it was with the events of daily life and the experiences of the people represented in the songs, Budapest also served as a canvas onto which these characters' shifting but predominantly depressed moods and more permanent emotional states became projected:

> Mr. Controller, I have neither cash nor a ticket
> And Mr. Controller, my bus pass expired
> and Mr. Controller, my sweetheart left me.
> (Balaton)

> Sleeping powder, sleeping powder
> Save me from this city.
> (Balaton)

In the early punk songs, simmering with disdain, anger, and hatred, the city took on more politicized meanings. In the following song by the Ultra Rock Agency, for example, it is renamed Betaville[21] to become an allegory of a totalitarian society:

> I was told a city is here
> I was told it's called Betaville
> I was told there's a festivity going on here,
> The unending jubilee of drill.

Related to this construction of the city is the notion of a morally degenerate social world. Drawing on a characteristic streak of male-

21. "Betaville" is a reference to the French film *Alphaville (ou Une Étrange Aventure de Lemmy Caution)*, directed by Jean-Luc Godard. The film is a dystopic vision of a police state struggling against terrorism.

defined Western literary tradition, some songs portray the city as a sinful woman. Succumbing to her pleasures is tantamount to the sex act:

> This city is a prostitute
> I hate when she satisfies me.[22]
> (Ultra Rock Agency)

Whereas the imagery of totalitarianism in the early punk songs implicated a distance from and disdain of the city by the sexist "angry young men" of those times, later songs, even by the same songwriters, adopted a softer and subtler insider perspective. From such a perspective the city and all its residents, including the songs' autobiographically conceived personas, were of the same mold. The city was a place where these characters not merely spent but expended their lives. Small and insignificant as this place seemed with its bleak streets, the city constituted not solely the context but the content, the very substance and fabric of its residents' lives. The hatred for the city's ways was by and large indistinguishable from the hatred of the rock community's own ways:

> Sin and shame hand in hand,
> I'm looking for my man.[23]
> . . .
> As if the world was waiting for some signal
> Music is pouring forth from a sinking city
> A dirty little story: someone will unearth it
> Rock'n'roll was just a killing joke.[24]
> (EPH)

Another important layer of meaning grafted onto the trope of the city had to do with the poignant and diverse expressions of existen-

22. Compare this to Péter Esterházy's slightly sarcastic take on the city's feminization: "Colleagues like to talk about their love for a city and about the object of their love as a woman (oh, well, a slight macho effect). More precisely, as a filthy slut who sleeps with everyone. She's no longer young, her makeup is ribald, etc., etc., it goes on as wittily as that, and yet, oh, yes, she's our eternal love. If Prague is Central Europe's heart, [György] Konrád wrote, then Budapest is its lap. Which seems to me a rather good sentence" (1994: 177).

23. Apparently a reference to the Velvet Underground's song "Waiting for My Man" in the album *Velvet Underground and Nico*, Verve Records, 1967.

24. A subtle reference to Killing Joke, a British punk group.

tial crisis and marginality. Earlier I dealt extensively with the experiencing of this crisis as spatial and temporal disjointedness. The city is portrayed as a microcosm on its own, a "distant planet," a "five-star mental ward," a place that "passes (away)," just like time and life itself. This place is cut off and is out of touch with what seems to be the only real domain, the imaginary, since history is "a rusty city." The city is perceived as dragging down the men and women of the songs; but it is also the place where fantasies of a different time or a distant place are woven.

In brief, the city is the most frequently used metaphor to convey rupture, the absence of anchoring values, a meaningful order, and transcendence in one's life:

On the Blaha, on the Blaha[25]
there my mother bore me
Each time I pass there
I burst into tear gas
This is a real, real tough, tough world . . . [repeated four times]

The music is no music
The words are not words
Nobody knows if he's comin' or goin.'
(Ultra Rock Agency)

In a more Dadaist and absurdist vein, the Committee evokes a similar idea of existential confusion, a sense of life's incoherence. The mention of the city right in the middle of the song "Vanilla Dream Cake" ties the representation of an experience to the place the subjects inhabit. "Budapest" is inserted as a referent to cultural identity:

Vanilla dream biscuit
tarirarira
this is the first act
the first act is on now
tarididida

25. Blaha is the popular name for Blaha Lujza Square, a major traffic juncture in the heart of the city. It is an area associated with petty crime and prostitution.

Vanilla dream biscuit
the second act follows
vanilla dream biscuit, Budapest
this is upsetting
this is entirely unprecedented
tarirarira

Vanilla dream biscuit
the fourth act follows now
the third one is omitted
the fourth follows
but there won't be a fifth act
surely won't be
tarirarira
(trans. Csaba Hajnóczy)

From Ghetto to *Depresszó*: The Significance of Creating Places in the City

In the heyday of the underground rock era specific rock venues were important and well liked because of the bands that played there. Groups such as Balaton, the Committee, and the Galloping Coroners gave luster to otherwise faceless clubs or venues run by schools, districts, or the city council. This trend was reversed by the end of the decade: new and exciting venues popped up, such as the Fekete Lyuk (Black Hole) and Tilos az Á (Trespassers W), to confer prestige and character on new bands. Underlying this reversal was a major shift in the social organization of noncommercial rock culture in Hungary: places rather than performers enjoyed star status in the music scene. These were places that musicians, as well as their audiences, felt to be their very own. The shift epitomizes the gradual and variably successful accommodation of the underground rock/art community to a new socioeconomic regime by establishing its own institutional spaces and places. If Szirtes's act of displaying his logo in the city center stood for the art community's symbolic reappropriation of urban spaces, thus making a claim for more prominence and prestige, the establishment of new venues—and later on a radio station, magazines, and so forth—marked the real and active reappropriation of such spaces.

In the process of social transition, places that enabled a previously cohesive community to get together for a musical event had extraordinary psychosocial and political significance. The economic and political dislocation endured by the underground community in the late 1980s called forth attempts to "relocate"—that is, to remake social life in new forms, to render creative and meaningful association possible under the altered circumstances of postsocialist Hungary. Subconsciously, musicians must have known that only by establishing physical spaces and places (primarily venues, but also radio and television stations, etc.) could they re-create affective spaces and places, which are the stuff and goal of music-based social events and rituals. The reconfiguration of the political-social space surrounding the community compelled it to seek stability in the building of physical places. This territorial approach to renewal seemed indispensable for many members of the underground if they were to retain a minimal sense of continuity with the past and regenerate a sense of collective identity. As we shall see, these places were also sought out by new generations of young people interested in alternative culture.

Martin Stokes (1994: 3) writes: "The places constructed through music involve notions of difference and social boundary." The passion with which new venues and clubs were built, worked and struggled for, used, and represented in cultural and political disputes underscores the potential of these places to draw and redraw boundaries when previous ones had lost their validity or effectiveness. Such interest also marks the capacity of places to renegotiate the differences among various youth groups and between them and mainstream society.

The burgeoning interest in clubs and venues was manifested in the sheer proliferation of places of entertainment in larger cities after 1989. This process paralleled the explosion of record labels and book publishing firms that cropped up right after the market had been freed. Many of the alternative clubs, like the publishing companies, waned and went out of business. Yet more relevant than the numbers is the attention the clubs and venues received from journalists, filmmakers, musicians, and visitors. In order to create a contempo-

11
Cult figures: János Gasner of EPH playing in front of a Stalin portrait. Photo by Tamás Ligeti Nagy.

rary feel, local movie makers made sure they included scenes in one or another alternative place (Nagy n.d.).

For several years *Magyar Narancs* ran a section where old and new coffeehouses, bars, and music clubs were described at length, including their interior design, offerings, prices, and clientele. The founders of new places found great pleasure in defining a new space in the cultural life of postcommunist Budapest and gave the venues humorous and imaginative names, such as Tilos az Á (Trespassers W, Piglet's door sign in A. A. Milne's *Winnie-the-Pooh*);[26] the ironic Egocentrum (Ego Center), and the Na+na Depresszó,[27] or the politically playful Marxim (a pun combining Maxim, the night club's name,

26. Generations of Hungarians have read *Winnie-the-Pooh* as a cult book in the exquisite translation by Frigyes Karinthy.

27. "Depresszó" is a pun: *presszó* is both espresso and the facility where it is served. *Depresszó* is pronounced only slightly differently from *depresszió*, "depression."

with Marx; and see Fig. 11). These attempts to attract the potential guest's attention were more than merely a commercial ploy. They replicated the exuberance, if not the radicalism, with which rock bands, especially punks, had invented the most bizarre stage names (Orgasm, Galloping Coroners, Spinach) to shock or amuse the public a decade earlier.

Venues in Postsocialist Budapest

The Black Hole

Founded in 1987, the place called Fekete Lyuk (Black Hole), or simply Lyuk (Hole), was emblematic of the entire underground-turned-alternative music scene.[28] Designed and actually rebuilt in voluntary community service (*társadalmi munka*)[29] by the members and friends of the rock group Balkán Turiszt (Balkan Tourist),[30] the Hole became, as one of my informants said, "the place that everybody had wanted for a long time in Budapest."[31] Its founders defined it less against a disintegrating official culture than against crass commercialism.

The Black Hole's building had originally been a major industrial plant. In the 1970s the Communist Youth League took it over. After it had been empty for years, Balkan Tourist and three other rock groups had an opportunity to remodel the place according to

28. Ágnes Molnár, a student at Eötvös Loránd University, generously provided me with the typescript of her interview with the club's program director (*népmüvelő*), Gyula Nagy, as well as other published and unpublished materials pertaining to the history and workings of the Black Hole. The following description draws on her compilation.

29. If work and community life in socialist Hungary were to be depicted with a set of key concepts and phrases, *társadalmi munka* would certainly have to be included. Officially, it meant centrally organized volunteer work for employees of a workplace or students; in reality, participation was mandatory. The work "volunteered" was usually, though not always, seasonal agricultural work (harvesting, for example), for which no labor could be organized through the existing mechanisms. Employees worked on weekends, students during regular school hours. Mandatory *társadalmi munka* gradually waned as the Hungarian economy moved away from planning and its attendant flaws. By 1989 the term resumed its original meaning of voluntary community service.

30. Named after the notoriously ineffective state-run Bulgarian travel bureau. Since it was a national monopoly, whenever Hungarians traveled to Bulgaria, they had to do business with this company. The satirically tinged name, like Trabant, is a marker of Eastern European cultural identity.

31. Ágnes Kamondy. See also "Alternatív rock," *Magyar Narancs*, Nov. 8, 1989, p. 12.

their liking. By then the district council of Budapest controlled it. Even though the opening of the Hole preceded the actual collapse of the party-state, its bold visual design[32] along with its unusual and innovative policies epitomized the gradual loss of the socialist cultural establishment's grip on its own facilities, followed by enthusiastic self-organization of social groups at the onset of the transition.

The club served primarily as a place for the founding musicians' regular appearances and rehearsals. In its ambition to become a top-quality Central European center of alternative music it displayed a flair for cosmopolitanism. The Hole hosted numerous foreign bands and built up its reputation quickly. Additionally, it nourished the new generation of local talents. After 1988 Fekete Lyuk became a recording label too, as the club built its own studio and management bureau.[33]

From the beginning the underground rock culture had been connected to the avant-garde fringes of film, theater, and visual arts. The venue emphasized this link by keeping on its program experimental films and videos that were not shown elsewhere and by arranging exhibitions of works produced by members of its regular audience. Meanwhile, the management made special efforts to serve the neighborhood's poor working-class youth, the punks, most of whom had come from broken homes and abused drugs. Entrance fees were kept low and hours were accommodated to the needs of those who could afford only mass transportation. The club also provided work opportunities for this underprivileged group. In brief, while the management encouraged self-expression and self-organization among its varied constituency, it championed the explicit goal of keeping the

32. Gyula Nagy (n.d.) describes how the club's designers and builders embraced the punk aesthetic of ugliness, with the walls painted black and covered with graffiti. "What was marvelous about the design of the rooms was that they became renovated in their original, natural form. Where there had been a hole, it remained there; where there'd been a crack, we left it there. What was nice remained in that form, and what was ugly became underscored too" (16).

33. The director of the label was Feró Nagy, the icon of the early punk movement and one of its few "working-class heroes." In the late 1980s, at the time he was running the record label Black Hole, he was a supporter of the Alliance of Free Democrats (AFD). A few years later, however, he changed political colors as a vocal mouthpiece of the ultraright Hungarian Party of Truth and Life (MIÉP). It is rumored that Feró literally sold out to the party (András Siklós and Tamás Szőnyei, personal interviews, 1993).

punks off the street and turning the club into a place where they could feel at home.

For some of these kids, the club's avant-garde art profile and its bohemian ambience represented a specific taste and lifestyle they identified with a higher class status and embraced with enthusiasm. Others, however, did not or could not mingle with the bohemian crowd and clung to their identity as punks. The coexistence of punks and alternatives (the "arty" crowd) was not without conflict. The management was compelled to decide which group's needs should enjoy pride of place.

Early on the founding rock musicians were pushed out of the club's management because, as a so-called professional supervisor (*szakmai felelős*) put it, "problems arose in terms of their human, professional, and moral conduct."[34] Written in a characteristically cliché-ridden woodenspeak full of omissions, the supervisor's document provided neither a factual account of the events that gave rise to such an accusation nor a fair representation of the clashing interests of the musicians and the cultural officials.

Even after the removal of Balkan Tourist, the club retained the Hole's original profile for a while. In the absence of repeatedly requested financial support, however, the punks' needs proved easier to control and capitalize on. Gradually the club's varied and intellectually vibrant cultural style gave way to a more straightforward and commercially exploitable style defined by the punks and metal kids. A musician of the art crowd, Ágnes Kamondy, complained that the Hole, which had been "our kind of place," became one kids attended only to go wild. Each turn in the club's policy entailed the removal of previous managers and staff. When I had a chance to visit the place in 1993, its physical outlook and program policy only vaguely reminded me of what the Fekete Lyuk had started out to be a few years before. One interviewee in the music business, Ferenc Bródér, asked me to turn off my tape recorder as he updated me about the Lyuk and its suspected ties with the criminal underworld.

Egocentrum (Ego Center)

"If it hadn't been shut down by the police, it would've gone bankrupt," Péter Magyar, the drummer of EPH, said when we discussed

34. Quoted in Molnár's collection; see n. 28.

the fate of the short-lived club called Egocentrum. It operated for only a few months in 1992 and 1993. Like the Black Hole, this place was rented, renovated, and run by half a dozen musicians and organizers, including Péter. Some of them joined this enterprise when they became disillusioned with other projects that had gone sour. They worked day and night for several months in the club. They invested 200,000 forints of their private funds (about U.S.$2,000 at the time) in Egocentrum, an amount that would have sustained any one of them for about a year. They lost all of it.

The club was owned by the Federation of Young Democrats, who at the time still advocated alternative culture and politics, so the rent they charged was very low. Despite this advantage, the club was not financially viable. Péter admits that nobody had an inkling of how to run a business. They hired no accountant, and without a permit to sell alcohol, they could not net enough money. The project was doomed from the start.

Egocentrum's problems, however, were more than merely financial. Like many other alternative clubs and bars, it was a constant irritant to the residents of the area. Péter says that the local district government received thousands of letters, most of them complaining of the noise level, asking it to restrict the club's hours or simply shut it down. The club management adhered strictly to the regulations, but to little avail. Once, Péter remembers, just a month after it opened, a large contingent of police burst in, acting as rudely as in the old days of state socialism. Péter and his friends were baffled.

> [The police said], "Get out of this place right away!". . . This sparked a heated quarrel 'cause they wanted *me* to announce in the microphone that everyone should go home. I told them I wouldn't, it's their job. And then a conversation began between the audience and the policeman with the mike. A rock'n'roll. It was neat. People took the mike and passed it on to one another. The police seemed scared because the atmosphere got inflamed. They ordered more police backup, fearing that something was about to happen. . . . The main problem was their tone of voice. It was offensive. "All right," we said, "but where's your permit to raid this place? Technically, it's a democratic state [*jogállam*] we're livin' in, isn't it?!" . . . "No permit, but leave right away because the residents" and so on. . . . Well, on those grounds, then,

> anything can happen at any time. So we insisted on seeing their permit. But no. . . . You know, there were far too many of them and we didn't want any mayhem. Finally, the next day they produced a permit.

Péter suspected that party politicking may also have played a part in the shutting down of Egocentrum. The enemies of the Young Democrats in the local government may have used Egocentrum to undermine the party's credibility. Whether or not his suspicion was grounded in fact, the FYD leaders refused to support a club with such a tumultuous reputation.

Péter's story exemplifies the confusion in which the former underground community found itself during the transition, as they faced an intricate web of social and political forces. At one time the only real trouble they had to worry about came from some representative of the party-state, from a venue's director, the local police, or the Central Committee of the Communist Party. The new force field of political battle appeared far more opaque and the outcome of the battle as unpromising as ever. Now the onslaught came, at least in part, from below, from ordinary citizens who claimed their right to peace and quiet. And the sponsors of Egocentrum, a relatively large political party, perceived this social group as potential voters for whose ballots they sacrificed their former allies, the rowdy alternative crowd made up of people who, unlike FYD politicians, refused to grow up to wear ties and suits, and who ignored and even subverted the rhythm of citizens' everyday life.[35] Thus the resentment against the music played in the club had to do with its appearance as noise in a physical as well as a metaphorical sense: as Attali (1985) so lucidly explained, it acted to disrupt the workaday social order.

It was the police intervention that Péter found most disturbing. Underlying his frustrations were questions he could not answer. Whom did this allegedly new type of police represent—the angry neighbors or merely themselves acting out of the routine they had been socialized to follow in a police state? If the neighbors, how

35. Despite the shared cultural and political roots of the FYD and the rock underground, it became clear soon after the elections of 1990 that the politics and principles of alternative culture could not be attuned to the FYD's increasingly professional style of politics, targeting the mainstream.

could they represent those people without considering the rights of the bohemian crowd? Where are the boundaries drawn in the new system? Where does the protection of one social group's interests turn into the oppression of another? And considering the situation as a whole, who pulled the strings on which Egocentrum's existence depended—the FYD, its political enemies, or a far too autonomous police force? Who, after all, controls the city's spaces that the dedicated architects of Egocentrum wanted to make their own?

Tilos az Á Trespassers W)

"A cellar room plus upstairs bar on a quiet central square. Open 7 days a week. Normally 6 days live music. Small upstairs disco. No specific programming on certain days of the week. Quite varied programming. . . . Owned by 4 private partners. Not run as a strict business. Important meeting-place. Problems especially with noise that may cause it to be closed down soon" (Hobbs 1993). This is a British concert organizer's succinct description of Tilos az Á, or simply the A (pronounced Ahhh), the place that embodied what was defined as alternative culture in Hungary in the 1990s. Throughout its existence it managed to retain its hip character in its visual design, program policy, and mode of operation. The A carried the aura of social transition in that its predecessor, a restaurant called Bakony, had hosted the meetings of the newly formed Federation of Young Democrats and other liberal organizations and proto-parties in the late 1980s.[36] Among the A's program directors one could find, for a short time, László Kistamás, founder and designer of the Black Hole and Egocentrum. Until it was shut down in 1995, the A fared better than both: unlike the Hole, it no longer was constrained by socialist proprietors, and was run exclusively by alternative-minded young entrepreneurs. In contrast to Egocentrum, the A acquired a license to sell alcoholic beverages, which contributed to its viability. Greater specialization in administration—the people who looked after legal and business affairs did not interfere with musical matters—also helped to ensure that the place was run more efficiently.

For some of its organizers and employees, the club served as a testing ground for a new type of noncommercial culture. They at-

36. See *Magyar Narancs*, Apr. 18, 1991, p. 11.

tempted to accommodate the club to the new free-market economy without letting it be driven by the profit motive. The alternative character of the A was based on its similarity to alternative music clubs in Western cities in management style, program policy, and physical appearance. "Originally," a journalist wrote, "the so-called Memphis style was predominant, with walls painted harsh pink. The cosmopolitanism of the joint was marked by, among other things, signs on the bathrooms in no fewer than eight languages."[37] A few years later the Memphis style was gone, replaced by old signs from socialist establishments—characteristically mixing satire with nostalgia—and frescoes depicting the New York skyline. Interestingly, despite its infatuation with images of American popular culture, the A was often compared with its Dutch counterparts, largely because Hungarians were more familiar with the cities of Western Europe than Memphis or even New York.

The program policy of the A was also admired for its wide range of musical styles: boogie, blues, jazz, avant-garde; the new hybrids of the music industry, such as hard core, and heavy rap; and a growing variety of ethnic music, from Gypsy through klezmer (Eastern European Jewish) to Turkish (played by a Hungarian group, Üzgin Üver). A monthly program booklet listed performers from Australia, Yugoslavia, Slovakia, Austria, and France. The club was known for its active interest in other Central and Eastern European groups largely unknown or inaccessible to Hungarian audiences earlier. Unfortunately, László explained, they could not pay enough to cover the minimal expenses of such groups' travel. And while Western alternative groups at least owned a minivan to take them on tour, the Eastern European musicians often had to decline invitations from abroad for lack of a means to get there.

A new balance was struck among local musicians as well. Now a significant portion of the A's performers came from the provinces rather than from Budapest only.[38] Even more important was the equitable quality and appreciation of the music produced by young provincials. The A selected new local talent on the grounds of originality rather than musical proficiency alone. Musicians were sup-

37. Ibid.
38. *Magyar Narancs,* Aug. 5, 1991, p. 21.

posed to tap into a taste culture whose boundaries were becoming increasingly vague. Bands playing "cover songs" (imitative renderings of music composed and performed by others) could not make it to the A's stage. But László also admitted that "countless times friendships of all sorts play a role."

From 1991 on, the A's management was busy fending off government attempts to close it down. The story sadly parallels that of Egocentrum: the neighbors' complaints about the noise level played into the hands the Hungarian Democratic Forum (HDF), then the majority party in Parliament. Their efforts to ban the club surely won a few extra votes for the party's district representative at the next elections. Among other complaints, the A was allegedly a threat to the morals of the students attending the neighboring schools. During the four years of the conservative government of József Antall, the culture war against Anglo-American popular culture was so fervent that the A's felt compelled to highlight folk music in their program profile.[39]

Conclusion

Rock music's relevance lies not only in what kind of music is made for whom and in what media but also *where* the music is made. In Central and Eastern Europe the years 1988 to 1990 encouraged new ways of organizing the rock/art community, and in the reorganization urban spaces and places gained unusual prominence as sites of self-assertion and self-expression. Revolutions and major political upheavals not only invite people to the streets, to protest or celebrate; they also provide, however ephemerally, new symbolic and literal spaces for popular artists to engage in street art and subcultural lifestyles. Did rock musicians' efforts to build alternative music clubs serve merely to compensate for the loss of their musical voices as public intellectuals? Alternatively, did these efforts demonstrate their creative vigor and resourcefulness at a time of crisis—a crisis of identity and collectivity? My data allow for either argument to be made (although I lean toward the latter), but there are far more interesting questions to be asked: Why did these exciting new places and

39. "Aaaaaaa!!" *Magyar Narancs*, Apr. 18, 1991, p. 11.

spaces fail? In the longer run, what could be realized of the visions, innovative ideas, and building efforts that went into those first alternative clubs? In broader terms, how could noncommercial culture adjust to the crystallizing economic, legal, and political structures of postsocialist Hungary? An in-depth look at the record industry's transformation will take us closer to the answer.

4

Clients and Entrepreneurs

The Shaping of a Capitalist Recording Industry

With the arrival of the postcommunist era, the last barriers to the pluralization and privatization of the recording business fell. The structure that developed was quite similar to its Western counterpart, with large-scale commercial and small-scale or independent music production. The withdrawal of the state from the management of cultural production made possible what Habermas called a public sphere. The last bulwark of state control was the mass media, a major battleground of the conservative coalition and liberal opposition during the early 1990s. The so-called second public of the state-socialist system became integrated into the new public sphere of the evolving postsocialist society. In this process the avant-garde arts, music especially, figured significantly. Finally, the growing share of Western media and entertainment conglomerates in the production of local music and the supply of the local market with Western cultural products lifted the previously existing barriers between local and global musical production and consumption.

Cultural Thaw and the Fall of State Monopolies: The Case of Hungaroton

To some extent popular music had been commodified in the Hungarian version of state socialism. With the effort to meet public demand, the state-run monopolies began to break down as early as 1980. Yet, while it was not difficult to secure approval from the Ministry of Culture to self-publish a book, unless it contained material that was deemed politically subversive, no such permission was forthcoming in the field of music. The party-state had circumscribed popular music primarily by monopolizing the right to issue recordings. In 1986 Hungaroton ceded its exclusive right to disseminate music first to other state-run megafirms such as MAFILM, the national film production company, to Hungarian Radio, and eventually, in 1988, to newly formed independent record publishers.

From the mid-1970s Hungaroton had been among the few relatively well run and internationally respected Hungarian companies, owing especially to its classical music repertoire. Yet because it wielded so much power, which it inevitably abused, Hungaroton was remarkably unpopular among rock musicians and their following. Some of them virtually demonized the institution. In the early 1980s a punk band called CPG was prosecuted for a hate song targeting a prominent manager of the company for his rigid political labeling and screening of lyrics. Others resented Hungaroton for its poor organizational culture: its sloppiness and lack of expertise with regard to studio work, promotion, and marketing. Most musicians never had a chance to try their luck outside the socialist markets. The few who did tended to receive less than adequate professional and financial support from Hungaroton. Many musicians nonetheless dreamed of international stardom (Dám 1987).

Underground bands did not insist on this kind of success. They developed their own networks, embryonic as they were, in the international alternative scene. Yet the underground too resented the national recording industry for ignoring their domestic popularity and critical acclaim. Unlike its Russian counterpart, Melodiia, which until glasnost and perestroika had not even recognized the existence of rock music (Troitsky 1987, Cushman 1995: 43–45), Hungaroton thrived on producing a variety of mainstream rock styles. It even released a few underground rock albums. The company's policy was erratic and uncertain. It typified the country's wavering official cultural policies in regard to expressions of dissent and artistic innovation. Péter Iván Müller recalls an episode with Hungaroton in 1987:

> P. I. M.: We prepared an almost two-hour demo tape because they invited us to produce a record. Then the record was banned but the demo had been done almost in its entirety. . . . Then they called us back again and so we recorded it . . . using very sophisticated technology. Only the mixing and the final recording of the last two songs were missing. And then they stopped us with the excuse that the budget had been used up. . . . I. W. [a label manager] got scared somehow and made us terminate the whole thing.
>
> A. S.: Do you know what may have scared him?
>
> P. I. M.: I can only guess. . . . In the song "You Can't Trust Anybody," which starts with spoken lyrics, it goes like this: "A paramedic's hitting a man, a nurse is attackin' another one, an Ami jet's approaching with Albanian markings to bomb the Chain Bridge[1] to the ground," which all means that you can't trust anybody. They said we'd better leave this out. . . . I said I wouldn't change anything about the lyrics. . . . So that's why this second record crashed.

What, indeed, explained Hungaroton's odd behavior? While some of the industry's personnel were ready to put out subcultural music, they were constrained by political taboos. Within a few years, however, the taboos were brought down. At the end of his career, Hungaroton's profoundly unpopular director (the one who had provoked CPG's hate song) began to act not merely as a shrewd businessman—he had done that before—but as one unaffected by previous political considerations. In 1985 he unexpectedly offered a contract to EPH, which his colleagues had consistently turned down. I wondered aloud how and why the group had come to accept the offer from a person so thoroughly despised in the musicians' community. I'll call him P. E. Jenő Menyhárt answered, "You know what?

1. The oldest and most spectacular bridge over the Danube in Budapest.

I'm yearning for P. E. now [*visszasírom E.P.-t*]! There were a couple of those tough guys. He was one of them, a censor like the others. . . . I had a lot of experience with those types in the record company and in the film company. Everybody in a job like that was a censor. P. E. just happened to be assigned a symbolic status or something." Then he told me about receiving an excellent contract offer from him:

> He phoned me one day . . . saying, "I want to talk with you. Come in [to my office]." I was very apprehensive about what the heck he might want from me. I went in and he says: "You'll be surprised, so you'd better sit down. I'd like to put out a record with EPH." I retorted, "It won't be easy," and we began to negotiate. It turned out that the provisions were totally fair. I don't think rock stars in the West get such good offers! We were to prepare our material and they were obligated either to accept it the way it was or we'd withdraw it. In other words, they wouldn't dicker with us about this word or that verse. We received more than enough studio hours and could design the cover insert ourselves, too. There's nothing like this anywhere else. Maybe in fairy tales. A first-record act, as we were, we could spend four hundred hours in the studio!

Because of the complex sociopolitical situation in which it occurred, this offer was an unforeseen, peculiar, and historical moment in the EPH's career. Their delight was not spoiled by the disgruntlement of their audience. "Everyone thought," Jenő continued, "that this record was an outrageous betrayal, since we left out the old songs. They thought we did it because of censorship." But it was not P. E. that demanded new songs, it was the group that wanted them. They thought that recording their classics years after they were written would be to play Hungaroton's game of covert censorship. Hungaroton liked to publish material that was provocative enough to serve as a safety valve for the fringe elements but dated enough to attract minimal attention elsewhere. EPH's more recent songs had far less political edge than the old favorites.

But this time EPH's tactics to avoid Hungaroton's covert censorship were no longer necessary because the company all but gave up on containing underground rock. EPH was free to decide about the contents of the record simply because Hungaroton was no longer concerned about ideological precepts. The company's approach to underground musicians coincided with Gorbachev's coming to power, even though "no one knew, then, what that meant," as Menyhárt commented. Nor could cultural administrators such as P. E. be fully aware of its implications. Only his death in 1989 put an end to EPH's business dealings with Hungaroton; the company collapsed soon afterward. "At the time a huge match was played every day: political parties were formed, the Republic was declared, and there was this big [pandemonium]. The company closed down entirely. When P. E. died, no one knew what was going to happen. I dropped by three weeks later and the company didn't exist any more. So our [new] album *Szavazz rám* [Vote for me] could never come out." Hungaroton was resuscitated, but its story exemplifies the confusion, favoritism, and disruption that surrounded the privatization of former state monopolies. Much of the struggle centered on whether or not to allow foreign owners to buy stock in Hungaroton.[2] The company's full privatization in 1995 ended a six-year struggle in the course of which it drastically reduced its output, lost 90 percent of its market share, and finally declared bankruptcy (Szőnyei 1993).

Meanwhile, most of its former staff sought stock or employment in new ventures or with the local affiliates of Western labels. Hungaroton's chief director established a firm of his own called Quint, which subsequently merged with the British-based EMI Music. Hungaroton Gong, the company's popular music label, was sold off to the wealthiest veterans of Hungarian rock music, pioneers of privatizing the rock business who had established the first private recording studios, production teams, and so forth to compete with Hungaroton back around 1980.

2. This ideologically saturated conflict was amplified by the Antall government's endeavor to place its own cadres in key positions. The removal of the former head of Hungaroton angered classical musicians and the predominantly liberal media. This educated and smart technocrat, disliked by many people on the right and the left alike but especially by the rock community, now was represented as a talented and successful expert unjustly replaced, a victim of the new political elite's favoritism and corrupt practices (see, e.g. "Exhumálás," *Magyar Narancs*, Apr. 18, 1991). Paradoxically, the first democratically elected government's intervention in cultural production and the media coupled with its cadre policy seemed to many observers to have more in common with harsh communist practices than with the softer policies of the late socialist era.

The fall of Hungaroton, the bulwark of the socialist music business, removed two major boundaries structuring pop music in Hungary: the line between officially supported or tolerated music and the underground and the line between national and international music. Popular music production and consumption came to be rearranged by the dominance of the marketplace. New types of actors emerged on the music scene: self-publishers, independent labels, and the local affiliates of entertainment conglomerates.[3]

Wedding Rock and Underground Rock: The First Generation of Independents

In the major cities of Hungary around 1989–90 even the casual visitor could immediately sense a breakthrough. Streets, pedestrian underpasses, and parks were crowded with vendors selling books and music tapes.[4] The music being offered was dominated by a craze in Hungarian pop music called *lakodalmas* rock (wedding rock).[5] Actually, rock fans would see the term as a misnomer: wedding rock had nothing in common with conventional understandings of rock. It was entertainment music originally played, as its name suggests, on festive occasions. Stylistically, it combined the electronic synthesized sound and rhythm of modern urban dance music (disco) with a distinctly rural local idiom. Lyrics emphasized the themes of love and

3. The only sector omitted from my discussion is self-publishing. There is only one musical subculture, ultranationalist skinhead rock, where self-publishing is prevalent (Szőnyei, personal interview). Groups such as Magozott Cseresznye (Pitted Cherry) and Egészséges Fejbőr (Healthy Scalp) have their own British-based fashion store, a few venues where they perform regularly, and sponsors in ultraright political parties, but up to the mid-1990s they lacked a record label of their own.

4. On the political significance of the book supply, see Szemere 1992a: 624.

5. Although Barbara Rose Lange (1996) provides important observations about this style, her social and cultural analysis of the music contains some unsubstantiated assumptions. She says, for instance, that *lakodalmas* rock expresses the values of Hungarians "who were villagers before World War II and then formed an urban 'working class' under Socialism" (80–81). Since *lakodalmas* was played and enjoyed predominantly by middle-aged and younger people who were born or grew up after World War II, this point is certainly mistaken. Second, Lange's argument that the local elite's disdain for this music style was based on a "disgust for the facile" and an idealized notion of "folk art" seems about as one-dimensional as the citation with which she apparently agrees, according to which the attraction of *lakodalmas* reflected "a general national need."

sex in a manner bordering on pornography. Wedding rock corresponded to a widespread obsession with pornographic images, a short-lived trend that peaked in the early 1990s in postcommunist Eastern Europe (see, for example, Kürti 1991b, Meštrović 1993: 72). Its eruption into prominence coincided, interestingly, with the rise of several related music styles in the Balkans, such as the Bulgarian *chalga* (Levy 1998) and the Serbian "newly composed folk music" (Vidić Rasmussen 1996, Gordy 1999: 125–65).

The massive outburst of interest in wedding rock in Hungary indicated a previously unrecognized popular taste suppressed by the socialist cultural establishment. The same officials who vacillated about the political propriety of underground rock had refused to produce wedding rock on aesthetic grounds. The music, not merely its lyrics, was disdained as tasteless. While this harsh folk-pop style was more conspicuous than any other genre, the old and fresh repertoires of the former underground performers also started to surface. Occasionally the same company that profited from wedding rock published these recordings as well. Proton was one of them (Szőnyei 1993: 106). The two former outcasts of the socialist cultural policy, which could not be further removed from each other, aesthetically and socially, now came together in Proton's listings. This was the firm where EPH continued its recording career after they left Hungaroton in shambles. Jenő Menyhárt remembers the band's dealings with Proton:

> J. M.: New companies sprang up in the market. So did Proton and we made an awesome contract with them. [The cassette] came out in 4,000 copies, and by the time I could go in and collect the money, the company had gone out of business. . . . As they'd come out with a lot of profitable stuff . . . they [thought it best to] declare bankruptcy, switched to a different name, and have been operating ever since.
> A. S.: Didn't you see any money from them?
> J. M.: Only the advance.
> A. S.: Are they still producing records?
> J. M.: They pocketed lots of dough on it. But now they're putting out cassettes only. They published our new cassette recording. No longer by the name Proton, though. . . . Many [entrepre-

neurs] acted like this, making huge profits on recordings in four months. And we were screwed.

Szőnyei's interpretation of Proton's activity is less harsh. He states that the company "overproduced" in an increasingly saturated market, and its inability to sell its products led to its bankruptcy (1993: 106).

Listening to the musicians' stories about their encounters with the new companies, I kept hearing the same accusations of exploitation, adventurism, negligence, and incompetence. András Márton transferred with his band from Hungaroton to a company called Holdex as soon as private labels were instituted: "It was like I was disappointed right from the start, because I thought here's a private company, they'll publish our cassette on a private label. If they chose to open a private business, they'll surely set an example of how to do it, since everyone bashed the dysfunctional socialist economy. First of all, they didn't want to sign an entirely correct contract." András, a finicky musician with considerable business experience, formulated the eight-page contract himself. The Hungarian Copyright Office (Szerzői Jogvédő Iroda) believed that the text was so accurate and well worded, Márton proudly claims, that they asked to use it as a blueprint for future transactions with other clients.

A. S.: Did they eventually release your record?
A. M.: They did, but they weren't a correct company. We had many problems with them. They didn't deal with distribution or promotion, so they were no better [than the socialist predecessor].

Márton places this experience in a broader context of economic and social change:

Just because an economic system broke up, it doesn't mean people's mentality has changed too. Something is about to develop that before would have made people sigh: "Oh, how good it'd be for me in Vienna!" Well, now here's Vienna for them [in Budapest], but their attitude is as slipshod as ever. And as selfish as ever. This is the bottom line. So the system doesn't operate any differently. You need to stumble kind of accidentally into small companies that are can be trusted.

A less experienced musician, Tamás Kocsis of the band Sexepil, who attributed the release of their first recording to the emergence of a pop market freed from political surveillance, told me about his encounter with another new independent called Ring.[6] The founder of this company came from the popular music department of Hungaroton. Ring, like so many new enterprises of the postcommunist economy, was established, to draw on Bourdieu's theory, with the underlying purpose of converting their owners' social and symbolic capital, primarily their social networks and professional experience obtained in the socialist pop business, into economic capital.[7] Apparently Ring had cash-flow problems and delayed paying royalties to their recording artists, including Sexepil. Sexepil, unlike many Western recording artists, did not have a lawyer to help them handle such matters. They set up a small street demonstration demanding their royalties in front of Ring's office. Reporters from Hungarian Radio and Television were invited to the event. Finally, after lengthy disputes, the company settled its financial obligations with the artists. The band's manager, Péter B. György, thought Ring failed to invest sufficient time and work in the production. He also generalized on Ring's example: "They made the mistake that companies involved in the music business will be making for a long time to come. Under the illusion that this [Sexepil's commercial success] can be achieved real fast, they wanted to pump up things in a single year rather than, as usual in the business, working hard on it for five to six years." These musicians' accounts reflect not merely their feeling of helplessness in the face of a chaotic recording business that lacked the proper legal framework and the infrastructure necessary for its day-to-day operations.[8] The stories exemplify also a conspicuous trend in private and public discourses surrounding the business world in postsocialist

6. The Hungarian meaning of the company's name is "boxing ring," but like other new ventures, it was apparently named to appeal to English speakers too.

7. For an extended argument, see Róna-Tas 1994; Eyal et al. 1998.

8. Some characteristics of the transition from socialism to capitalism bring to mind Max Weber's claim that the rational structure of law is integral to the formation of the capitalist enterprise (1989: 25).

Hungary, which is typically cast in a moral framework. Complaints of "ruthlessness," "lawlessness," "carelessness," and the "Wild East" predictably recur. Today's entrepreneurs, according to a widespread belief, are desperate to make as much money as fast and with as little effort as possible. Business, from this perspective, had become indistinguishable from crime.[9]

While the musicians may have had a right to complain of disempowerment, their emphasis on entrepreneurs' moral failings tended to obscure the structural difficulties with which businesses had to grapple. Most new companies that dealt with popular music were short-lived in part because they could not compensate for the deficiencies they inherited from the pop business, especially the lack of distribution networks and regulation. (The publishers that delayed payments to musicians were occasionally themselves left without payment by other actors in the market, such as distributors.) This first generation of independent record companies were run by people outside of the informal or subcultural network of the musicians they contracted. And more often than not they were indifferent to the content of their releases as long as they sold. The former underground musicians they signed were clients in much the same way they used to be clients of the socialist music enterprise. The second generation of independents, by contrast, came from the subculture. In the world of pop and rock music, the term "independent record company" (an indie or minor) is associated with interest in or commitment to minority, marginal, underground, or alternative music.

Indies—Are They Indeed Independent?

According to the conventional wisdom, independent record companies are the true nurturers of the innovative and provocative in modern popular music. They are "independent" because they record, manufacture, and market their products without relying on the services of large companies or entertainment conglomerates—the "ma-

9. The capitalism unfolding in these stories recalls what Weber calls pariah or adventurist capitalism. It is driven by social actors' desire to grow rich rather than by the disciplined work ethic Weber associates with Protestantism. Interestingly, the lack of a work ethic in the rock community was addressed and resented by several musicians.

jors"—so presumably the music can stay intact, aesthetically as well as politically, safe from the exigencies of the marketplace. Rock critics tend to emphasize that all the shakers and movers—the promoters of the rock'n'roll of the 1950s, the counterculture of the 1960s, the punk movement of the 1970s, the grunge of the late 1980s, women's rebel rock in the 1990s—were such small, flexible, and committed companies run by people who were themselves often rooted in the subculture. Because of this strong association between small companies and youth movements, independents are believed to be more honest in their financial and artistic dealings with their musicians than the big commercial companies, which are routinely represented as exploitive. When a rock performer transfers from an indie to a major, some fans and critics immediately write them off. Such bands are "sellouts," the argument goes, and whatever they end up producing will predictably be heard by the hard core of alternatives as diluted and commercial (Negus 1992: 16).

Closer inquiries into the workings of the Western recording business have proved these assumptions to a large extent unfounded. Simon Frith (1981) claimed that most of the so-called independents depend, at least partially or covertly, on major companies, especially for dubbing and distribution. It seems fallacious to infer a company's financial honesty or generosity from its size. The relationship between majors and minors is more convincingly explained as a symbiosis rather than a confrontation. Not only do the minors rely for their survival on various forms of collaboration with the major companies; the majors also depend on the indies to spot trends and talent. Only independent companies have the flexibility to cater to a specific minority segment of the audience. The contemporary recording industry may be best construed as a web of small and large companies that complement each other (Negus 1992: 17–19).

While the romanticized antagonism between the supposedly non-exploitive, oppositional mavericks and the profit-driven, hegemonic majors cannot be upheld, it would be a mistake to dismiss a specific kind of alternative music producer committed to a music style or set of styles. If the music itself is political, the ideals and values embodied in it may underlie the company's business practices as well. Many independent labels, however, come to be formed only for the purpose of putting out material that cannot be released by a large company

(Negus 1992, Gray 1988) or can be produced less expensively because smaller companies have smaller overhead costs. To some degree, then, it is the logic of a stratified market consisting of minority and mass taste groups that sustains the dual structure of the music industry.[10]

Miklós Sükösd's distinction between two types of alternative cultural practice fits the structure of the record industry too: one based on the market position of the medium, the other on the values and contents of the material it disseminates (1993: 80–81). Proton and numerous other first-generation record companies in postcommunist Hungary were the first type of independents. In the following discussion I suggest that we view the second generation of record producers as value-based rather than positional alternatives. But within this broad category, as we shall see, they operate along distinctly different principles.

From Clients to Entrepreneurs: The Second Generation of Independents

Alternative Rock as Art: Bahia

The best-known alternative music label with the largest catalog in the postcommunist domestic pop business, Bahia, operates in conjunction with a chain of stores that carry records and fashion items; the chain also distributes merchandise directly to other retailers as well as the Bahia stores (Hobbs 1993). The label is a nonprofit organization supported by the proceeds from fashion sales (Szőnyei 1993: 107–8). In the early 1990s Bahia grew remarkably, so that by 1995 it had three stores in Budapest and more than twenty others in the provinces.

Csaba Hajnóczy, one of the two A&R (artist and repertoire) persons—the other is one of the owners—is responsible for the publishing profile of the Bahia label. His wife, Gabi Kenderesi, is involved in distribution. Both Csaba and Gabi are active musicians in the renowned alternative band Kampec Dolores, formed in 1986. KD is one of the several descendants of Kontroll Csoport, with which Csaba used to play bass guitar. He was associated with the under-

10. I thank George Lipsitz for helping me formulate this idea.

ground in other ways as well. Csaba has a strong theoretical bent. As a musicology student at the Liszt Ferenc Academy of Music, he wrote his dissertation on rock'n'roll as an aesthetically worthwhile form of contemporary music. His choice of topic and perspective provoked bewilderment and resistance among his professors. Csaba shared his impressive knowledge of the topic on radio, too. He ran a series that familiarized his listeners with the international history of punk and new wave music at a time when access to recordings, videos, and music magazines catering to such specialized tastes was extremely limited. He also did more than most musicians to tie the local underground movement to the international circuit of alternative labels, management bureaus, and concert organizations.

Besides music making, which he considers his primary focus and vocation, working with Bahia, he regularly writes on alternative and serious contemporary music for magazines. I asked him about the circumstances of establishing Bahia and the motives for his involvement with it.

> [The owners] are partly the guys who used to run the Ráday Club and later Club 2000 at Almássy Square. They were still university students then, and as I see it . . . , they traveled really a lot at a time when cheap flights were available from Warsaw, Moscow, places like that.[11] They traveled all over the "exotic" continents and somehow figured out how to import exotic clothes and jewelry. . . . Being familiar with the musicians' world . . . , they issued a cassette by the Kontroll [Csoport] in 1991. There were about four occasional releases that they'd been talked into and that they funded.

Csaba was not particularly interested in becoming involved in the music industry. He realized, however, that it was extremely difficult to produce and market KD's recordings as an individual. A parenthesis on the changed status of recorded music in the postcommunist era is in order here.

11. During state socialism, public transportation among Comecon countries was subsidized. Flights from some Eastern European cities to Cuba and other socialist countries enabled young people to reach a number of Third World destinations through complicated itineraries but for affordable airfares.

Until the end of the 1980s, as we have seen, musicians' presence in the underground subculture depended fundamentally on live shows. When the legal barriers to record production were removed in the 1990s, that was no longer the case. Technically, anyone could record and circulate music. Given the constantly lowering costs of recording technology, printing facilities for cover inserts, and so forth, it was no longer impossible for musicians to put out their work even without recording deals or significant capital investment (see, for example, Robinson et al. 1991). Several of my very alternative interviewees expressed great satisfaction over the fact that they finally were free to prepare recordings and circulate them, typically on cassettes, even if the number of copies was small and the profit nonexistent. Even musicians who were less motivated to make recordings felt pressured to do so. In the 1990s, musicians' presence in the music scene, whether alternative or mainstream, was assessed on the basis of their recordings. Live shows, no longer politically charged rituals and thus no longer the dominant medium of subcultural expression and cohesion, became complementary to or a marketing tool of recorded music.

Problems arose when musicians intended to sell enough copies of their recordings to reach the break-even point or even make a profit. Audience expectations concerning sound quality and packaging have risen significantly. Once the music's special aura deriving from its ghettoization dissipated, bad sound quality could no longer be excused. (This recognition is reflected in the self-effacing irony of the name chosen by András Wahorn, a former Committee member, for his short-lived label: Bad Quality Records.) Once the technologically more sophisticated Western pop music became ubiquitous, it reshaped the public's perceptions of what is a "good enough" musical sound. Thus despite the availability of lower-priced recording technology, countervailing factors keep pushing up the level of financial investment and effort necessary for musicians simply to stay afloat. Csaba's Kampec Dolores is one of the few alternative bands that enjoy domestic as well as foreign recognition.

> C. H.: Kampec Dolores produced the album *Levitáció* with the help of English funds. We arranged for the manufacturing, the distribution all on our own. It cost us a tremendous amount of work.

A. S.: How did you raise the money?
C. H.: From Recommended Records.[12] [The album] was in fact on an RR label. They paid a manufacturer in Hungary, which involved all sorts of complications. We had immense manual and bureaucratic work with it. But it turned out that it's impossible to go with publication on such a basis. It was awful. And then came the idea of founding a continuously operating company with me doing all the arrangements and two distributors. In other words, we'd run a company ourselves. They'd [Bahia] give the money and would participate in whatever they want to.

The arrangement has been working out well for both parties. Csaba and Bahia's owner work side by side as A&R persons. Because of the relatively tight budget and low sales figures (anything between a few hundred to a few thousand per release), Bahia dubs most of its titles on cassettes, although at the time of my research there was a marked increase in the number of titles on compact disks as well. The CDs were manufactured in Prague, where Bahia received a better deal than from the only CD manufacturer in Hungary (Hobbs 1993). While Bahia expanded its catalog impressively, there was some concern about the declining sales of individual releases, a trend felt in the entire field of domestic pop music production.[13]

Bahia typifies the independent company committed to musical standards and styles that appeal to a relatively small public. Their idea of independence does not prescribe the nature of their relationship with other actors on the market in any straightforward manner. They do not shy from deals with majors; the local affiliate of BMG, for example, distributes Bahia recordings. But neither does the label serve as a trend spotter or talent scout for large companies. Bahia's idea of autonomy consists of determining and conforming to the criteria by which it selects and signs up recording artists.

12. Recommended Records is a prestigious British independent label.

13. According to Szőnyei (n.d.), this trend may be explained by the combined effects of the vastly expanded supply of available music and the economic recession, which curtailed consumer buying power. The national recording industry acknowledged this state of affairs by lowering the sales figure for the gold record awarded to best-selling local recordings from 100,000 copies in 1980 to 25,000 in 1995 and to 20,000 in 1996 (personal communication from Ágnes Müzinger and Tamás Ligeti Nagy, and from an anonymous distributor for the record company BMG Hungary).

Bahia's present identity and character are rooted in the countercultural past. A large part of its catalog consists of the underground music of the 1980s. Old demo tapes were given a face-lift and a package, and post-1989 nostalgia concerts of the temporarily reunited bands of the former subculture were recorded and released. Yet the company is not a nursing home for the old underground. It does not attempt to sustain the appearance of a collective identity that no longer exists. And, more important, Bahia's identity, while formed in the past, is molded increasingly by its adherence to the contemporary standards and values of the international alternative music community. Some bands close to Bahia's musical standards and taste chose to sign with foreign labels. These are groups that established their international reputation as early as the mid-1980s and still have an audience. The success abroad of several other local underground bands faded when they could no longer be perceived as exotic oppositional musicians from behind the Iron Curtain. Acts such as Vágtázó Halottkémek (Galloping Coroners) belong to the first category. They do not record with Bahia because more advantageous deals are available to them from foreign companies with better equipped studios and better distribution facilities.

Other star performers of the 1980s underground declined to sign with Bahia because they no longer saw themselves as alternatives. They sought a broader audience and more financially agreeable deals with the newly formed local majors. With marked disdain Csaba calls their music "popular" (*populáris*) or "mainstream,"as opposed to the music he considers truly valuable. As a publisher and a critic he applies the musical criteria of excellence prevalent in the global alternative music community.

One might call Csaba elitist and cosmopolitan. The value of music, in his view, is unrelated, if not antithetical, to large-scale popularity. Uniqueness is music's most precious property, but it is not to be mistaken for any form of local color that would articulate the local with the exotic. In Csaba's own words, "The [foreign alternative] organizers who, as entrepreneurs, are genuinely interested in signing us up will pay us for doing something that's hard to compare with anything else. (This may not be the reason why the larger public likes us, though.) We're not imitative of British or German bands. In other words, within the frame of this alternative musical language,[14] we do something one of a kind. This is not true for the [alternative] mainstream bands." He views the more massive domestic appeal of certain bands as incompatible with the kind of uniqueness foreign alternative labels and organizers, like himself, look for in musical acts. He dismisses large-scale popularity at home as derivative—that is, imitation of Western bands and styles—or attributes it to extra-musical factors, such as the salience of the lyrics or the musicians' charisma. Implicitly, in separating out lyrics and charisma, Csaba confines aesthetic/musical value exclusively to the musical sound.[15]

Also, by equating local relevance with mass domestic popularity and inferior aesthetic status, he delegates the authority to make aesthetic/musical judgments to people outside the local music community. Csaba thinks that if the "popular" alternative musicians were willing to work harder, they could obtain recognition abroad, since a transnational infrastructure encompassing the domestic scene is already in place. He overlooks the fact that not all musicians feel driven to trade their success in Hungary for the rewards that membership in the intercultural community might provide them. Some musicians claim that their songs cannot be translated into English, and even when they are translated, the entire gamut of meanings is lost on foreign audiences.

Despite Bahia's elitism and modernist universalism, its cultural policy is relatively open-ended and culturally plural. It offers a site where several members of the old underground experiment with new sounds, styles, and group formations. It also serves as a test ground for fresh talents that conform to Bahia's standard; expands the frontiers of the alternative music culture to encompass the infrastructurally backward provinces; and breaks down the isolation of

14. The current language of alternative music may be described as an assemblage of idioms and styles, including contemporary experimental music, folk, ethnic or world music idioms, jazz, and classic rock. It is interesting to note that some of its currents (postpunk, no wave, noise, and ambient music) are hardly more accessible to persons outside the subculture than the most esoteric streak of experimental music in the serious contemporary tradition, and the audiences they attract are small. Several musicians engaged in alternative music have a background in classical music. The reason they claim their music belongs to the realm of the popular or rock deserves a separate cultural analysis.

15. On the multitextuality of music, see Born 1995 and Negus 1992.

the local scene from the transnational community of experimental and other fringe musicians.

Mark Slobin (1993) introduces the term "interculture" to capture the interaction of musical subcultures and the unique entity it creates. Interculture may involve the music industry and the mass media but not necessarily in a substantial way. Border crossing is common to all of its types, including what Slobin terms diasporic and affinity intercultures. While the former "emerges from the linkages that subcultures set up across national boundaries" (64), the latter refers to "music cultivated across boundaries without appeal to shared heritage or without being commodified." He goes on to explain: "A city, a festival, a shop can create a musical world without frontiers, one that seems to exist across, or somehow suspended above, national lines" (69).

The idea of interculture helps us to comprehend the alternative music scene of postcommunist Hungary in the context of global music structures and processes. The subcategory of affinity interculture is particularly relevant to Bahia's work. First, as a nonprofit indie with its own distribution network, Bahia attempts to neutralize the exigencies of the marketplace. Second, with its growing local infrastructure and connections with foreign counterparts, the company is an active agent of the kind of interaction that is the stuff of a supranational musical world. The industrial interculture created and sustained by major entertainment conglomerates tends to jeopardize the existence or distinct character of local music cultures (for example, Born 1993). Bahia's activity, however, participates in a small frontierless musical world in a manner that strengthens and promotes creative efforts in local music.

Treading a Narrow Path: Human Telex

If Bahia's work contributes to an affinity interculture crystallized around a set of aesthetic values, another type of independent rock label on the present-day scene, Human Telex, is enmeshed in the production of what Slobin defines as industrial interculture, "the creature of a commodified music system," a hegemonic power intervening in local musical worlds (1993: 61). While this form of interculture is molded primarily by the majors, the picture is more complex than it seems. As I pointed out earlier, the antagonism between majors and minors has given way to a complementary or symbiotic relationship. Human Telex is both the product and local promoter of reconfigured structural conditions in the pop business based on a new kind of relationship and cooperation between these two types of music producers. It is no wonder, then, that the ideas about independence and alternative culture that guide Human Telex's practices differ radically from Bahia's.

Like Csaba, the owner and director of the Human Telex, Péter B. György, has a long history in the counterculture. For ten years before he established his record company, he organized concerts for local and foreign alternative bands. In the late 1980s he began to work as Sexepil's manager and sponsor.[16] His career became inseparable from that of the band and the label, which, despite its temporary deals with a few other bands, was established to develop and promote Sexepil.

Sexepil was one of the hottest bands of the 1980s underground but was not among its most celebrated. It seems more than a coincidence that toward the end of the decade, as the party-state started to crumble and the underground's cultural and political status grew nebulous, the members of Sexepil felt ready for a change. On Péter's advice, they replaced their former singer and front man with a Dutch musician who began to write their lyrics as well. With the addition of Mick Ness, Sexepil assumed a new singing voice, a new singing face and poetic style, and a new singing language (English). The substitution of a single band member thus transformed the very identity and character of the band.[17]

An English-language singer—a Westerner "with a perfect English accent"—promised Sexepil easier marketing in the West. By this move, the band also distanced itself from the former underground, where the accessibility of lyrics to the local public was taken for

16. The band originally spelled its name by separating its syllables: Szex-e-pil, thereby adding new layers of meaning. The *e*, as a phonetically spelled version of the French *et* (and), connects "sex" with "pil," referring to the British postpunk group PIL (Public Image Limited). PIL was formed from the legendary Sex Pistols, just as Sex-e-pil started out as a punk band named ETA, which in turn paid tribute to the organization of Basque separatists.

17. On the importance of the singing voice as the embodiment of personality, see Frith 1987: 145–46 and Laing 1985: 54–59; on the relevance of the lyrics in Eastern European rock, see, e.g., Troitsky 1987 and Cushman 1995: 103–7.

granted. The ambition of making it abroad became central to the new Sexepil, which, with Péter's sponsorship and complex business arrangements, began to target the Western alternative rock market. Rather than merely releasing tapes, as Bahia did, Human Telex, with its associated business units, comprises a management and a production company as well.[18] In his detailed analysis of the contemporary pop business Keith Negus explains:

> A number of management companies simultaneously operate as production companies signing artists and financing the development of their music to a point where it is in a form suitable for public consumption. This can then be released through a 'production and distribution' deal with a record label. . . . The production company is therefore formed to develop the artist a stage further. This may be taken a step further again, and the company may develop into a hybrid management/production/record label, publishing the material themselves and operating through various licensing, production and marketing arrangements with larger companies. (1992: 43–44)

Human Telex is the first music producer in Hungary to assume such diverse functions. Péter takes pride in his company complex as pioneering in the domestic pop music scene. A regular reader of trade papers, music magazines, and books dealing with the daily workings of the pop industry, he consciously cultivates a professional image fashioned on Anglo-American models. To him, professionalism entails a systematic search for talent, persistent hard work with the acts, and generous investments of time and money in the production of the recording, publicity, networking, promotion, and marketing. Whereas Bahia emphasizes the uniqueness of the musicians' creativity as an aesthetic value, Human Telex's emphasis is on production value. Péter conceives of music as a peculiar kind of commodity: "I noticed recently that the more serious this thing becomes, the more it resembles any other kind of enterprise. We need to work

18. Péter created a number of economic associations in order to work as effectively as possible in his diverse jobs as music producer, record company owner, and rock manager. These business units bear a confusing array of names but all are essentially functional parts of the same enterprise. Besides Human Telex, which is the company's name, I came across the name T3 (his record label) and PG Productions (his management bureau).

out marketing and strategic plans as in any other business. The difference, simply, is that one works with more personal material. We don't deal with toothbrushes but with things created by humans. So the uncertainty factor is greater, but that's what makes the task so much more beautiful." Interestingly for an alternative rock entrepreneur, Péter refuses to recognize a contradiction between aesthetic value (the "goodness" or "authenticity" of the music) and commercial success. On the contrary, he believes that anything worthwhile in pop and rock is bound to break through to a mass audience if it is produced, promoted, and marketed according to the highest professional standards. In his view, the commodity status of pop and rock does not curtail the music's aesthetic quality but rather facilitates its wide diffusion. Making good music accessible to a variety of audiences, moreover, has the additional merit of contributing to the formation of a more sophisticated and tolerant public taste.

Péter's argument has several curious elements. First, by referring to music as a potential tool for educating "the masses," he revives a rhetoric that originated in state-socialist cultural policies.[19] Second, he adds a twist to it to justify market-oriented behavior, which typically is accused of being driven by self-interest and catering to the lowest common denominator of public taste. Third, Péter challenges the countercultural notion of co-optation, which implies that commercial success corrupts rock by rounding off its counterhegemonic edge. Peter reverses the argument: it is not the character of the music that changes as a result of broad popularity, he says, but the character of the public. Two U.S. bands, Nirvana and Red Hot Chili Peppers, exemplified for him the kind of alternative properties in music to which, given the structure of the music industry, audiences of the most mixed kinds could and did respond:

> Look at Nirvana. I organized a concert for them. Two hundred people came. Now [in 1993] they're still the same kind of guys they used to be before they'd broken through. And they're classi-

19. The rhetoric of socialist cultural policies has its own bourgeois antecedents. Drawing on Norbert Elias, Lawrence Levine (1988) describes, for example, how the construction of classical music, previously undifferentiated from the popular, as a "noble" art form was viewed as a civilizing force in nineteenth-century North America. Culture was synonymous with order. The elitism with which classical music thus became imbued was paralleled by the upper classes' genuine desire to reach out to the masses with the aim of refining what they perceived as a crude and materialistic culture.

> cal embodiments of . . . nonconformity. The same is true of Red Hot Chili Peppers. One day their time arrived and they became sought after. If someone had told me two years ago that the guy selling groceries on the corner, with the gold bracelet and rings, would be listening to Nirvana and RHC, I'd say it's stupid, that couldn't possibly happen. But it did. You hear these improbable types blast this music and you don't know what's happened.

Actually, he knows and explains to me what has happened. The structure and politics of the international music business have been transformed since the 1980s. The major companies have split their financial and creative divisions. In order to keep up with emergent trends, companies began to hire young and musically competent A&R people and gave them considerable autonomy. There is no significant difference now between the majors' and the independents' business style and policies in regard to selecting and dealing with recording artists. The independent music business dissociated itself from alternative music as long as the alternatives associated themselves with a nonconformist attitude, political commitment, or any particular musical style. In fact, the very idea of alternative music lost its meaning as the majors bought up college radio stations and independents turned into trend spotters or development bureaus for the majors.

Péter's explanation echoed contemporary ideas prevalent in pop journalism and in the sociology of the entertainment industry. He emphasized that the relationship between the majors and the minors is complementary and interdependent rather than oppositional. The only legitimate meaning of "alternative," Péter claimed, is originality or relevance. In order to survive, the majors must demand as much originality and relevance as the minors do. Hence the cooperation between them.

Creativity, originality, and all the other virtues of musicianship were far from sufficient to enable Human Telex to mold Sexepil into an international star band. The music was treated as raw material to be carefully processed before it was marketed. Like Csaba, Péter needed financial resources to produce, manage, and promote his group. As a well-off director of the magazine *Magyar Narancs*, he claimed to have invested his own money in Sexepil, which had yet to yield a profit when we spoke in 1995. All the same, Péter trusted his

Western-style "methodology," which he starkly contrasted with local practices:

> P. G.: The methodology I use is absent even with the major Hungarian companies. Our normal practices are exactly what a Western company considers normal. I mean, we don't try to save on our material [resources]. We give material to the press and so forth. I can't tell you precisely now, but I guess we've sent out more than a hundred and fifty [promotional] packages to the world. Each contained press material, a video tape, a CD, and a T-shirt.
>
> A. S.: It must have cost a lot. Most bands simply lack the financial resources to do that.
>
> P. G.: Exactly. But I believe one has to invest in something in order to take anything out of it, and the group is aware that while they give their patience and musical skills, I invest my money, because that's what I have. I don't have it, actually, but I try to produce it out of my other jobs.

Another aspect of Human Telex's professionalism is the specific collaborative ventures and deals made with other companies. In order to obtain better distribution, Péter licensed one of Sexepil's albums to Polygram Hungary, but his own PG Productions kept the music publishing rights and part of the copyright revenues. In their deal with another major, Warner Hungary, PG retained the management rights as well, in order to keep control over the band's visual image as it was projected in photos, album covers, and video clips. Warner's part was restricted to manufacturing and distribution; that is, to the capital- and labor-intensive aspects of record production.

Reliance on Hungarian-born westerners is common in the business life of postcommunist Hungary. They are expected to combine interest, empathy, and cultural understanding with business acumen and expertise. In the export of a cultural commodity such as rock music, this combination of attitude and skills is particularly valuable. Sexepil's manager, too, prefers to work with emigrants. He hired a Hungarian-born American "with excellent connections in the music business" to handle the band's "international development." Sexepil appeared at a number of prestigious festivals and clubs all over the United States. The group is also among the very few local bands that Music Television Europe has featured on several occasions. The key to this accomplishment, according to the manager, is his reliance on a German Hungarian to produce their videos.

Never has popular music depended on sounds alone for its power and meaning. It is a multimedia text, dependent on pop video, DVD, CD-ROM, satellite and cable television, the Internet, and what Negus calls media synergy, a strategy employed by entertainment corporations "of diversifying into directly related technologies and areas of entertainment and using the opportunities that this provides for extending the exposure of specific pieces and music" (1992: 5). He goes on to argue that the makers of popular success rely so heavily on the promotional use of visuals, concerts, interviews, movies, and so forth that by now music as sound has been displaced from the center of focus. Artists are positioned in complex "entertainment packages," and the media personnel who acquire, develop, and promote them play a remarkably important role in their creation.

The sophisticated technologies Péter and his partners employ in their effort to fashion the first Hungarian international star band fit very well with the concept of the entertainment package, a multimedia construction in which music is just one element. It does not mean, however, that the musical sound must fall by the wayside. Much of contemporary rock, rap, and other popular musical sounds are appraised less on the grounds of the actual music material than on the basis of the styles and technologies of recording—a highly creative act in itself—and the mixing and mastering to which the original tape is subjected (Rose 1994; Goodwin 1992, 1998).

Sexepil recorded one of its albums in a local studio but with help from a U.S. producer. The mixing and the mastering took place in what Péter deemed to be the most outstanding U.S. studios for alternative rock. It was not merely the technologies and expert skills that Sexepil sought in the United States but also the creative atmosphere that rock producers and studio technicians are seen to bring to their work. Producers temporarily act as members of the bands they work with, shaping the songs' structure and delivery, the lyrics and so forth (Hennion 1983). This "producer system," Péter and other pop music practitioners claim, is traditionally absent from the Hungarian music industry. The title is merely formal. At a recording session, he says half-jokingly, sound engineers do nothing but push the knobs up and down on the mixing table, and the loudest of them will proclaim himself the music producer.

Since foreign critics dismissed the sound of Sexepil's earlier album as "obsolete," the company turned to Western production facilities and personnel in an effort to attain that distinctive yet elusive acoustic quality that Western pop listeners identify as "contemporary" and "alternative." Sexepil selected a studio in Madison, Wisconsin, and another one in New York, both of which nurtured one-time alternative but hugely successful and famed acts, such as Nirvana, the Irish U2, and the British Dépèche Mode. Important as it was to produce the "right sound," it did not hurt to combine it with the prestige of celebrated pop professionals.

Independence and Ideological Work: Human Telex and the Alternative Music Scene

Given the complex pop machinery set up in the pursuit of mass success, it sounded paradoxical that Péter classified the operation as "independent." To the outside observer it seems anything but independent of major entertainment corporations. The highly calculated manner of inserting themselves into the workings of the transnational music business suggests that Sexepil is indeed a producer of and participant in the industrial interculture. In what sense, then, may this production team be viewed as independent?

Independence, for Human Telex, means autonomy, the freedom to cultivate their own thing in their own way. This freedom entails dissociating and distinguishing themselves from the two power centers in the alternative music scene: the local affiliates of the majors and the old underground-dominated indies represented by Bahia. Since Sexepil's target is the Western pop market, they have to cooperate with the majors. Cooperation poses two problems. First, voicing a widespread idea, Péter argues that the transnational companies established their offices in Hungary with the primary goal of marketing their own international stars rather than promoting local musicians abroad.[20] This practice, commonly referred to as cultural im-

20. Unfortunately, the national recording industry figures collected by MAHASZ, the Hungarian branch of IFPI (International Federation of the Phonograph Industry), do not include data concerning the export of local music to Western markets. Many of my inter-

perialism, is exacerbated by a specific form of the star system employed by the domestic divisions of the majors. According to Péter, this system is unimaginative and obsolete, imposing managers' "secondhand visions" on musicians. Since several of these offices came to be staffed by the personnel of the defunct socialist pop industry, this perception is not without basis. By maintaining control over the artistic work and management, Péter wants to make sure that Sexepil remains unaffected by the damage allegedly afflicted by Hungarian star-making practices. His description of it fits with the prevalent discourse of the 1980s and early 1990s, which equated Western ways with professionalism, up-to-dateness, and creative freedom.

> My situation is rather unique because I have insight into the corporate strategies of both the local and the foreign offices of major companies. It's become common sense in the West that stars can't just be created, say, by me sitting at home in my living room and deciding we ought to have the local equivalent of [the group] Faith No More, so then I just go about creating it. . . . There used to be such practices over there, too, but by now, in making a star, they rely on the artist's talent and on how that could be developed best with respect to his or her own individuality. One can't say that Madonna is being "created." She is herself.

If a star like Madonna is not an industrial product to be manufactured, then first she has to be spotted. But a Madonna, Péter contends, would never be spotted in Hungary, where A&R people rarely

viewees see the goal and nature of the operations of major companies as a form of cultural domination that threatens the ability of local musicians to be heard not only abroad but even at home. Musicians' and media people's everyday perception of a one-way flow between Western and domestic markets seems correct: the number of local musicians who even attempt to target international audiences is negligible in comparison with the overwhelming presence of Western music in Hungary. Statistical figures, however, do not justify the musicians' anxiety concerning the threat of Western pop and rock to their popularity at home. Legitimate (that is, nonpirate) sales of foreign pop did not exceed those of domestic music until 1994. Even then the difference was small, 2.7 million units for foreign music and 2.6 million for local music in 1991–94. The years between 1995 and 2000 did not alter the direction of this trend. Even though more foreign than local items were sold, their respective shares remained in balance (Tamás Ligeti Nagy, personal communication, based on MAHASZ statistics).

take the trouble to attend concerts and clubs in search of new talent, as they do in the West. Aside from the absence of the producer system and effective promotion, the local pop industry is dragged down, according to Péter, by the persistence of the old boys' network, which cues directors as to whom to sign. Péter portrays his team's values as clashing so sharply with those of local majors that effective communication is impossible: "We're talking about the same thing in two languages and don't understand each other." I wondered how Human Telex had secured the indispensable cooperation of these remodeled yet sluggish mammoths. He said it had used its extensive foreign networks and professional credibility to achieve recognition at home so that it could bargain for favorable deals with Polygram and Warner Hungary. It took advantage of the corporate hierarchy: the center advised the periphery about the creative potential it saw in Sexepil. Human Telex thus played on the tension between the core (center) and the periphery: between the more dynamic Western-style pop business and its emergent capitalist imitator struggling with the legacy of the noncompetitive organizational culture of the 1970s and 1980s.

Human Telex's struggle for autonomy not only required it to distinguish itself from the local practices of major music corporations; it also had to demarcate itself from the old underground in an attempt to construct a credible identity for the renewed Sexepil and to present the entire commercial operation as a respectable project.

Earlier I touched on how Human Telex's aesthetic ideology and policies diverged from Bahia's. Whereas Bahia articulated the familiar elitist underground indie philosophy, Human Telex challenged the opposition between alternative/underground values and commercial viability. Bahia idealistically attempts to keep market forces at bay; Human Telex pragmatically embraces those forces. While Bahia celebrated the pre-1989 countercultural movement as its roots, Human Telex turned away from it to sculpt Sexepil's new image. Péter's rejection of Bahia and the old underground's social and artistic world seemed essential to the image-reconstruction work demanded by institutional and political change.

In his discussion of the postglasnost Russian underground rock scene, Cushman (1995: 277–97) describes how the collective identity of musicians forged under communism was shattered along a fault line of social and cultural factors, such as professional role divisions, generational conflicts, attitudes toward Western versus national culture, and attitudes toward money. The controversy between Bahia and Human Telex threw into relief another factor that caused fragmentation. As the subculture dissolved in the late 1980s, a painful division developed between the most successful and the second- or third-string musicians, who were usually younger and enjoyed less respect. Péter worked with the latter groups. His scathing commentary on the underground may be viewed as an attempt to cover up the bitterness he felt when he and Sexepil were left behind as new interest groups were forming. Or perhaps his bitter criticism served as psychological justification for his denial of the underground's core values and his turn to a market orientation. As an observer of this complex scenario, I am not in a position to determine which explanation may be closer to the truth. It may not even be important to do so. Instead, I will examine the perennial themes and debates in rock-'n'roll that Sexepil's dispute with the old guard brought to the surface and reworked.

Popularity in rock music is a highly ambiguous and politically loaded concept (Cohen 1991, Frith 1981, Middleton 1990, Fiori 1985). Stardom has always been part of rock mythology (Vermorel and Vermorel 1985), but so has disdain for commercialism and mass success. Moreover, in rock's day-to-day reality it is hard to separate musicians' narcissistic desire for popularity from their wish for material success. Rock is a mass cultural form par excellence, yet fans make subtle distinctions between what music is and is not good enough to fit the category of rock'n'roll. From the outset the ideology of rock-'n'roll has had an elitist and a populist strand. The contradictions and debates between these two strands articulate the increasing social differentiation and cultural heterogeneity of the audiences for the music, while the category itself has lost its clear boundaries (Fornäs 1995).

As a populist Péter charges the former underground with having no ambition to be popular. By creating and staying in what he calls a style ghetto, they can avoid testing the attraction of their music. Their aesthetic, resting on the elitist canon of hard-core alternative music (Straw 1991, Kruse 1993), merely rationalizes a lack of effort to make better (read: more successful) music. To challenge Peter's view,

I hinted at Kampec Dolores's reputation abroad, appealing to Péter's unconditional respect for Western standards. He then shifted his ground with a snide remark about the smallness of KD's audience. He expressed extreme frustration with what he considered the dilettantism and confusion of Bahia's business dealings. He blamed that, too, on the old underground's conceit. Again, Western counterexamples helped him make his case:

> [The likes of Bahia] in the West at least are aware that even if they think differently [from the mainstream], this music is still a commercial enterprise. And that there are structures. Even if you don't hook up with the majors, you have your own structure with proper decision-making mechanisms, since the aim is to create something that works. Here the idea coming from an elitist stance is that things will work by themselves. "Because I'm a genius, my ingenuity will move the whole thing." This is stupid. It won't move anything.

In my efforts to understand Péter's perception of Bahia and the ideological work of which it forms a part, I find Bennett Berger a good guide. Berger's (1981) idea of ideological work rests on the assumption that under the pressures of everyday living, material circumstances, and interests, people's ideas and beliefs are rarely congruent with their observed behavior. Ideological work is an intellectual process through which we adjust our professed ideas and values to the exigencies of the real-life situations in which we act every day. Yet even in our own eyes the ideologically reworked ideas never cease to appear autonomous.

The conflict between Human Telex and Bahia brings up several enduring themes and issues in rock music: the eternal tension between rock as art versus commercial enterprise (elitism versus populism); the nature and measurability of success; the relationship between musical value and success; the meaning and content of professionalism and independence in a capitalist industrial setting; the stylistic or textual requirements for being alternative or underground (the legitimacy of a canon), and so on. The changing social context of the debate within the former underground required social actors to continually reevaluate and readjust their ideas in an attempt to comprehend and interpret their reconfiguring environment. They needed to envision their appropriate place in this new environment. Their interpretations and ideas became subject to other actors' evaluations and interpretations. Societal transition requires far more intense ideological work than is usual when social life is stable. Such work not only involves constant readjustment of ideas, the structural conditions of life, and new material interests; it also requires constant checking against the ideas of others—fellow musicians, friends, industry personnel—as they distance themselves from some social relationships and enter into new ones. Nothing seems stable. Whenever structures, institutional habits, or ideas do seem unchanged, they appear anomalous or anachronistic.

To Péter, virtually everything about Bahia seemed anachronistic: their musical taste, their style of doing business, even the way they connected with the past. If Bahia's status rests, as it does, on their founders' and artists' countercultural past, Péter called into question the kind of legitimacy offered by that past. While acknowledging the historical merits of the 1980s underground, he spurned its members for failing to build the foundations for an independent infrastructure of their own; of lacking musicianship and relying too much on the political message they wanted to communicate. Therefore, when political opposition lost its urgency, Péter argued, it became obvious that the underground had consisted of poor musicians. He implied that the political thaw of the late 1980s not simply undermined the musicians' maverick status and identity but revealed them as having been incompetent from the start. According to this logic, not even good politics can justify bad musicianship. A very biting comment indeed, and one I heard repeatedly from a circle of musicians, the rejects of the movement.

Péter and Sexepil, however, were insiders throughout the 1980s. They wouldn't have been if they had believed at the time that politics and musical competence were mutually exclusive in rock'n'roll.[21]

21. In fact, Sexepil and its manager still cared about politics and a politically correct image as defined by the liberals in the early 1990s. Few people knew, Péter said, that in the media war, which was at its most ferocious at the time of our first interview, Sexepil organized a protest among rock musicians. The initiative involved joining writers, composers, and other intellectuals in withdrawing their works from programming as long as the government and other right-wing forces pursued their antiliberal interventionist policies on state-run radio and television. To set up yet another contrast between themselves and the old

Less famed than some of their peers who later gathered around Bahia, they felt pressed for a radical shift in profile and attitude. Sexepil had less clout to help them weather the consequences of sociopolitical change. In Bourdieu's terms, their accumulated symbolic capital was not sufficient to convert into postsocialist success.

Péter's case was different. As an organizer who, in his own words, had continually asked for and done favors over the previous ten years, he gained considerable business experience and social capital in the form of extensive networks at home and abroad. These networks enabled him to start a whole new kind of alternative pop business, treading the narrow and inherently controversial path of market-oriented alternative music. Sexepil and Human Telex had to rationalize their isolation from former friends and peers. The institutional and artistic autonomy Péter emphasizes so forcefully vis-à-vis both the majors and the old underground may most easily be seen as a hard-worked-for and difficult ideological position, taken in part by default. It was an elaborate answer to the disillusionment with a subculture where, in Péter's words, "there was no way to bring the groups together to support and help each other." Ironically, despite his respect for the market, he echoes the bitter complaint of many other musicians I interviewed: "Money intruded in the movement real soon."

The Orthodox Independents: Trottel

As Mihály Rácz, a journalist with the rock fanzine *Ordító Egér* (Howling Mouse), noted, "it is characteristic of the company [Trottel Records] to select acts on the basis not only of their music but of what kind of people they are. This, I guess, is not a negligible point today when people's value systems have been shaken."[22] Trottel

guard, Péter was quick to point out that a certain musician, idolized in underground circles—someone who had recently returned from a decade in the West—was reluctant to participate in the action for fear that his new release would not get sufficient airtime. Again, the truth or falsity of this charge is less pertinent than the light it throws on the complex and bitter struggle between former peers and the ideological work in which individual musicians engaged to achieve a stable identity.

22. "Trottel Rocords: Still the Same Story Goes On '94," *Ordító Egér*, no. 4 (1994), 26. The English name of the label reveals the company's orientation to the international underground music scene.

Records was founded in 1992 by Tamás Rupaszov, the leader of the punk band of the same name. The record company shares Bahia's commitment to serious experimentation in production and publishing, as well as a disregard for commercial gain. But Trottel is peculiar in its concern with political and ethical issues.

The rock group Trottel belonged to the lesser known second wave of the pre-1989 underground. Its career started just a year before record production and dissemination were liberalized, so systemic changes did not disrupt the group's life and public face in any major way. On the contrary, Trottel was a product of structural changes in the culture industry. At the beginning of his career, Tamás Rupaszov issued a series of three tapes comprising some local punks' musical repertoire. The technology Trottel Records employed corresponded to the radically rudimentary music aesthetic and do-it-yourself philosophy of the punk movement (Laing 1985, Hebdige 1979, Vermorel and Vermorel 1978, Greil Marcus 1989). If musicians were not expected to be able to play more than three chords to form a band, as the saying went, it seemed entirely appropriate to reproduce the tapes at home with such low-fi facilities as two-tape recorders and to prepare and copy the cover inserts by themselves. What distinguished Trottel from the rest of the underground was that Trottel circulated their homemade tapes as a business before such operations were fully legal. Trottel was literally an underground enterprise, and a moderately lucrative one at that.

Like Kampec Dolores and the Galloping Coroners, Trottel actively built its reputation abroad within the interculture of alternative rockers. Through promotional tapes sent to foreign fanzines, record labels, organizers, and musicians, it became part of a network that provided touring and recording opportunities in Europe (Szőnyei 1993: 105). Ferenc Bróder, one of the two members of Trottel Records' staff, was formerly a musician in an experimental noise band called Hidegroncs (roughly Nervous Wreck)[23] and a writer for *Howling Mouse*. He tells me that it was the Trottel group's positive re-

23. This name is an untranslatable pun combining the words *hideg* (cold) and *idegroncs* (nervous wreck). The cold metallic and distorted sound as well as the monotonous, sustained dissonance the two-member group elaborated in its music well explains both components of the chosen name.

ception abroad that persuaded them to come aboveground. They sold so many tapes at concerts outside of Hungary that they could no longer carry enough of them in a suitcase to satisfy the demand. They had to get official permission to sell tapes in order to avoid violating customs and sales tax regulations. Trottel Records (TR) is proud that their predominantly local catalog includes a few Western acts too. Still they have retained the ethos of an underground operation. In the company there are no fixed roles and no division of tasks. Ferenc says, "We determine that the next task ahead is, say, to pick up the cassettes of *X* band from the pressing plant. One of us agrees to do this. He brings the cassettes home and we throw a big dinner party, open three bottles of wine, fold in all the five hundred cover inserts, put the tapes inside, and put them all in a big box."

Ferenc believes that Trottel operates in an atmosphere of solidarity. It uses friends' and spouses' help for a variety of services it could not afford to pay for. For promotion and advertising the company relies on sympathetic journalists and media people who seek out Trottel's latest publications and catalogs on their own. Ferenc's girlfriend used to be an editor of *Howling Mouse*. She is no longer involved directly in the musical life of the underground. As a full-time business person, however, she shares her expertise and skills with Ferenc to help his business move ahead. This working method and style certainly corresponds to a low-profile operation. Ferenc explains: "Usually we dub a portion of five hundred copies. There are a few titles that don't sell even that many, others don't sell at all! . . . We issue a minimum of five hundred and reorder as long as they sell. The largest selling [title] was over three thousand copies."

Distribution poses a great deal of difficulty. It is costly and inefficient to carry such small numbers of tapes to retailers. Trottel Records wants to stay the least expensive music provider in the market, so it must put considerable effort and time into making deals with individual retailers. But TR is short not only on capital but on the time their minuscule staff can spend: both Tamás and Ferenc have full-time jobs outside the music business[24] At the time of our in-

24. Tamás is a printer; Ferenc studied to be an electrician, and later to be a printer.

terview they considered changing their distribution and marketing strategies. Their practice was to sell their tapes to a wholesaler on commission, and the wholesaler would resell them to retailers who were willing to take them on commission. The commission system is used for handling tapes whose sales are predictably very small. Nonspecialist stores therefore are not keen in adding these items to their stock. Even when they do, Ferenc explained, small-scale providers such as Trottel are the easiest to cut off in case of financial difficulties. In brief, as a business partner TR is quickly pushed aside by other actors in the marketplace. TR therefore decided to switch to direct distribution by mail order. In this way they hoped to lower their costs and consequently the prices of their releases. Their main targets, Ferenc stressed, are not the well-off young people in Budapest who can afford to go to rock concerts but the poorer ones in the economically most backward eastern parts of the country, who are also quite radical in their musical taste.

Mail-order distribution seemed to suit Trottel Records' political outlook as well. Not only does the company nurture direct, informal, and friendly relations as a working team, but it is also intent on personalizing their relationship with their audience. This is not the marketing ploy it would be for a mainstream pop publisher. Ferenc found that corresponding with over a thousand people who are interested in the label is exciting, even as the intensity and intimacy of the relationships vary widely. Sometimes discussions about the music prompts intriguing conversations on a variety of political and cultural issues with a sociologically and demographically diverse group of people. While the majority of them are young, age does not appear to affect the intensity of their dedication to Trottel's music. This came as a surprise to the Trottel staff, men in their late twenties. Ferenc told me, "There was a guy I kept talking to on the phone for a very long time when he revealed himself to be a grandfather. Another one was a daddy [*apuka*]. Daddy, a computer expert, happened to be a Nervous Wreck fan too. . . . Then I was corresponding with a lady in Slovakia whom I addressed informally [*tegeződtem vele*]. We talked on and on about politics and then she said she was a forty-five-year-old school principal."

From the perspective of Human Telex's market-oriented professionalism, Trottel's version of independence is anachronistic, too. It eschews any compromise when matters of money interfere with dignity, friendly relations, or musical taste—and this at a time when money became the central player in noncommercial rock culture in Hungary. Perhaps the single most important aspect of change in the character of this music scene has been the development of an institutional environment that compels performers and organizers to redefine their relationship to money, whether in the form of profits, taxes, performance fees, corporate or noncommercial sponsorship, studio rental fees, recording costs, royalties, or subsidiary fees. Many of these financial items were not visible or simply did not exist in the cultural life of the socialist era. Those that did exist, such as recording costs and performance fees, were not negotiable by the musicians, who invariably were cast as supplicants. The space of the underground especially had been so restricted that the money to be made from music was too little to matter.

With the onset of the 1990s financial questions intruded in TR's everyday existence in a variety of forms. Like most other alternative musicians and publishers, they needed sponsors to cover rental fees for concert venues and the costs of production and promotion. Among the several sources of support, commercial sponsorship has become a necessity. Young alternative bands playing in front of Pizza Hut or Coca-Cola signs are by no means an unusual sight. The TR staff, however, was especially reluctant to set up deals with big businesses.

The venue where TR's bands were to perform received support from the Trident corporation, but still TR was charged for part of the rental fee. This arrangement entailed the risk of losing money on the concert if it failed to attract a sizable audience. Ferenc and Tamás insisted that if their musicians shared the stage with advertising for Trident, Trident must pay the rental charge. When Trident refused, TR canceled the performance. Nobody seemed to understand, Ferenc says, why they did not compromise. "In Hungary it's become the norm to hang around [*odacsapódni*] large corporations 'because they give so much money.' We're not interested in how much money a corporation throws around if they don't pay us right. I won't take risks for the sake of their business if I have to stand under any kind of logo. . . . If a company expects me to advertise for them, I won't go crawling to them." Trottel Records goes against the grain in taking this position. Most people in the music business, Ferenc contends, are willing to humiliate themselves for what amounts to pennies for a corporation like McDonald's or Trident.

The episode, as Ferenc recounted it, suggests that the small-scale entrepreneurship that empowered people in alternative culture when the free market was introduced did not save them from sliding back into the position of supplicants for economic survival. The place of socialist bureaucracy has now been taken by the all-powerful multinational corporation, eager to expand its market in Eastern Europe. Marlboro, for instance, targets a large youthful population of actual or potential smokers by sponsoring three-day rock talent search festivals. Trottel's principled response to what they perceived as the arrogance of multinationals is not common, yet it also signals the rise of anticorporate sentiment in postcommunist Hungary: "They're the ones who advertise and make profits—these essentially exploitive companies—so why should I lower myself?"[25]

Another site of confrontation for TR is the emergent bureaucratic-legal apparatus of the capitalist music industry. The regulations set up to protect publishers from illegal reproduction and distribution of their releases left musicians powerless to negotiate for a better share of the profits from their recordings. It was difficult for them even to ensure that companies carried out their obligations and paid the agreed-upon royalties. The whole arena of music production and reproduction was in a state of chaos.

This turbulence subsided significantly as the five major transnational companies gradually acquired local affiliates: the Japanese-based Sony Music, the German-based BMG, the Dutch-based Polygram, the U.S.-based Warner Music International, and the British EMI Music. (The latter three fused with or bought up domestic labels.) By 1995 the estimated share of these five companies in the local

25. As I have suggested, it would have been difficult to anticipate the rapid resurgence of this kind of leftist rhetoric, especially among young people. Many concepts frozen into the stock phrases of Marxist dogma had become abused and, in a sense, contaminated by the previous political system's discourse. Esterházy reflects on this type of linguistic damage: "Words, meanings, consensual understandings, intentional misunderstandings were floating, circulating, sniffing one another like dogs in spring; magic formulas like workers' power, proletariat of the world, objective, international situation, socialist patriotism were whirling in the wind" (1994: 25).

(legal) market reached 89 percent.[26] No wonder they have made major efforts to minimize black-market operations. The majors had a significant role in founding MAHASZ, the Hungarian branch of IFPI (International Federation of the Phonograph Industry). In 1995 MAHASZ comprised twenty-six music publishers and record companies, none of which specialized in alternative music. The relatively high annual membership fee effectively excluded small-scale producers striving to recoup their investment rather than aiming at profits. These producers felt that MAHASZ set the fee this high to shield its members not only from piracy but also from the competition posed by the alternative music business.

MAHASZ's less popular measures included the tightening of copyright regulations and restrictions on trading activities. Trottel would not have incorporated itself if MAHASZ had not required producers and distributors to secure permission to export and import recorded music. Another measure requires record producers to obtain authorization from the Copyright Office to have their tapes reproduced. Copyright fees were to be paid when the tapes were released. These fees were such a significant item for Trottel Records that they had to make special arrangements to pay only after each recording sold rather than at the time it was issued. (It should be noted that the company's financial situation is in part a function of its unusually royalty payments: TR shares 50 percent of the profits, if any, after each release [Szőnyei 1993: 107].)[27]

TR is particularly resentful of the introduction of a symbol, the "nodding giraffe," to legitimate the tapes and disks issued by the five majors. Since piracy poses no threat to a small independent label, TR pays dearly for protection it does not need. Yet the big companies' advertising campaigns convey the impression that the "nodding giraffe" is the only guarantee of a recording's legitimacy, and that the public should refuse to buy products without the label. TR's

26. Ágnes Müzinger, legal representative of MAHASZ, personal communication, April 1995.

27. Although contracts vary widely, bands that haven't displayed great earning potential usually receive a royalty of 10–14 "points." Points are percentages of a recording's sales revenue minus the advance paid to the band (Negus 1992: 42–44). Small producers like TR don't pay advances.

philosophy—cooperation at the expense of competition, informality rather than professional business relations—does not fit the realities of the capitalist culture market, especially when its major players don't seem to play a fair game.

Conclusion

Since rock music is primarily a mass medium, the reorganization of this sector after the collapse of the party-state holds central importance for the shifting social status and inner makeup of the former underground subculture.

In the recording industry the structural transition was gradual and was marked by curious twists and turns. In the late socialist era some musicians enjoyed remarkable political freedom and generous material support by Hungaroton, which was going through its own identity crisis. Capitalist rearrangements in the music industry initially produced a state of disarray, leaving musicians vulnerable to a legally unregulated market that favored adventurism. Yet the introduction of the free market did offer former counterculturists an opportunity to create their own recording companies.

Engaging in business opened up new cultural spaces at home and abroad; it allowed for new forms of creativity and gave a sense of autonomy to those involved in it. At the same time, the autonomy that entrepreneurship has provided to commercially nonviable popular music is extremely precarious. Because of their need for sponsors, few musician-entrepreneurs are capable of controlling the conditions under which they produce, perform, and sell their music. The evidence indicates that without multinational or other corporate support, alternative music's share of the pop music market would be even smaller than it is now. But as the plight of Trottel Records demonstrates, quite often this support can be negotiated solely from the position of a humble client before a powerful patron.

The widely varying entrepreneurial structures, styles, and ideologies among the three indies testify to the breakup of alliances within the former underground community and to its replacement with a fragmented and vaguely defined alternative music scene. Whereas some of the organizing values and policies of these companies are complementary and represent cultural differentiation and diversity, others articulate and rationalize a conflict of interests. Such a conflict arose in response to the differential symbolic and social capital the musicians and entrepreneurs brought with them from the counterculture. Curiously, the contestation over what it means to engage in alternative music revived perennial debates about rock's controversial politics and complex identity.

5

The Countercultural Past:

Symbolic Capital or a Sacred Domain?

In 1993 a unique stage performance called *Songs from Central Nirvania* premiered.[1] "Nirvania" in the title immediately defined the program's theme and character: in an early punk song composed and performed by the Spions, Nirvania was a metaphor for state-socialist Hungary. Perhaps the only well-known song as subversive as the original "Nirvania" was the Sex Pistols' "God Save the Queen." "Nirvania" was banned, of course, but not before it became a hallmark of Hungarian underground rock.

Songs from Central Nirvania was conceived and performed by an old-timer of the post-1968 avant-garde, Ágnes Kamondy (Fig. 12), who had made her name in the folk revival and amateur drama movements and subsequently landed in the rock underground. For *Central Nirvania* Kamondy rearranged the most widely known and cherished songs of the underground legacy, peppered with her own compositions. Diverse in expressive style, ambience, and message, these songs were to invoke what Kamondy called the "ghetto," the feel of a place and an era as insiders knew them.

1. In Hungarian, *Dalok Közép-Nirvániából: Szabad Variációk barátaim és magam dalaira, tizenöt év távlatából.* Director: Róbert Vörös. Conductor: István Silló. Premiered at Egyetemi Színpad (University Theater), Budapest, May 23, 1993.

12
Ágnes Kamondy. Photo by Tamás Ligeti Nagy.

The self-reflective protagonist of EPH's song "The Tourist" is having a hard time situating herself in the bleak realities imagined as "moving pictures in black and white." The antihero of URA's somber and hallucinatory ballad "The Unknown Soldier" changes from the "innocent who hasn't killed" into the "innocent who's already killed." Even though "he barely understands the news" and has "zero chance for victory," he is well aware that the system destroying him must be destroyed. Sziámi's hard-edged and cynical song "You'll Die Too" challenges our belief in the possibility of moral integrity in "nowhere land," where "the law itself is sinful and punishment needs to be punished." The cat-fearing reclusive mouse in Balaton's "Faustian Moment" is trying to make sense of her cosmic angst and emptiness. In EPH and Balaton's irony-tinged "It'll Go Away" the languorous subject finds pleasure in pain and reveals self-pity underneath the suffering. EPA's "It's Gonna Be Good for Us" transports the lyrical subject and his lover from the real and apparently uninhabitable social world of 1980s Budapest to the rarefied privacy of "alien stars," a trip that turns out to be beyond human history.

By the 1990s these and many other underground songs attained the sacred status of classics. Even the youngest teenagers demanded them at concerts, and they and their elders readily bought them as soon as they were commercially available. Lines from the lyrics made their way onto school kids' backpacks,[2] into satirical cartoons, into political, personal, and even commercial advertising. The musicians both fostered and exploited the songs' sacralization. They reunited for nostalgia shows; Bahia remixed and reissued concert programs that had existed only on amateur recordings. For the first time radio shows gave exposure to the favorites of the 1980s. Journalistic and academic accounts, even university dissertations, on the merits of this subculture proliferated (Nagy n.d.; Szőnyei 1992, 1993; Sükösd 1993; Apor 1994).

Musicians and critics talked about their desire to finally "document" (*dokumentálni*) the musical output of the early 1980s. Why did musicians and music lovers use such an unwieldy term, more appropriately belonging to the vocabulary of librarians and lawyers? I figured that they wanted to imbue these songs, symbols of the counterculture, with a more acoustically adequate and pleasing form. The old poor-quality tapes may have reminded them of the technically poor and politically adverse performance and recording contexts to which the music was confined under the previous regime. Not only the musicians and their audiences were victimized in this way, but the music as well. The desire to touch up the music and make it widely available, then, had more than merely commercial or even artistic motives: it had the aim of redressing and substantiating the countercultural past.

What role did these musical pieces, traces of a bygone era, play

2. A young friend of my family's, for example, scribbled on her backpack the motto on the Committee's first LP, *Up to Adventure!* (Hungaroton, 1983). Because it is a play on words, my translation only roughly approximates the original meaning: "Everybody worries so much, and all that worry is such a worry that there's no need to worry!" (Mindenkinek annyi baja van, az annyi bajnak annyi baja van, hogy annyi baj legyen!).

in the musicians' efforts to relocate themselves in the social and cultural spaces of postcommunist Hungary? Did the community have control over the meaning and uses of the legacy? What questions of ownership and authorship did the legacy pose?

Making Sense of the Countercultural Past

The relegation of the former underground and its songs to the past marked people's awareness that the political change had thoroughly transformed the social conditions and the political character and effects of the subculture's music. Some musicians emphasized the loss they felt as the music lost its exhilarating public appeal and became a largely private matter confined to the aesthetic domain. Others explained how the music scene needed to reinvent itself as it shifted from an oppositional space to a position defined by commerce. Ágnes Kamondy, who likened the underground to a ghetto, talked about the dilemmas individual musicians faced as they emerged aboveground to redefine their place in the wider community. "Either you reassess who you are as a person," she said, "or you live the values that were forged in the ghetto."

Cushman claims that rock subcultures are interpretive communities. They share "common definitions of reality and rules for interpretation of meanings of cultural texts" (1995: 114). People who, "in their well-protected and self-enclosed space," as Ágnes put it, "circulated slogans, habits, boyfriends, and girlfriends among each other," faced the challenge of making sense of the surrounding social world without being able to negotiate it in intense and affective interactions with musicians, friends, and audiences. With the wearing away of the fabric of shared ideas, habits, and sentiments, with the dissolution of a common lifeworld (Habermas 1981–87, 2: 113–90), members of the former community experienced further difficulty in interpreting the not yet crystallized operation of power in their everyday lives. The once relatively transparent links between the political, ethical, and material aspects of subscribing to the alternative culture turned opaque, ambiguous, and contradictory.

According to the cultural theorist Philip Corrigan, refusing or opposing particular social practices and relations requires our imagination to identify who and what exactly we want to refuse or oppose (1990: 274). Several musicians suggested that their new adversaries were far less easily locatable than they had been in the socialist era. If the forces and spirit of capitalism seemed frightening and alienating, that perception did not spring from the unbridled rule of the market alone, although no doubt it played a part. It seemed equally troublesome to identify the apparently distant and impersonal social forces at play. "To be sure, one could find out where the center from which power operates is, but not from my perspective and not even from yours," Jenő Menyhárt said to me resignedly. This interpretive crisis, which also surfaced in Péter Magyar's story about the failure of Egocentrum, is a crucial yet often overlooked element of what it takes to regain one's voice as an independent or alternative artist in new circumstances. The literary scholar Péter Balassa (1994) imagines himself in a wrestling match to express the general sense of unease typically felt by intellectuals and artists:

> In the old regime, in the last stages of its existence, it was no longer the political system per se that abused the artist, the scholar, or the intellectual. Things worked more complicatedly and problems could not always be attributed directly to the mechanics of the system as such. But now it seems the very intangibility of the system is plucking on our nerves—as if we were confronted with a wrestler who spread too much oil on his body to prevent us from getting a grip on him. (1994: 48)

This subtle form of disempowerment, coupled with the loss felt as a network of friends and fellow artists fell apart, made the imperative to redefine oneself and the direction of one's work a constant pressure. The former community, moreover, grew into a terrain of conflicts, as demonstrated by the rock musicians' imbroglio with other elective communities and by the sharp confrontation of cultural values in building up an alternative music business. Ideological discords and unequal economic and career opportunities redrew the map of former alliances and friendships, arousing bitter competition and suspicion where a sense of unity had prevailed. Even though new subcultural alliances developed in place of the old one and a diverse alternative cultural scene was emerging, in the process several musicians broke away from the community or were left to their own resources. In the individual and collective attempts to negotiate, benefit from, or step beyond the countercultural past, intriguing facets of the identity work in which musicians engaged came into view.

Symbolic Capital and the Renegotiation of Marginal Identity

Pierre Bourdieu (1980, 1984, 1993) developed his theory of symbolic and cultural capital to explain the reproduction of inequalities in bourgeois society through the differential social valuation of symbolic forms and practices that social actors appropriate through socialization. Symbolic capital is integral to the economy of cultural production in that it bestows honor and prestige on cultural works. In the long run, symbolic capital can be turned into economic capital. Bourdieu understands cultural capital as a set of skills and competences associated with the production and consumption of works of "legitimate culture"; that is, those endowed with symbolic value by the cultural elite.

Existing analyses show that the ideas of symbolic and cultural capital are pertinent not only to the institutionalized mechanisms of reproduction under stable societal conditions but also to the reformulation of class and status hierarchy in the context of structural change. Ákos Róna-Tas (1994) described how members of Hungary's former elite used their cultural (educational) and social capital to stay atop the social ladder even as the contents and titles of their jobs changed. What possibilities did the change in regime open up for rockers with symbolic and social capital acquired as underground artists under socialism?

To apply Bourdieu's conceptual framework to the predicament of the oppositional avant-garde is uniquely interesting. First, obvious contradictions are involved in the conversion of symbolic capital derived from countercultural activities into economic opportunities and advantages. Second, structural changes in the economy and politics in Eastern Europe intersected with a major and ongoing shift of global scale in the field of art production: the transition from modernism to postmodernism. This process became most visible, as I argued earlier, in hybridization and cross-overs between "high" and "low" cultural practices and in the creation of new cultural spaces that defy traditional classification (Walker 1987, Frith and Horne 1987, Huyssen 1990, Zolberg 1990). The postmodern turn problematized fundamental assumptions and value judgments about art, and this process had a bearing on Hungarian intellectuals' and artists' ideas of cultural value as well. Did the socioeconomic transition facilitate the legitimization of new cultural spaces?

Let me first address the question of why the conversion of underground musicians' symbolic capital is intrinsically contradictory. Unlike such political dissenters as the democratic and nationalist opposition, the rock community had no specific political agenda or goal programmed into its activities. Musicians emphasized political themes that tied their art to the contextual realities of postwar Hungary. But they also borrowed themes and ideas from the countercultural tradition of Western rock, which, as Frith and Horne pointed out, had been inspired by oppositional avant-garde art. The Control Group, for example, directly addressed political taboos such as the presence of Soviet troops in Hungarian territory but enacted subversion on other semantic levels too, by incorporating such perennial rock'n'roll themes as sex and drugs.

Because these musicians and artists refused to turn music into a tool in the service of politics, the breakdown of the party-state did not obviously and directly undermine their desire to transgress existing rules, conventions, and boundaries. Whether they opted to stay marginal by re-creating the margins, however, or tried their luck in the pop mainstream or in global alternative culture markets, the newly unfolding structural conditions of music making recast their position as well as their public image. Postsocialist society called into question the performance of marginality.

Whose Dissidence? Whose Business? The Story of EPH

EPH enjoyed a high reputation within the subculture and beyond it. Even in 1993 their concerts attracted full houses with a core of loyal fans. In drawing their act closer to the mainstream, they expected to benefit from their long-standing star status.

In 1990 a former manager of Hungaroton, at the time working for EMI's Hungarian affiliate, Quint EMI, proposed to EPH that they put out an album in a series he wanted to launch under the title "Banned Songs"—that is, the songs banned in the communist era. The series was to be modeled on a television program about the banned movies of the same epoch. Ironically, the former manager of Hungaroton happened to be one of the people who had banned the songs. Marketing the dissident voices of the past regime appeared not only chic but also lucrative in the years 1989–91. Shocked by the former censor's apparent amnesia, Jenő had to figure out how to respond to the offer. Given EPH's relatively solid but dwindling popularity, how would the rejection of the offer affect the band's long-term relationship with the music industry and, by extension, their chances of commercial viability in a progressively narrowing local market? And how could one deal with this most absurd form of co-optation and selling out of dissidence? How would accepting the offer affect the band's image, its self-respect, its political and artistic integrity?

Eventually the "Banned Songs" project never materialized, but EPH's newest recording was issued by Quint EMI. The conditions under which the recording was made added insult to injury. The manager and other record company personnel repeatedly reminded the musicians that even back in the 1980s their music had attracted only a small audience. And because "the world has changed since then," their music would no longer sell very well. In Jenő's words:

> The same I. W. who . . . back in 1983 kicked me out because of my [incendiary] lyrics keeps making the excuse that now, given the ruthless laws of capitalism, we're not really marketable. . . . Nevertheless, I managed to squeeze out a record contract from him, but I guess that contract will one day be required reading at the Department of Robber Baron Capitalism [*vadkapitalizmus*]. It basically states that we are to prepare a recording [at our own expense], and any proceeds coming from it will be theirs.

EPH had to come up with the money to cover their own recording costs. To find a sponsor, especially for rock music projects, was never easy in Hungary, where elitist assumptions about art and pop culture prevailed. It took Jenő a year and a half to scrape together the money—a little here, a little there—to prepare the master tape. The recording sessions came to a halt each time the money ran out. Meanwhile, Quint EMI was pressuring the band to complete the recording. Yet when they did, the company proved sluggish and inefficient in dubbing, promoting, and marketing the album. Even though Quint was affiliated with a Western company, it displayed, according to Jenő, carelessness and a lack of professionalism and business acumen.

One of the several agencies EPH had approached for funding was the Budapest Municipal Council. At that time the council was administered by the Alliance of Free Democrats (AFD), then the largest party in opposition to the right-leaning nationalist coalition government.[3] The Free Democrats' image still reflected and reiterated the ethos of dissident politics.[4] Remember that as the former democratic opposition, these dissidents had intimate ties to the underground rock of the 1980s. Therefore EPH was not surprised when one day an AFD representative showed up during a rehearsal to ask if AFD could use the song "Deliver Me from Evil,"[5] an anthem of dissent and alienation, to advertise pre-1989 issues of Beszélő. Jenő notes that the band did not particularly resent AFD's inability to pay them.

About a month later Jenő submitted EPH's application for funding to the cultural department of the Municipal Council. There EPH found itself competing with established classical musicians. Having received no response after what seemed to him a long time, Jenő contacted the office in person only to learn that their application had been turned down. The explanation truly humiliated him. "Only" 75 percent of the requests could be granted, and even the big-time classical music conductor had to make do with less than what he'd asked for!

This story highlights a number of issues central to the plight of popular musicians, and more broadly, it reflects the irony and para-

3. The elections of 1994 brought great gains to the Hungarian Socialist Party, which formed a coalition government with the Free Democrats.

4. For instance, the party continued to publish the formerly persecuted samizdat journal *Beszélő* (Jail Talk), initiated and produced by AFD's founding members under the same name, leaving its format largely unchanged. Only in 1993 was the journal's logo adjusted to the new political realities by removal of the bars representing the imprisonment of speech under state socialism.

5. The song is quoted and discussed in Chapter 1.

doxes involved in people's transactions with their symbolic capital. Despite EPH's wide recognition, they could not capitalize on their status as icons of the counterculture. Even though in the 1990s audiences learned of their upcoming concerts through huge posters rather than word of mouth, even though they were making more money with their music than they had ever made before, the transition disempowered them. In order to have their music more widely disseminated, they had to handle some of the major contradictions of the emergent political economy of popular music in Hungary.

To their disadvantage, the band was faced with the simultaneous operation of several different logics of social transaction. EPH's former censor tried to take advantage of them in his new role as a market-conscious manager of a capitalist corporation. He offered them an opportunity to convert their moral/political capital—their countercultural past—into financial capital. But his own political credentials rendered this bargain morally degrading for the band. The recording contract that EPH eventually signed with Quint EMI reinstated the old pattern of client-bureaucrat relationship. Even though postsocialist relations ensured EPH the freedom to produce and sell their records (once they obtained funding), their case points to the dominance of the big-time music industry over the pop artists, the same pattern that had prevailed before the transition.

EPH's need for sponsorship rendered the musicians vulnerable in their dealings with their former allies as well. Initially, when the AFD's representative asked for EPH's song as a ploy to sell their publication without paying the group for it, he took the musicians' support and solidarity for granted. EPH indeed acted according to the values of the ghetto, ironically in the entirely different social context of commerce. Occupying a powerful position, the Free Democrats managed to do what the rock group could not: convert their moral/political capital as former dissidents into financial gain. In the meantime they exploited the band.

When EPH later sought reciprocal support from the party, the musicians acted on the assumption that they had moral, cultural, and political capital to offer. They had reason to believe that the Free Democrats would appreciate not only their countercultural credentials but their recent support of the party's publication. Whatever capital they may have had, it did not prove convertible by the party officials in the city government. To the band's surprise, the officials applied conventional aesthetic criteria, according to which rock-'n'roll ranked lower than classical music. It simply did not count as cultural capital. And by adopting the conventional elitist system of artistic classification, the new government replicated the conservative practices of the socialist party-state toward rock music as an illegitimate cultural form.

EPH's story thus indicates how the transition gave rise to different systems and logics of capital conversion, and how difficult it was for the former celebrities of the underground to predict the particular logic in effect at various sites of the postcommunist marketplace of aesthetic, political, and cultural values.

Songs from Central Nirvania, or Who Owns the Countercultural Legacy?

The issue of how ownership of the underground legacy operates as symbolic capital, sacred or profane, in the postsocialist music business highlighted the musicians' complex relationships and conflicts with cultural actors outside their own circles. Controversies, however, arose not only between the musicians' community and the new cultural and political apparatuses; disputes about the status and property rights in the countercultural legacy divided the community itself.

In the 1980s gender rarely, if ever, surfaced as a problem in the rock community. A shared disdain for and defiance of institutions of the party-state obliterated it.[6] After the golden age, however, some of the most independent-minded women of the former underground ventured to articulate a distinctly female sensibility in and through their work. The men's response was to formulate a sensibility of their own. The new fault line between the sexes found expression in gendered theories of art; that is, in the construction of aesthetic theories built on concepts of male and female and reflecting divergent perspectives along gender lines. These theories were not explicated in any systematic manner, but even in their implicitness served as tools for understanding and coping with everyday life.

6. On the politics of gender, art, and transition, see András 1999.

Let me return to Kamondy's show *Songs from Central Nirvania,* which she subtitled *Free Variations on Her Friends' and Her Own Songs from a Span of Fifteen Years.* In addition to reviving the themes, concerns, and attitudes that prevailed in the 1980s art community, Kamondy introduced a new voice and altered the songs' overall texture and sound. The typical rock stage gave way to a theatrical setting where she appeared as a cabaret chanteuse. Through the ambiance of her whole performance, she projected an intimate, mature, and feminine image that was a sharp departure from the punk-derived, macho, youthful character of underground rock ten years earlier.

Re-presenting some of the most poignant pieces of the era, Kamondy made a statement about the past and its significance at a time when that past was just becoming a different country. As theorists of collective memory have warned us, the stories told about past events and experiences are not merely instruments of remembrance but means of understanding those events and experiences. "The past," according to Michael Schudson, "can be transmitted to the present in ways that maintain emotional connections or in ways that modulate emotional intensity, seeking to secure a knowledge of the past while reducing the intensity of its grip on us" (1992: 127). Kamondy was the first person in the art community to tell a coherent and emotionally captivating story about the counterculture of the 1980s in order to reduce the intensity of its grip. Hers was the first act of looking back to an era that in calendar terms was recent but virtually overnight had become reclassified as history.

Several circumstances made Kamondy's act provocative and painful for some of her fellow musicians. Most poignant of all were the pace and profundity of social change that destabilized individual and collective identities. Second, the music constituted the counterculture of state socialism, so it soon became identified with a bygone era in the same way the old street names did: Lenin Ring Road, People's Republic Avenue (Esbenshade 1995). Hundreds of streets reverted to their old names, but what about the specious and painful memories and the creative vigor associated with late socialism? How to part with those aspects of the past?

Rarely do popular cultural movements or styles become relegated to history so quickly and so abruptly as did Central and Eastern Europe's rock culture after the fall of the Wall. The community that Kamondy drew on, portrayed, and addressed had had no time to adjust psychologically and socially to those societal shifts that had turned the recent past into a far country in a few years. With her new rendition of the past, she tried to negotiate an ever-widening gap between personal and collective experiences; between the past-turned-history and the not-yet-formed present; between the political and the artistic aspects of the music; and finally, between the ghetto community and the new, disjointed alternative scene of the 1990s.

Kamondy raised the thus far latent issue of gender to the surface of group consciousness. To the male-dominated world of rock and politics, she brought her self-consciously female voice and produced an original narrative woven of songs that had been, for the most part, composed and performed by men. Thus not only did her chronicle of the past fifteen years reflect a female appropriation of those songs; at the same time she claimed ownership of the songs: a right to determine the value and relevance of the countercultural heritage.

Sir Ágnes Kamondy and Yesterday's Train

Many critics as well as the general audience received *Central Nirvania* with enthusiasm. The performance ran for two years and was issued on CD under the Bahia label. Curiously, however, the composers/performers of the songs, to Kamondy's dismay, felt uneasy about the show. This is how Kamondy recalls their reactions:

> A. K.: Despite the fact that I'd asked [the authors] to allow me to rework their material freely . . . , I thought I did respect the spirit of what I rearranged. But I was free in my treatment. I changed the harmony here and there.
> A. S.: You seemed to have filtered it through your personality.
> A. K.: Absolutely! I asked everyone to give me creative license but I don't think it harmed [the songs]. Yet apparently the authors had an awfully hard time dealing with it. . . . I ran across Jenő [Menyhárt] about three times those days [right after the premier] and had some tremendously good talks with him, but he couldn't utter a single shitty word about my performance. We had such superb exchanges with each other! I sat in for their

> rehearsal, we were sitting next to each other at the press conference for the Diáksziget Festival, and he simply couldn't get himself to say one shitty word about it!
> A. S.: Did you prompt him to do so?
> A. K.: No, hell, no! I'd wait till he said something. I put out the program, so "now it's your turn, Jenő," I thought. But no, he didn't say anything at all. I've also met with Miska [Mihály Víg] since. I was sittin' in a bar and he walked in from the street. He saw me, came up to me, kissed my hand, and said: "It was OK" [she caricatures him with a grimace], but he wasn't thrilled either.

The men whose behavior Kamondy found so hurtful shared the sense that she did not merely rearrange the pieces but transformed them into high culture. Péter "Sziámi" Müller, for instance, playfully dubbed the artist "Nirvania's savior."[7] His words reeked of irony and ambiguity:

> It's not usual to celebrate the urban folk style called rock'n'rot [*rock'n'rohadj meg*]. . . . Dear Ági, it's a huge honor/purification (*megtisztultatás*)[8] for me to have entered that serious and classical world in this manner, that is, by way of the Central Nirvania Monument, where the simple shout gets musical instrumentation and articulation; where there's a conductor, woodwinds and brass, strings and percussion, light, sound, and director; and where there's my favorite fixture, the usher lady. . . . You may have worried about how we surviving composers and performers would react to our own costly marble monument, which one might just as well call apotheosis. Rest assured, I liked it two [*nekem is teccett*] and polled others. All of them did two [*mindenkinek is*].[9]

7. See Péter "Sziámi" Müller, "Kamondy Ági lovag, Nirvánia megmentője" (Sir Ági Kamondy, Nirvania's savior), in the booklet accompanying the compact disk of Kamondy Ágnes, *Dalok Közép-Nirvániából* (Bahia, Budapest, 1995).

8. *Megtisztultatás*, Müller's brilliantly ironic lexical invention, conflates two words: *megtiszteltetés* (honor) and *megtisztulás* (purification). The latter is in the unusual causative mode, suggesting that the act was imposed by some exterior agent.

9. Here Müller slides into a playfully ungrammatical mode. He also intentionally misspells *tetszik/tetszett* as *teccik/teccett*. My own misspelling of "too" as "two" attempts to capture his feeling and style, reminiscent of John Lennon's.

Müller suggested that the honor of elevating street art to the status of high culture is highly dubious. Laci Kistamás rehearsed a similar idea, claiming that Kamondy had reworked the songs into museum exhibits. Menyhárt believed that any pretension of art and culture meant to be written with capital letters is anachronistic. "Here everybody sticks by certain cultural traditions. Kamondy is also tinkering with those [outmoded traditions], which is a fundamental error. The art of the 1990s . . . is somehow linked to the media, and categories such as 'alternative' and 'commercial' are losing their meaning." Aware that cultural values and lifestyles have become fluid over the past few decades, he presumes that artists would need a whole new creative approach to stay in touch with present-day realities. "Kamondy tried to convey so-called important ideas in an important fashion. This is how she musically adapted them, put them onstage, performed them. . . . These are, in fact, old ideas . . . that in this present form are not meaningful." Menyhárt sees Kamondy's alleged failure to catch up with the here and now as indicative of an entire community's inability to synchronize with history. With the end of the Cold War, Hungarian society entered a new era, yet it shows no signs of recognizing this transition or being able to handle it.

> J. M.: Budapest is a city outside of time [*nemlétező idejű város*]. If you come here, you won't sense that it's the '90s now. If you travel to Amsterdam, though, you'll know within a week where you are in time. Or what time it is. If you come here, you'll figure out where you are but not when you are. The whole city is like that. The way they relate to chicks [*csajok*], to the environment, the way they dress, the way they are, the outlook of business people, of the culture, you simply don't know when it is now. . . . The present time has no spirit. There's a confused city here that has nowhere to go. . . . Here the politicians in Parliament want to win World War I!

With his final witticism Menyhárt refers to the territorial claims against Romania and other neighbors resuscitated by the center-right regime of József Antall after 1989 and lingering on the right's agenda ever since. But his sarcasm targets much more than political thinking. It is aimed at the Hungarians' character and mind-set in various social milieux, the rampant male chauvinism, the insensitivity toward the environment, the arrogance in business. It is in this broad cultural and political context that he dismisses his fellow avant-gardists' artistic outlook: "In comparison with this, to reach back five years [as Kamondy did] is not so [absurd], but something got entirely lost here. . . . From Budapest it's still difficult to see onto the world. Starting with the language barriers. . . . In this place theories dating back ten to thirteen years prevail. . . . Here it's yesterday's train that's late." This last aphorism could well have found its way into one of Menyhárt's lyrics. He continues on this more general plane:

> I think that since 1990, when the Wall was demolished and the whole system that had been in power globally broke down, things seem to have been operating fundamentally differently in the entire world. . . . These days culture is dominated by microworlds and the personal. . . . This is no longer a time . . . when you proclaim something but when you . . . kind of contemplate. And you don't want to resolve anything but make a statement in a subtle way. . . . It's not to be some sort of universal statement but rather your highly personal comment. . . . Kamondy's mistake is that she doesn't dare to be personal.

Menyhárt's and the other men's critiques were symptomatic of an arising postmodern sensibility in the local art community. The art critic Edit András's (1995) observations echo, expand on, and contextualize Menyhárt's ideas. András also claims space for a more personal voice in the Hungarian art scene. Ironically, she does so from a feminist perspective. She starts out with a discussion of the fertile blending of feminism with postmodernity in the international scene:

> By the 1990s . . . the '70s slogan "the personal is political" became modified to become "the personal is the only political." This is to say that we are so much locked into socially manipulated roles and are so vulnerable to the inscrutable workings of power; our actual space for action is so limited that only the personal, the ephemeral and nonrepeatable life experiences have come to be

> considered real and credible in the arts. This is the mind-set that characterizes the third and youngest generation [of women artists] who attempt to find their distinctly female voice and establish a form of women's language required for self-expression. (1995: 35)

András is keenly aware that this encounter between feminist and postmodern sensibilities has not yet taken place in the domestic art scene.

> It is . . . the legitimacy of the personal approach or the personal voice as a metaphor for artistic expression that meets with the most obdurate resistance locally. This may be the consequence of our socialization, traditions, historical experiences, and notions of art. Hungarian women artists working abroad . . . have a natural way of incorporating aspects of the body, their autobiography, and personal preferences into their artwork as part of a historical or aesthetic problem. Domestic artists, especially women, however, strictly abstain from every personal gesture as incommensurate with art, according to the prevailing consensus. (36)

András's analysis of the local art world's imperviousness to fresh contemporary movements is in line with Menyhárt's disparagement of it. Its parochial and anachronistic features András traces to the region's political history. The highly politicized underground art of the communist era was embedded in modernist tradition. Because it was isolated from Western culture for so long, it failed to recognize the erosion going on everywhere in the world. Unable to come to terms with major political and philosophical landslides, the movement was equally unable to reflect on its own anachronism. She holds that "all forms of minorities, subcultural identities were forced to be subordinated to the fight against political repression by the existing regime. Multiculturalism fell victim to the unofficial underground art movements' fight against the official art in Hungary" (27).[10] Women, along with ethnic and sexual minorities, could not even come close to articulating

10. Translated by Zsuzsa Gábor.

their distinct group interests and perspectives, owing to the male-dominated underground's monopoly over the definition of resistance and difference.

Now there is a huge paradox here. With *Nirvania* up steps a woman, Kamondy, to re-present an essential segment of this tradition in an admittedly personal fashion, only to be dismissed as anachronistic and old-fashioned by her postmodern male fellow musicians. Why and how did this happen? Why was Kamondy's reworking of the underground songs a target for such criticism? How did Kamondy's unique blending of discursive and interpretive traditions cause the validity of her performance to be challenged? And what extra-artistic factors turned her, in her fellow musicians' eyes, into a kind of Don Quixote, embarrassingly out of touch with her times?

"This Is How Things Are Born"

Peter Manuel notes that "urban subcultures . . . may have inherent inclinations toward postmodern aesthetics, while at the same time retaining ties to modern and even premodern cultural discourses. The syncretic popular musics created by such subcultures may reflect these multiple cultural orientations by combining postmodern and more traditional characteristics" (1995: 227). Eclecticism has always characterized the local rock musical underground. The theme of political protest and self-marginalization is quite pertinent to early modernism (Huyssen 1990: 241–47, Goehr 1994), as well as to its reappropriation in the art of postwar socialist societies (Forgács 1994, András 1995). Therefore underground rock displayed an elective affinity with modernist (or neo-avant-garde) notions of art. Ideological and aesthetic references to classical avant-garde movements such as Dada and Surrealism were instrumental in the creation of countercultural spaces and identities (Hajnóczy 1983b).

This was made evident by István ef Zámbó, of the Committee and Zámbó Happy Band. In Zámbó's account of a happening more than two decades earlier, it is intriguing to see how an event allegedly not intended as political came to be defined by the authorities as a problematic combination of political subversion and mental disorder.

I. Z.: I was jailed for half a year for an [art] action that the authorities misunderstood. . . . [It] was an artists' rally [*megmozdulás*] called in support of a friend I'd worked with a lot, who was also drafted [like me], and . . . was incarcerated in the closed wing of a mental hospital. When I heard this news, I organized an action in his honor in the central square of Szentendre. . . . The action, true to the spirit of the times, was entirely misinterpreted. But then, because I was a child, so to speak, it didn't even occur to me that it could be misinterpreted. . . .

I'd been a night guard at the camp site at Szentendre and I knew the actors and actresses who'd been living there and performed on the stage that was set up every night at the square. There lay an empty stage during the day. On this stage I assembled my friends, to whom I read out one of my surrealist lectures titled "The Last Song, or Don't Commit Lovectomy" [*lovektómia*, a nonsense word that sounds much like "lobotomy"]. But it makes no difference at all [*tök mindegy*] what the title was. This was an abstract thing and indeed was a poetic text. Then we offered gifts to the tourists there and to ourselves, such as various radio tubes and children's sandbox toys and so forth. It was a kinda Dadaist gig [*buli*]. At the time men with beards and long hair were persecuted everywhere in the world. This was the case here too. And when a policeman who just happened to come by asked for someone's ID, this was being watched by several other men with beards and long hair. A small crowd was gathering around the policeman, and another policeman . . . decided his colleague had gotten into a critical situation, so he called for backup. . . . A jeep showed up with ten policemen. They jumped out and arrested everyone with a beard and long hair. And then the investigation began. "What was this?" and "Who was that?" and "What poems were recited?" and "What ideology [*milyen eszme*]?" and so on. And then followed the closed wing of the mental department.

The point was that they thought it was a political demonstration. In fact it was far from it. It was an artistic happening. In this sense this was a total misinterpretation. As a result, the whole affair was investigated for six months. . . . The whole story ended like this: At the time it wasn't customary for the

> police to apologize. So they trumped up an indictment. The gist of it was that the action was "a felony committed by collective will" [*akarategységben elkövetett garázdaság*]. This meant to imply that no one had done anything criminal individually, but the way it came across was conducive to a scandal.

Whereas the starker and more directly political face of avant-gardism was also recognizable in rock music, several other expressive devices associated it with a postmodern aesthetic: the blurring of the boundaries between the serious and the playful, high and low culture, professional and amateur musicianship, everyday life and its artistic representation; the use of blank irony, pastiche, the recontextualization of old pop musical clichés within more contemporary idioms such as minimalism, industrial music, and punk. The Galloping Coroners' musical ideology and practice exemplified the postmodern use of ancestral—that is, premodern—poetic traditions (Milun 1992). Manuel's description of urban subcultural music fits precisely the Hungarian underground rock scene, whose most interesting feature was that "it at once celebrate[d] meaning and meaninglessness, play and nostalgia, pathos and jouissance, in a synthesis that goes much deeper than the paradigmatic dualities of . . . 'commercialism' and 'authenticity'" (229). Kamondy's Nirvania also drew on a wide array of modernist, postmodernist, and folk-based idioms and performance styles. Even her persona was ambiguously constructed and fluid. It combined diverse voices and vocal styles, such as the wistful and confidential tone of the chanteuse, the assertive and declamatory tone of the bard, and the raspy blues vocal representing the "girl gone wrong." On purely musical grounds, then, her fellow musicians' attack on her as an old-fashioned modernist was hardly justifiable.

Where Kamondy does appear to be a highly serious modernist is in her interpretation of artistic intentions. She indeed desired to elevate the musical output of the ghetto to the status of Art, out of her commitment to a transcendental aesthetic. In rearranging the songs she attempted to demonstrate that they had latent artistic qualities, which she made manifest by her rendition. This idea would not be interesting in itself, in view of the local art establishment's persistent investment in hierarchic and universalist approaches to art and skepticism about multiculturalism and feminism. Kamondy's conservative discourse is intriguing and unique for the way it is bundled with religious and healing metaphors. For her, art gains its power from its ability to purify and heal the body and the soul. The rebirth of ghetto culture as high art ensures, Kamondy intimates, the metaphoric rebirth of those who seek to establish a new identity outside the ghetto. The glorification of the ghetto songs helps her externalize the hurts and traumas of the previous era:

> Á. K.: For me, [*Nirvania*] was an act of concluding something. I'd like to forget the ghetto.
> A. S.: Really forget?
> Á. K.: Yes, very much.
> A. S.: When you say it's art . . .
> Á. K.: (*interrupts*) But art's already a resolution! That's no longer the ghetto.
> A. S.: Does it become art as it gets released from the ghetto?
> Á. K.: Yes. At least, I guess I succeeded in experiencing and conveying it as art. . . . Perhaps those friends of mine who created these [songs] can't come to terms with the fact that what used to be grim realities [*véres valóság*] become art. . . . I see this as narrow-mindedness because what's so fantastic about art is that it gives absolution even as the grim realities surface in it. . . .
> A. S.: And this absolution didn't occur when the songs were first created and performed?
> Á. K.: No, no. We let off steam, we shouted it out, something was expressed, the truth perhaps. But telling the truth is not the same as when Oedipus blinds himself when he confronts the truth. Then you weep and get absolved at the same time. . . . The absolution, you understand? That's very important for me. . . .
> A. S.: So that things get in their rightful place?
> Á. K.: Yes. So that they gain their rightful place and rest in peace. So that we have a sense that this is how things are born. . . . Out of tremendous suffering.

Kamondy's metaphors of rebirth, regeneration, redemption, resolution, and remembrance resonate oddly with themes and acts central to the public political life of Hungary—and of the whole region—during the transition. "Like shed skins," the anthropologist Katherine Verdery points out, transitions are mostly about death and new life (1996: 231–33). She describes "a veritable parade of dead bodies," both flesh and bronze, that symbolized the collapse of state socialism in the former Soviet bloc. Corpses were "exhumed, shuttled from New York to Budapest, from Washington to Warsaw, from Paris to Bucharest, dug up and turned over, exiled from the Kremlin Wall to more lowly sites" (232). The definitive moment in Hungary was marked by the rehabilitation-by-reburial of Imre Nagy, the prime minister at the time of the 1956 uprising. And in 1993, even Miklós Horthy, the notoriously undemocratic head of state in the interwar years, found his way back to his native Hungarian soil.

But what does underground rock culture have to do with the fate of politicians' corpses and statues? In fact, Kamondy's performance also embodied an attempt to reassess the past by changing the underground's symbolic location on the cultural map. Especially revealing is the imagery used to illumine her motive for rearranging the songs: "so that they gain their rightful place and rest in peace." Verdery explains that "people seized and revalorized the past in the service of a new future by seizing and revalorizing the dead bodies of persons once and now newly significant" (ibid.). When Kamondy transported the music of the ghetto into a high cultural setting, she also seized and literally revalorized those pieces. Instead of dead bodies, she moved about dead songs that represented resistance to a defeated social system. She thought that a new life, indeed an afterlife, could be rekindled in those pieces if they were removed from their original context and, like a Shakespeare play, given a distinctly new and personal rendition. No longer merely textbook documents of collective hurts and degradation, the music of the ghetto then would become an open-ended body of art susceptible to repeated reinterpretations. Eternity in association with an artifact reclassified as art is anything but art's mummification. On the contrary, Kamondy considered it the only viable procedure through which texts produced under a certain set of circumstances could stay alive and meaningful in a new context.

This perception, as we have seen, is in stark contrast to that of the male musicians who had gained their fame with those songs. The original meaning and spirit of the songs, they suggested, had been ruined in a setting defined by plush orchestra seats, conductors, and usher ladies. From their postmodernist or populist stance, Art with a capital A fits comfortably in its traditional bourgeois setting. It connotes status, respectability, passivity, and a disciplined audience (Levine 1988: 171–242). Nor is it presumed to carry more profound and transcendental meanings than what Müller wittily called "rock-'n'rot," the music of the outsiders.

Kamondy's conscious motives in producing *Nirvania* did not include sacralization. Ironically, she blamed the men for precisely what they found fault with in her. If the men thought that Ágnes had killed the living essence of the pieces by erecting an artistic monument to them, she contended that the men mythicized the pieces by insisting that only in their original context would they remain meaningful. Kamondy contrasted her own approach to the songs as open-ended, living, malleable, and reinterpretable artifacts with that of her critics, who saw them as closed and immutable texts eternally frozen in their performance context and, by implication, in their original performers. For Kamondy, they were in effect mythicizing the ghetto. She opposed art as a living entity with mythology as a form of closure; the former connoting openness, flexibility, and femininity, the latter rigidity and masculinity.

The genderization of an essentially aesthetic argument suggests that the men musicians' dislike of Kamondy's show was based on more than purely aesthetic considerations. It reflected and furthered a growing tension between men and women in the alternative community of the 1990s.

Women, Gender, and Sexuality in Alternative Rock

Kamondy's proto-feminist stance underlay the entire conception of *Nirvania*, a deliberate recoding of the gender subtext of the old songs: "These songs had mostly been sung by men. And it was also interesting for me to see if the songs could be relived, performed, reinterpreted, and transmitted by a woman."

Punk and its musical offshoots in the West conspicuously supplanted stereotyped images of male and female, and thus opened up new possibilities—roles, voices, and images—for women as well as men musicians. (Laing 1985: 88–94, Greil Marcus 1989: 77, Juno 1996). "Punk was the first form of rock not to rest on love songs, and one of its effects had been to allow female voices to be heard that are not often allowed expression on record, stage, radio—shrill, assertive, impure individual voices," wrote Simon Frith and Angela McRobbie (1990: 384). The explosive effect of this music on women's presence in musical production as well as on their sexual identity was not felt in the Eastern bloc, where gender politics, especially the politicization of the private realm, met with resistance even before it had had a chance to be properly formulated (see Funk and Mueller 1993 and especially Goven 1993). Existing discussions, scant as they are, of women's status in Central and Eastern European popular music point to rampant male chauvinism, seen in both women's lack of prominence in the music scene and their degrading representation in song lyrics (Cushman 1995: 184–85, Kürti 1991a). Indeed, even in the local punk-influenced underground of the 1980s women's space was quite restricted.

Nonetheless, the underground music scene was a terrain where one could experiment with defiant images of women and gender relations, predominantly through irony, parody, and satire. The Committee's woman singer, double named Kokó/Mrs. Erzsébet Kukta Taylor (Szabóné Kukta Erzsébet) represented an oddly detached and alienated but quite prominent character, drawing on punk as well as absurdist/Dadaist aesthetics. Her alternately used names (one onstage, the other on concert flyers and cover inserts) created a harshly humorous effect in their conflation of two incompatible identities: the impudent eccentricity of punks (Kokó) with the ordinariness and invisibility signified by Mrs. Taylor—an inconspicuousness that most women unquestioningly adopt along with their husband's name as a warranty of normal femininity.[11]

Unconventional approaches to love and sexuality in underground music underlay a whole series of songs that demystified or parodied romantic love and heterosexual desire. In the Committee's song "All This Is Me" (Mindez én vagyok) Kokó and her male part-

11. In Hungary the custom of identifying with the husband to the extent of assuming his full name (e.g., Mrs. George Taylor) still holds sway. Although in most informal settings women are called by their own first name, it is not uncommon to bear one's husband's name, even in semiformal contexts (in the neighborhood, at the workplace, etc.). There is a

ner, Laca, portray a sexual encounter that turns into horror. The female persona of the song systematically names the parts of her body, starting, in a seductive tone, with those that conventionally invoke the idealized and eroticized female body ("my eyes," "my hair," "my neck"). But her checklist continues with her inner organs ("my colon," "my stomach," "my lungs"), so what she ends up verbally displaying is a far cry from what had started out as the object of male desire. A real flesh-and-blood body is pictured for us. The male character of the song first responds with exaggerated gestures of sexual arousal, which give way to screams of horror as the sexual encounter turns into an act of vivisection. Kokó counterpoints her sliding repetitive melodic lines, chanted rather than sung, with a refrain in which every syllable of the phrase is forcefully accented: "All this is me / I'm givin' you all this."

The piece lends itself to several possible readings. Male desire giving way to horror over this unconventional spectacle of femininity may be read as a critique, a feminist objection to women's sexual objectification. But the transformation of male desire into dread may also be regarded as reiterating the dichotomy of the idealized/desired and the repugnant/fearful in women's physicality. Even if the song's meaning is ambiguous, however, it is unmistakably akin to endeavors in the visual arts that deconstruct the male-construed, repressive, and restricted notion of the feminine by exhibiting women's real bodily experience associated with pregnancy, menstruation, aging, sickness, and so forth (András 1995: 32).

Despite the occasional misogynist flavor of the songs, most of which were written and sung by men,[12] the incorporation of new perspectives and strategies in representing love, sex, and woman had a refreshing and liberating effect on this musical form. Typically, women in this branch of rock could probe forbidden identities (derived from punk's attraction to fetishist and lewd iconography) or

trend toward identifying a woman officially by the name she acquired at birth plus her husband's family name. Many professional women and artists, however, retain their birth name without taking on the spouse's name. In a country where feminism is just about to gain some limited legitimacy, this is a way for a woman to assert her own identity.

12. For example, "Hello, baby, you're a rotten bitch / I've never wanted a girl better than you" (EPH) and "No one's called me for days / Never mind, one of them's ugly, the other's cold" (Balaton).

dissect the dynamic of heterosexual relationships with a candor unprecedented in other domains of popular music.[13] As singers and lyricists, these women, few as they were, acted as creative partners in the bands and for the most part enjoyed the respect of their fellow musicians as well as of their audience.

Some women tried their luck as drummers, keyboardists, or guitarists, but the assumption that men were inherently superior at mastering instruments and related technical gadgets (Frith and McRobbie 1990) was so firmly and widely held that the few women pioneers in the bands were confined to peripheral and subordinate positions. Even though punk's investment in gender play challenged the taboo of women's taking to the guitar, the saxophone, or the drums, the barriers remained largely in place in Hungary. In fact, some of my most outspokenly independent female interviewees had absorbed the prevailing ideology that musicianship was male.

Ágnes Kamondy quit her brief membership in EPH, where she played keyboard, to form a rock band of her own. Orkesztra Luna, established in 1986, consisted of three men and three women. Since Kamondy wrote all the lyrics and much of the music, she admits a degree of female dominance in the group. When I asked if she had ever considered forming an all-female group, she vigorously rejected the idea:

> Á. K.: I don't like homogeneous things. I dislike female homogeneity. It bores me. . . . In my dramaturgy I build on contrasts and dialogues. If there are only women in a band, we have nothing but similarities. Basically. One can talk about many things, but the moment men step on the scene, dialogues develop, contrasts, forces and counterforces clash. . . .
> A. S.: With male groups, you don't sense homogeneity, or you just don't mind?
> A. K.: Well, this is a convention. In Miles Davis's band there's no woman, yet I don't have a sense of anything missing there. Maybe I'm also affected by prevailing conventions, but in an

13. This introspective and at times combative approach to heterosexual relationships may be likened to U.S. women rappers' confrontation with their partners in songs that convey a minidrama, such as those of Salt-n-Pepa. The difference is that rappers use their daily life experience in a more immediate and direct fashion in their songs.

> all-female group I always miss the male gender. . . . And another thing is that it feels somehow contrived when you see only women in a group. Or, more precisely, predetermined. There seems to be a conception there. And conceptions bother me in art.

Kamondy keeps her distance from any explicit feminist statement to be made in and through music. While an all-male group seems for her entirely natural, embodying all the potential richness of musical expression, an all-female group cannot help drawing attention to itself as simultaneously deficient—the male is absent—and ideological-minded. Male particularism is not perceived as such, yet its female counterpart in the arts, regardless of what it stands for and how, is always already political and therefore repudiated.

Ági Bárdos Deák confided similar hegemonic presumptions about gender and music. She is another woman musician renowned in the underground for her powerful talent and charisma. She had begun her career as a singer in the highly acclaimed Control Group, and after it broke up, she created a band of her own called Ági és Fiúk (Ági and the Guys). Like Kamondy, she single-handedly selected her musicians, exclusively male instrumentalists, and as a singer she has remained the group's core, while the "guys" have been coming and going over the years. Whereas the music is collectively composed by the band members, Ági writes all the lyrics, mostly in a confessional mode.

When I asked her if she had ever thought about including women players in her band, she answered that several women instrumentalists had been recommended to her, but none of them really came up to her or the guys' expectations: "Recently they proposed a girl, a bass guitarist. She's an American girl who's settled here in Hungary [*ittragadt*]. I saw her playing. But I'd need someone who's at a higher [technical] level than she is right now." She dropped another candidate for bass because her guitarist "may have found her too feminine," Ági reckons. She expands on this thought:

> Men do very hard physical work on the guitar. Or on the drums. On everything. But I do think that playing the guitar is very physically draining. We'd need a woman who would be

> comparably tenacious in her habit of practicing and playing. I have the sense that women can't abandon themselves to their instrument to the same extent. Women have a different relationship to it. Men's union with their instrument is so absolutely intense, as if the instrument was a woman.

Ági's observation goes against the common wisdom in pop music journalism and academic discourse, that men's treatment of the guitar or the saxophone as a phallic symbol is a form of narcissism (Frith and McRobbie 1990, Stewart 1981). Ági sees it as a simulation of heterosexual lovemaking. "The way men relate to their instrument, their infinite tenderness toward it, is entirely different from women's. Frankly, to me a female guitarist as a sight . . . is a bit unattractive. I'm biased in this way. Maybe it's because I've never seen one, but picturing a woman playing the sax makes me feel uneasy. . . . I can't help thinking that this instrument's been designed for men." Ági's reluctance to employ women instrumentalists finds its analogy in Kamondy's aversion to all-female groups. In justifying her dealings with women candidates, Ági lumped together essentialist arguments about men's endurance, their physical and sexual prowess. Interestingly, both women suspected that their ideas might be rooted in deep-seated prejudices and assumptions about the nexus between music making and gender roles. I suggest that both of them represent a kind of proto-feminist stance in that, first, they sensed and spurned obvious forms of sexism;[14] second, both emphasized and practiced their autonomy as women musicians by initiating and carrying out projects of their own; third, they both appeared keenly aware of their distinctly female contribution as integral to the overall musical product coming out of their collaboration with men. Remember Kamondy's characterization of art as feminine and open-ended and myths as masculine and rigid. Ági Bárdos voiced a similar form of gender sensitivity when she accused a male critic who had panned her last album of being unable to sense and appreciate the peculiarly female subjectivity conveyed through her art: "I felt

14. Ági told me with great indignation that her former husband, a fellow musician, asked on television what Ági had to say about the "empirical finding" that for every ten talented men there is only one talented woman. "I was so taken aback," Ági remembered, "that I quickly retorted, ''Cause that one talented woman is ten times as talented as the ten men!'"

that he didn't in the least understand that here a woman was singing about something. . . . My lyrical approach, if the distinction between men's and women's approach makes sense at all, is definitely a female one." Yet both Ágnes Kamondy and Ági Bárdos were leery of overt and collective manifestations of gender consciousness. Like so many highly educated women professionals and artists in Central and Eastern Europe, these best known and most defiant women of the local rock community stopped short of identifying with any clear-cut feminist viewpoint. For an explanation we must recall András's ideas about the legacy of the underground art world's antistate political agenda during socialism, which blocked the way for various social movements and ideological currents of the West, including feminism and postmodern thinking. Particularly pertinent is András's discussion of the reasons why the successive waves of feminist politics and ideology had difficulty taking root in the art community in postsocialist Hungary:

> The strongly left-wing character of the women's rights movement in the 1970s, with its militant and often Marxist overtones and utopianism, was regarded as highly dubious and inevitably aroused suspicion here in Hungary, where these categories had already been discredited. By contrast, the animosity and aversion with which the fundamentally changed feminism of the 1980s and 1990s have been received is rooted in its strong links with postmodernism. Strategies of modernism in this country had been handed down through generations and attained a dominant position only at a time when the entire intellectual construct had been deconstructed everywhere else outside this region. (1995: 28)

Thus women in the arts and professions felt pressured not to embrace any variant of feminist thought. Here lies the explanation for the ambiguity in the ways in which Kamondy and Bárdos, along with other women in the alternative music scene, experienced, constructed, and resisted aspects of their femininity. Strikingly parallel attitudes may be found among the youngest generation of women in the visual arts, whose works, according to András, display "a fresh air of change" but "still rely, for the time being, on the old and proven categories and schemes in their attempts to secure positions for themselves, not wanting to find themselves in opposition immediately" (39).

Since the underground music scene was always on the fringe of the modernist high art movement, the old guard's annoyance with both feminism and postmodernity is less forbidding for rock musicians than for fine artists. As the harshly obscene and humorous female-dominated group Tereshkova attests, young fine artists may enact a boldly rebellious gender identity more freely in their moonlighting roles as rock musicians. In contradistinction to rock veterans such as Kamondy and Bárdos, these women engaging in alternative music are no longer so eager to surround themselves with male instrumentalists, nor are they inhibited from using a feminist vocabulary in music, stage performance, and verbal discourse.[15]

They have come of age in a time and place where feminist ideas, while still limited to a narrow social stratum, are gradually spreading. Many universities and colleges offer courses in gender studies; *Magyar Narancs* has been regularly featuring articles on gender issues as well as sexual and ethnic minorities; and the Hungarian Women's Party and other women's rights organizations, tiny and relatively ineffective though they be, form part of the political landscape and raise important topics (abortion, spousal abuse, rape) for public debate.[16]

Since the late 1980s the underground/alternative music scene has exhibited a growing consciousness of and sensitivity toward gender issues. As the movement has expanded its influence and scope from Budapest to the provinces, from the bohemian elite to a predominantly younger and more socioeconomically mixed audience, women have gained more power in their relations with men, which has manifested itself in a more active, critical, and autonomous female presence in this scene.

Nirvania and Gendered Theories of Art

Having reviewed the differential and complex impact of postmodern and feminist currents on the artistic values and practices of the underground community, we are now in a better position to address

15. This observation is based on my attendance at a Tereshkova concert and on a lengthy interview with its leader, Kriszta Nagy, in June 1995.

16. The Hungarian Women's Party (Magyar Nők Pártja) was founded in December 2000.

the questions I posed earlier: Why was Kamondy's *Nirvania*, which drew positive responses from the critics and the public at large, rejected by her fellow musicians as a mistreatment of the countercultural legacy? And why did they criticize her from a populist/postmodernist point of view when in fact her performance displayed a postmodern sensibility?

My data suggest that Menyhárt and Müller deployed their populist/postmodernist reasoning strategically against *Nirvania* to offset their sense that their own popularity and public recognition were waning. Their attack on Kamondy's adaptation of the songs seems to have been fueled at least in part by their frustration when the apparent sacralization of their songs had no tangible social consequences for their status as pop artists at this stage of their careers. Kamondy's performance, despite the tribute she paid to them as persons, friends, and musicians, brought home the idea that, as key figures of the former underground, they were no longer indivisible from their own products. Four years after the change in regime they had come to be aware, as the story of EPH and many others testify, how limited was the symbolic value of the cultural capital represented by their past achievements. On top of the pain and disillusionment brought by this recognition, the new social situation raised difficult and divisive ethical, political, and existential questions about the nature of art and of politics, money, and success. One of Menyhárt's rap lyrics eloquently expresses this collective sense of losing ground:

> We still remember the past and reckon the future
> It's not even started yet
> But has already ended
> And we're to haunt here
> haunt each other
> each other's ghosts.[17]

Not unlike their Western counterparts in popular music, women in the 1990s display less insecurity than men, as the very concept, execution, and success of *Nirvania* exemplifies. "I've won the battle," Kamondy declared to me with a sigh of relief when her performance

17. Európa Kiadó, "We're Haunting Here," in *Itt kísértünk—Love '92*, CD, Quint EMI, 1993.

turned out to be well received by the general audience. The battle between her and the male core of the rock community had a hidden agenda other than a mismatch between modernist/elitist and postmodern/populist values.

Up to the 1990s, the rock community had sought and welcomed Art as a label for their activities. Contrary to Müller's allegation, it was far from uncommon for domestic underground concerts in the 1980s to be held in theaters with plush orchestra seats and usher ladies. Further, several professional and amateur (fanzine-type) writings, including a dissertation,[18] were determined to advance avant-garde rock to the rank of high art and stressed its kinship with experimental film, multimedia performance, and other related art forms. The musicians themselves were prone to theorize their music as a complex autonomous form of expression more or less divorced from everyday life or politics (as we saw in Chapter 2).

It does not follow that either of these musicians intentionally or cynically used populist arguments to discredit Kamondy's project. They may have felt genuine embarrassment with some of Kamondy's assumptions and certain characteristics of her performance. Moreover, the art scene of the late 1980s and early 1990s, as András perceptively observes, was a confusing space undergoing transition itself. Currents such as postmodernity, cultural relativism, feminism, and multiculturalism, especially their underlying philosophies, had a hard time infiltrating public thinking. With the removal of the intellectual hurdles around 1990, old and new information from the West and elsewhere began to flood the art scene. Yet the assimilation of these ideas and stimuli, which would require time as well as ongoing debates and dialogues, did not occur. Typically, therefore, elements of avant-gardist and postmodernist doctrines came to be inconsistently mixed in many critics' and artists' works (András 1995: 37).

This scenario explains why artist-musicians, especially such articulate ones as Menyhárt and Müller, could exploit such ambiguities and lapses in public discourse and maneuver with often contradictory facets of modern and postmodern thought in a self-serving,

18. Csaba Hajnóczy, "Rockandroll," M.A. thesis, Liszt Ferenc Academy of Music, Budapest, 1983.

strategic manner.[19] The conflict of interests underlying the *Nirvania* debate is evident in the use of gender terms on both sides. Tania Modleski (1986) pointed to the tendency in cultural theory to account for the rise of mass culture with reference to notions of femininity. Sentimentality, the propensity for formulas, passive and mindless consumption had been ascribed to women's inferior psychosocial needs and taste. Even postmodern theories reappraising and celebrating mass culture emphasize the masculine aura conveyed by modernist/elitist concepts of art as against the feminine aura attributed to pop and mass culture.

Curiously, the *Nirvania* debate turns this nexus of mass culture, art, and gender on its head. Not only does Kamondy regard serious art as feminine and distinguish it from "masculine" mythmaking. So does Müller, even though covertly and with opposing value implications. For him the principal referent to high culture is "my favorite fixture, the usher lady." In Eastern Europe the usher lady represents a highly unpopular social type, the disciplinarian and narrow-minded bureaucrat. She is usually a low-salaried senior citizen. To relegate art, as Müller does, to the domain of usher ladies is a barely concealed expression of disparagement. High art becomes redefined as old, authoritarian, and female, while rock'n'rot, by implication, is young, impudent, and male.

Müller intended his facetious act of knighting Kamondy for her *Nirvania* to be a gesture of honor and reconciliation with the "surviving composers and performers." Indeed, it symbolically reinstated the masculine ethos of rock'n'roll. Despite the disgraceful act Kamondy had committed by transposing the songs into a feminized environment, she was pardoned. Having been awarded a man's title, Sir Ági Kamondy could join their club.

Why was it so important for Müller to turn Kamondy into a man? At a time when the former celebrities of a suppressed but potent subculture found themselves solitary individuals to whom "nobody listens" anymore, it is easy to see why their anxieties were aroused by a woman artist who had never enjoyed the kind of prominence they had. This in itself rendered her handling of the

19. The strategic use of postmodern argument was more obvious in Müller's reaction to Nirvania than in Menyhárt's.

songs, symbols of masculine vigor, substance, and impudence, particularly irritating: *Nirvania* did away with the masculine subtext of rock'n'rot and mobilized in its opponents a deep-seated fear of losing ground, a fear they tried to conceal and dispel with a compelling but self-interested use of postmodern rhetoric.

Conclusion

The best songs of the countercultural movement came to be widely respected as symbols of the movement, as documents of state repression and resistance during the 1980s. This accounts for the commercial viability of nostalgia shows, the systematic re-issue of amateur tapes by Bahia, and the songs' cult status even among the youngest alternative music crowd. The aura of these pieces was powerful enough to generate interest in their re-issue by major record labels and to be used as advertising tools for the marketing of literature once termed dissident.

While the experience, social networks, and prestige the musicians accumulated in the counterculture had a perceptible impact on their ability to re-establish themselves within the reformulated alternative music scene, this impact was not directly related to the sacred status of the songs they had composed and performed in the 1980s. As the experience of EPH demonstrates, the songs did not secure for their creators new and fair recording contracts or government support. In other words, ownership did not become symbolic capital, especially not in the mainstream culture scene. A gap was evolving between the sacred status of the cultural legacy and the musicians' standing (unless they ventured into some new project), as well as between the musicians' old and more recent output. The discrepancy was symptomatic of their dwindling status and agency, which in turn fomented conflicts of interest and rivalry.

The status struggle manifested itself in the form of a curious ideological debate. The question as to who was allowed to deal with the underground legacy and how was integral to the musicians' sense of control in their dealings with outside actors in the postsocialist cultural life; to assess what constitutes a legitimate treatment of the legacy within the subculture was no less relevant. Kamondy's reappropriation of the songs in *Nirvania* was a highly personal way of coming to terms with history, memory, collective and individual identities. It provoked harsh criticism from the men once exclusively associated with the songs. The terms of the debate placed the issue firmly in the contemporary Hungarian political and cultural discourse. *Nirvania* produced a passionate, though not fully articulated contestation over high versus popular art, memory and myth, masculinity and femininity.

Particularly intriguing is the manner in which gendered theories of art were wielded to express and further a recent division between the men and the women in the former underground. The notion of doing "Art" rather than merely using pop music or politics to provide legitimacy in a repressive political setting arose to elevate this brand of rock as the successor of the local avant-garde art tradition.

In the 1990s the linkage between creative control and the idea of a transcendent art grew problematic. That idea was no longer effective in addressing pop artists' plight. An intricate interplay of internal and external factors that influenced the politics of expressive culture made musicians susceptible to fresh, nonhierarchical, and partial approaches to art, typically conveyed by women or ethnic minorities. *Nirvania's* male critics, however, deployed such populist and postmodernist arguments to discredit a feminine re-interpretation of the musical legacy, notably their own songs. In her defense, Kamondy combined her feminine sensibility with a transcendental concept of art. The *Nirvania* debate testifies to the complex, inconsistent, and contingent ways in which new ideas and movements become allied with conservative assumptions, typically for strategic purposes.

Conclusion

Albert Melucci opens his book *The Playing Self* with the following ideas about everyday life and its relevance for the study of history:

> Each and every day we make ritual gestures, we move to the rhythm of external and personal cadences, we cultivate our memories, we plan for the future. And everyone does likewise. Daily experiences are only fragments in the life of the individual, far removed from the collective events more visible to us, and distant from the great changes sweeping through our culture. Yet almost everything that is important for social life unfolds within this minute web of times, spaces, gestures, and relations. It is through this web that our sense of what we are doing is created, and in it lie dormant those energies that unleash sensational events. (1996: 1)

In rare historical moments great sweeping changes come close to the life of the individual. At such moments memories of the past and plans for the future become part of conscious efforts to make sense of one's life and rethink one's membership in informal and formal communities. The collective and sensational events of 1989–91 and their aftermath in Central and Eastern Europe brought about such moments for large numbers of people.

While the events and related structural and organizational processes have received a great deal of attention from the social sciences, relatively few studies have investigated the phenomenology of everyday experience as it pertains to social change. Patterns of privatization, election polls, the institutional structure and workings of new democracies and employment statistics yield crucial information about the transition out of socialism but next to no data about the ways people produce, experience, and adjust themselves to it. Without considering the cultural dimension of the structural processes, the nature of change—its components, its profundity, the underlying continuities with the past, the extent to which they are locally unique or parallel global phenomena—cannot be properly understood. My goal has been to explore this underresearched facet of social transition and, more generally, the interrelations between culture, politics, and the social process. I have followed the trajectory of a community amidst multiple ruptures in everyday life and in the social environment. The pop artists I have investigated worked outside, within, and across the institutions of a shifting cultural landscape. Their creativity waxed and waned as they chose new sites and forms in response to the decline of socialism and the public ferment as democracy beckoned, to the ups and downs of the bloodless revolution, and finally to the apparent consolidation of postsocialist relations.

How did they participate in all this commotion? Were they agents or victims of social change? How did subcultural life and its institutions mediate macrosocial transformation for the individual and the group? How did music activities encourage the construction and reconstruction of meaning and identity at a time of disorientation and discontinuity?

I have been arguing that the idea of cultural autonomy offers a useful approach to these questions. All the conflicts, schisms, and existential dilemmas we have explored pointed, in one way or another, to the contested issue of the nature of rock'n'roll as a popular art form. The tension between rock as art and rock/pop as fun or rock as politics versus pop as fad has accompanied the history of this popular form since the countercultural turn in the 1960s. Punk and the alternative music styles of the 1980s displayed peculiar affinity with the artistic avant-garde and through it with a high-art aesthetic. The ongoing polemic between fans and musicians, musicians and critics, subcultures and mainstream about whether to treat rock as art or pop culture is not at all unique to the Hungarian music scene, even though the high cultural aura of rock is far more prevalent in Central and Eastern Europe than in Western Europe and the United States (Cushman 1995, Gordy 1999). The existential and political stakes of such disputes, however, have rarely risen so high as in our particular case.

The individual and collective struggles involved in determining the aesthetic status of underground and alternative music formed an essential aspect of musicians' self-understanding as they negotiated the displacement of the subculture in a reconfiguring economic, social, and political space. Challenging or insisting on rock's relative separation from politics and ideologies came to be thoroughly intertwined with the musicians' most fundamental existential concerns, their collective and individual identities and career choices.

Bourdieu's theory of cultural fields, "habitus," and symbolic/cultural capital (1993) provides us with a propitious framework to capture the shifting sociohistorical ground, manifestations, and meanings of cultural autonomy, but it does so with certain limitations. It cannot satisfactorily account for aesthetic practices particularly relevant to historical change and the attendant transformation of cultural fields. His model is based on a relatively solid and bounded entity, the field of cultural production. We can expand his scheme to account for intense cultural and social change by discerning the discursive/ideological and the spatial dimensions of cultural production (a distinction assumed but not thematized by the theory of fields) and their shifting, reciprocally accentuated significance in response to the reorganization of the fields of culture, economy, and power. We must move beyond conceptualizing the discourse of autonomy as merely a means through which actors maximize their symbolic capital.

The concept of cultural field grounds cultural practices in the system of social relations. Any artistic field, Bourdieu contends, is "contained within the field of power, while possessing a relative autonomy with respect to it" (1993: 37). A field is autonomous if it has a principle of hierarchy and legitimation relatively separate from that prevalent in the field of power that comprises the market and state power. The more autonomous a field is, the more it operates according to its own logic. Central to Bourdieu's theory of artistic fields is the recognition of the reality of artwork as fetish within the art community. He argues that the shared belief that enables agents to treat specific texts as art underlies the field's existence and its mode of operation within the larger terrain of power.

Cultural fields in Bourdieu's schema are battlefields constituted by a structure of positions and a repertoire of possibilities that define the dynamic of the struggle between agents. It is through permanent conflict that a system of positions is created, sustained, and re-created. Position taking is a strategy by which agents try to maximize—not necessarily by conscious calculation—their cultural, symbolic, social, or economic capital. Such strategies are the products of the habitus, a system of lasting and transposable dispositions that generate and organize practices and perceptions (1993: 5).

The idea of autonomous field in Bourdieu's theory applies exclusively to high art, where legitimacy is conferred upon specific texts on the basis of other producers' aesthetic judgment. He calls this "restricted" production, in contrast to large-scale production encompassing the popular arts. The division is based on the role of the marketplace or other extraneous factors in determining the status and value of any one piece within a specific field.

Persuasive attempts have been made to extend Bourdieu's conceptual framework to popular art. Graham Vulliamy (1977) found that in contrasting "sincere" and "original" rock with "formulaic" and "commercial" pop, rock critics and fans mirrored the elitism of the critics of mass culture, who used a similar set of binaries to theorize art versus popular culture. Sarah Thornton (1996) introduced the idea of subcultural capital to interpret the ways in which young habitués of dance clubs create and justify distinctions and thus negotiate status within the framework of their own stratified subcultures. Paul Lopes's (1996) application of cultural fields to U.S. jazz illuminates how musicians between the 1930s and 1960s strove for legitimacy in the larger cultural field through a discourse of authenticity. As a strategy to improve the structural position of jazz in a hostile environment, they adopted a hybrid aesthetic with strong emphasis on jazz as "pure" and valuable art. Such an aesthetic stance was a smart and rebellious response to the constraints posed by the profit-based practices of the commercial music industry, as well as by the classical music establishment, which dismissed jazz as nonart or nonlegitimate culture.

Vulliamy and Thornton demystify the process, along the theoretical lines laid down by Bourdieu, whereby cultural actors strategize to secure symbolic value for specific popular forms and styles as they distinguish it from those deemed inferior in a field traditionally looked down on by the priests and brokers of high culture. Lopes departs from this track. Rather than viewing the consecration of a popular form (in this case, jazz) as an expression of its practitioners' search for domination through a reconfigured system of cultural stratification, he suggests implicitly that in attempting to advance jazz to the status of art, musicians merely sought to free themselves from the domination of the existing cultural establishment. Thus the struggle for jazz's autonomy in that particular era aimed at the emancipation of its producers and consumers, a socially and racially heterogeneous group of low social standing. Even though the entire history of jazz is more contradictory, calling into question Lopes's assumption of disinterestedness (part of the jazz establishment, for instance, was quick to disparage hip-hop as lacking creativity),[1] his implied distinction between cultural actors' quest for domination and their efforts toward emancipation by adopting the high-art paradigm is an important contribution to a more nuanced and historically contextualized understanding of cultural production and social change.

The U.S. jazz musicians' move was analogous to dissenting Eastern European rockers' response to the culturally conservative and politically repressive field of power called state socialism. The rockers' primary means of asserting their difference and freedom was the creation of texts that were subversive but that they nonetheless perceived as art rather than as politics by other means. In other words, an innovation in cultural form involved a new way of talking about it. The musicians' community also attempted to establish an under-

1. Mtume, the African American jazz producer-songwriter who at one time played with Miles Davis, called hip-hop "Memorex music" because of its reliance on record sampling (George 1999: 89–91).

ground infrastructure—concert spaces, a network for recording and distributing audio tapes, connections to other art media—which ensured a certain amount of creative freedom and sustenance of identity. The ideology of aesthetic autonomy enhanced the political economic space for the production of what were politically contentious texts and styles of performance. Part of the reason is that high art even in late socialist society represented greater symbolic value than pop culture, so the packaging of rock as a serious or complex intellectual endeavor enabled the agents of the field to collectively improve their symbolic capital within the state- and market-regulated field of power. Such use of the high-art aesthetic in that particular, broadly understood sociopolitical space nonetheless destabilized rather than reproduced the existing cultural and social order, in which popular music had been confined to mass commercialism.

With the transition the whole cultural political arena in which texts, meanings, and identities cohered into an underground art scene crumbled. It became very difficult to establish a distinctive marginal identity merely by composing and performing cultural texts. Rock and the arts, in general, no longer constituted a privileged terrain of critical consciousness at a time when, suddenly and excitingly, the political arena opened up to burgeoning civil-society activism, paving the way for the demolition of the one-party system. The rock underground at this point experienced a major crisis and began to redefine autonomy as space or infrastructure rather than as music or aesthetic ideology. The ideology of rock-as-art also lost much of its valence both within the community and between the musicians and the emergent institutions of postsocialist cultural life.

The controversy between the two postsocialist alternative music labels, Bahia and Human Telex, speaks to the two dimensions of cultural autonomy. Human Telex's pro-market pragmatism challenged Bahia's high-art aesthetic, whereas the positions they took in the alternative music field represented attempts to maximize their own socioeconomic and political spaces. Both facets of autonomy were implicated in EPH's trials and tribulations with the record industry and the municipal government: in order to attain economic autonomy, the group should have been able to present itself either as a commercial pop band for EMI Quint or as serious artists for the government. But the rock-as-art paradigm did not sound compelling to the jury of the local art foundation. Finally, there could not be a more transparent example for the strategic questioning of the modernist high-art ideology than the conflict over Kamondy's *Nirvania*, with its aim of redistributing the symbolic capital within the former underground along gender lines.

The dramatic nature of political and cultural change is best illustrated by the displacement of charisma from rock'n'roll to politics: if a couple of years earlier future politicians on the liberal side were flocking to underground rock events, now the rock musicians were mixing with the crowd at mass gatherings, live public debates, and election campaigns to listen to their former fans-turned-politicians. With the boundaries of the underground art field becoming increasingly blurry, its character and identity grew nebulous too. To hold onto aesthetic autonomy in order to maximize economic autonomy was of less and less strategic use for the musicians' community, yet the dominant mentality forged in the underground persisted. Several musicians still expressed a belief in some form of aesthetic autonomy. Tamás's and Mihály's contrasting experiences with the Fellowship of Faith indicated, however, that the rock-as-art paradigm was far from uncontested even within the subculture. These two men displayed different sets of dispositions, even as they temporarily occupied a similar position in the field. Bourdieu says that "artists endowed with different, even opposing dispositions can coexist, for a time at least, in the same positions. The structural constraints inscribed in the field set limits to the free play of dispositions; but there are different ways of playing within these limits" (1993: 66). The decay of the rock underground, I suggest, was in part the consequence of the increasing divergence of the musicians' habitus, which the shifts and realignments in the entire societal field of power rendered both more visible and more disruptive.

"Where shall I go tonight—to the disco or to church?" in the EPH's song expressed the community's predicament. Whether one chose the church or the disco, it was evident that the disco underwent substantial change before the turn of the decade. The capitalist/democratic transformation liberated it from its ghettolike existence, which led to the further differentiation of the underground field and to the development of a more loosely knit alternative cultural scene. Since one facet of the community's identity crisis was manifested in the musicians' low-key productivity, survival strategies focused on the political-economic preconditions of music life and the symbolic aspects of collective regeneration. Many musicians' wholehearted dedication to the establishment of new spaces and places in the city, as well as the creation of a plethora of independent record labels, alternative clubs and pubs, alternative magazines and a radio station, represented their desire for autonomy in this newfound second dimension.

Alexei Yurchak reports a strikingly parallel phenomenon in post-Soviet Russian youth culture. Taking advantage of the power and institutional void of the transition period, young people in the cities created what he calls "temporary autonomous zones"—that is, public places free of state or any other external control. Like their Hungarian counterparts, the occupants of such places experimented with new forms of entertainment, creativity, and social relations. Yurchak points out how and why these exciting but short-lived places served as catalysts for "a quick cultural and social transformation of the late socialist system" (1999: 102).

It may be assumed that the growth of a market-based but not profit-oriented genuinely alternative scene served to make up for the evaporation of countercultural music's charisma in these countries. At the same time, these new spaces embodied a missing yet much desired aspect of subcultural music making under socialism: having your own clubs (radio stations, magazines, record labels) designed and run by and for the community. The fact that these expectations were thwarted by financial and political factors before long is another story. Essential to my argument are the ways in which the two aspects of autonomy, discourse and political economic space, which previously existed in close interdependence, diverged in reaction to rapid and profound change in the outer field of power and forced a community of cultural producers to reinvent itself as a field.

This curious dual pattern of enacting or striving for autonomy is not exclusive to the experience of postsocialist Hungary and Russia. As Gordy observed, cataclysmic change had a reverse and more somber trajectory in the former Yugoslavia, especially in Serbia. The once internationally acclaimed, cosmopolitan, and multifaceted rock culture that thrived in the shared political and economic spaces and developed infrastructures across Yugoslavia's republics suffered an almost fatal blow with the rise of ethnonationalist isolation and the ensuing war. Hardest hit was the rock community of Belgrade, where Slobodan Milošević's authoritarian regime and its aggressive promotion of synthetic folk music ("turbofolk") drove this recalcitrant rock far underground. Interestingly, as local rock had to adjust to shrinking and marginal spaces, its mainstream sounds vanished, and avant-garde and esoteric styles, with an attendant high cultural attitude, became predominant. The severe circumstances evidently amplified a serious voice in rock in implicit opposition to state-sponsored folk, disdained as "primitive" and "Balkan" (Gordy 1999: 103–40).

The Serbian rockers' resort to the discourse of authenticity and their apparent elitism as they redefined their music's identity in response to the loss of previous political and economic spaces reinforces another central theoretical idea distilled from my case study: the cultural ideology of authenticity borrowed from high cultural discourse and associated with disenfranchised groups' or individuals' quest for autonomy may have empowering and potentially disruptive rather than reproductive political effects. This is not an argument in defense of artistic autonomy per se, a reification of "art," nor is it a recourse to Romantic and modernist assumptions about authentic culture. Instead, I propose a radically contextualized and historically situated understanding of autonomy, which in the realm of expressive culture is fought for by diverse and shifting means with diverse and shifting effects.

In the same way that the sounds, words, and images of rock and other popular musics produced under the same style category (punk, hard-core, rap, alternative, folk, etc.) have different nuances of meaning in different temporal, national, and sociocultural settings, aesthetic discourses that producers, critics, and audiences adopt or reappropriate in order to make sense of their art or to (re)position themselves have diverse ideological inflections. Such discourses do not operate in a vacuum independent of other currents of thought circulating within and across social groups, within and across national and regional boundaries. Nor are these ideas and beliefs unaffected by particular, often diverse and contradictory art practices, political ambitions, status struggles, and existential concerns. While the hybridization of cultural forms, practices, and meaning systems is a ubiquitous reminder of globalization, the instability of ideas and practices as well as their often improbable, unique, and dissonant blendings are more conspicuous in the fluid and spectacularly fragmented culture of postsocialist Eastern Europe than in Western society (for many fascinating examples, see Berdahl, Bunzl, and Lampland 2000; Barker 1999). As the *Nirvania* debate exemplified, residual (elitist, transcendental) concepts of art could easily blend with an emergent articulation of feminist issues. By the same token, the concurrent rise of a populist postmodern aesthetic is about as likely to undergird the male chauvinist agenda—in the rock community as well as in the society at large—as to promote the nonhierarchical coexistence and multiplicity of subcultural and intercultural sounds.

It is a curious twist to the story that while the modernist high-art paradigm became marginalized in the rock community by the mid-1990s, it had secured the status of official ideology in the postsocialist fine art establishment. The changing of the guard entailed the recruitment of a new elite from the formerly suppressed avant-garde/underground art world. Their continued emphasis on formalist aesthetics and the reification of quality at the expense of difference articulated along the lines of gender, sexuality, or ethnicity rigidified the art scene, making it difficult for the younger generation of a different persuasion to find their voice, let alone carve out their own discursive, political, and economic spaces (András 1999).

The reappropriation of the high-art ideology in popular culture is thus bound up with a search for autonomy. The relationship between cultural actors' and a cultural field's autonomy, however, is complexly entangled, temporally unstable, and contextually determined. The autonomization of a cultural field involves the use or reappropriation of the high-art paradigm. This recourse to "art" may work in both directions. It may be part of a strategy that reconstitutes a system of distinctions, and through it a hierarchic cultural and social order, either across the increasingly porous boundaries between high and popular or within the realm of the popular. But what appears to be the consecration of a particular popular form may be embedded in broader cultural and social struggles to restructure the entire field of production in a way that empowers its producers and consumers without implying a culturally inferior other. Thus from my position I see popular culture as a multidimensional social space in which it is difficult to draw a clear line between the reproductive and disruptive effects of the discourse of cultural autonomy.

Gil Eyal, Iván Szelényi, and Eleanor Townsley (1998) contend that cultural capital is more important than economic capital in the reformulation of class structure in postsocialist societies. The trajectory of the Hungarian underground community supports this argument. The symbolic (ethical, political, cultural) and social capital accrued in opposition was instrumental in the re-creation of a viable status and identity, even if the logic and terms of its use within and outside the community were far from transparent and the outcome was unpredictable. One might want to argue that in the restricted field of marginal culture, it was always symbolic and social rather than economic capital that organized the internal stratification of the community. But as soon as the community was left without the symbolic space it inhabited before 1989, its members needed to vie for positions in a commodity market, restricted as it was. Therefore, the cultural and social capital of individual actors came to be measured in terms of recording contracts, media exposure, concert and touring opportunities, and government grants, as well as the nonmusical awards and creative opportunities that were now essential for economic survival. In the absence of a solid and calculable institutional system, the strategic aspects of position taking, of playing the game, became more intense and more visible than ever before.

And yet Bourdieu's central metaphors, reducing culture to a form of currency whose value is to be negotiated in and through competitive game playing, leave us with an unexplained excess of human dilemmas, affective investments, and existential struggles. What happens to the individual whose identity, not merely his field of activity, is falling apart? Why do cultural producers cross over from one meaning system to another while being constrained by their habitus? How can one play in a field of positions and with a repertoire of possibilities without knowing the stakes in the game and the meaning of the contest? What regenerative resources does one's creativity and a belief in its symbolic value offer at a time when all cultural fields and the field of power are in flux?

One way of answering these questions is to suggest that assumptions about art, its complexity, its relevance, its location above the everyday, its ineffable qualities, and its capacity to provide a sense and site of freedom (definitions provided by my informants) constitute a set of beliefs that enable its adherents to use art less as a source of distinction than as a tool of introspection, and thus a source of empowerment (not domination), deeply interwoven with one's identity work and most profound and personal existential concerns.

Rock and other subcultural music styles may be analytically viewed as texts, a set of practices embedded in institutions, and a particular lifestyle (for a classic account, see Becker 1963). The innermost core of the Hungarian underground art community lived rock rather than merely produced and consumed it. And the more the community lost its creative edge and public renown, the more rock-'n'roll as a lifestyle degenerated into a downward spiral of nihilistic self-destructive behavior. The crisis of the field involved a loss of viable aesthetic paradigms, along with the musicians' difficulty in producing new and successful music. As we have seen, a variety of individual and collective responses arose to redeem this situation.

Some musicians restarted their creative careers abroad. Others (though very few) sought the intensity and provocation once provided by underground music in the service of the incendiary rhetorics of ultraright politics, even at the risk of losing face with their previous audience. The solution for musicians like Tamás and Mihály lay in engagement with an alternative religious community. But unlike Tamás, Mihály did not sever his ties to the art community. His most personal quest for freedom and integrity became completely intertwined with, in a sense symbolized by, the freedom of the artwork that he insisted on producing in defiance of the Fellowship of Faith. He did not strategize to maximize his social status in adhering to the high-art paradigm but rather lived it. Struggling with and for his art, he sought to regain his autonomy, both as an artist and as a person. Similarly, Ágnes Kamondy's quasi-religious faith in art as a means of re-membering, redeeming, and burying the past clearly testifies to the noninstrumental aspect of her aesthetic position and practice. Many other musicians' reflections on their own and other musicians' creativity in the transition made me understand the impossibility of reducing such positions and practices to game playing and jockeying for position.

In Bourdieu's framework a theoretical shortcut is made between cultural practices and cultural capital, between habitus and position taking in the field, between cultural distinctions and social hierarchies. In other words, the uses and meanings of culture are not interrogated apart from their entanglement in the social structure of power and prestige (see also LiPuma 1993). Therefore an important dimension of the meanings and uses of expressive culture and its surrounding discourses remains unaccounted for. This dimension is more noticeable, though certainly not restricted to, moments of social dislocation and social actors' ontological insecurity. In times when previously embraced meaning systems and ideologies lose their valence, expressive culture and its symbolic place in one's life become seriously scrutinized—assessed and reassessed—for their ability to anchor one's identity.

In his highly original essay on how aesthetics may be integrated into contemporary cultural studies Ian Hunter (1992) theorizes the work we do with art as an essentially ethical practice of the self. Moving away from paradigms of culture as commodity or symbolic capital, Hunter identifies the ways in which aesthetic practices, through the constant and systematic problematization of the self and the social world, of experience and conduct, contribute to the building and modification of subjectivity. The peculiarly aesthetic practice is defined as a technology rather than easily accessible pleasure or a form of knowledge.

Hunter's model has several advantages. First, in its emphasis on aesthetics as cultivated sensibility and a way of life, it encompasses both cultural producers and consumers, since the producers (in this case, the underground rockers) are also critical and active consumers. Second, by defining aesthetics as a technology deployed for ethical purposes, the model erases the divide between popular culture and art. Any text may be used as an object of aesthetic reflection.

Such a construal of the aesthetic has some curious implications for the study of the popular. It accounts for the persistent attraction, however small in scale, of esoteric subcultural music styles and practices that are neither immediately accessible nor profane, let alone popular in the sense of being widely listened to. The history of Hungarian underground rock not only gave birth to legends but registered many moderately popular performers, periods when productivity lagged, and dead-end stylistic experiments. In looking at these instances as acts of composing or reconstituting one's self (both individual and collective), one can make a case for the critical relevance of such music for its practitioners without claiming authenticity (political, artistic, or other) for the music or its participation in the regime of symbolic distinctions. Finally, without depoliticizing culture (critical interrogation is essential to the aesthetic "work"), Hunter's model theorizes creativity at a remove from its political and ideological effects. In this way, it allows for a better grasp of the entangled and individuated quality of meaning making.

One might regard musicians' active questioning and intensely self-reflective relation to art as the distinctly aesthetic dimension of expressive culture. Engaging in it, the Hungarian underground musicians dealt not only with the formal properties and meanings of individual artifacts or genres but also with the manner in which their art, placed in the temporal perspective of continuities and disruptions, seemed to them meaningful or meaningless, important or valueless, exhilarating or painful. Reflectively living their art was a means of rebuilding their personalities and musical personas, a process overdetermined by the complex interplay of macrosocial change, the micropolitics of group life, and individual biography.[2]

Although the upheavals associated with the change in regime tore away the fabric of the Hungarian underground community and re-created it as a very different musical formation, the story offers more general insight into subcultural life and its intriguing dynamic. First, it complicates arguments about the political effects of subcultural sounds and conversations. Does playing the game necessarily imply the acceptance of its most fundamental rules, whereby distinctions are made solely to reproduce systems of inequality and domination? Or does the restructuring of the field as a result of subcultural "noise" include moments of emancipation and the sustenance of spaces where nonhierarchic differences can thrive?

2. Such uses of expressive culture, especially popular music, are not confined to moments of cataclysmic social change. They are easily discernible in the intense affective and intellectual investment young people make in the music of their choice as they select, analyze, criticize, and abandon musical styles, personalities, and subcultures in the process of growing into adulthood. The psychosocial role of popular music is well known in the literature on youth but is often subsumed under a model of resistance or manipulation.

While it is possible, with the help of a sufficiently nuanced contextual analysis, to assess the ideological effects of a particular discursive and artistic move, in the messy terrain of musicians' everyday struggles to create a voice and make that voice heard, moments of resistance and innovation are enmeshed with those of conservation and repression. The macropolitics of noise is about as contradictory and unstable as its micropolitics: in-group competition and confrontation are no less intrinsic to subcultural communities than loyalty and solidarity. And no serious analysis can overlook micropolitics in the interpretation of the big picture.

Popular music is not, however, as closely intertwined with politics as most academic treatments of it suggest. Greil Marcus noted that "rock is seen as . . . an ideological drama of, at its most positive, manipulation and cooptation and resistance."[3] Indeed, in the service of representing rock as ideological drama, the academic vocabulary has overpoliticized the concept of identity, displacing such ideas as self, personality, and persona, all of which are central to the aesthetic and especially the musical experience. Future research should assign more autonomy to the distinctly aesthetic dimension of using and producing art and popular culture. Reconstituting the aesthetic and the personal moment in the sociological study of culture would contribute to a far richer conceptualization of the mediations between music and politics, individual and community, and to the ways in which selves and identities participate in cultural and social change.

3. Blurb on the jacket of Frith 1996.

references

Adorno, Theodor W. (1941) 1990. "On Popular Music." In *On Record: Rock, Pop, and the Written Word,* ed. Simon Frith and Andrew Goodwin, pp. 301–14. New York: Pantheon.

Anderson, Benedict R. 1991. *Imagined Communities: Reflections on the Origin and Spread of Nationalism.* New York: Verso.

Anderson, Ellen. N.d. "Trabantalia: Of Cars, Consumption, and Culture." In *Cultural Policies, Practices, and Debates in East Central Europe,* ed. Eric Gordy and Anna Szemere. Forthcoming.

András, Edit. 1995. "Vízpróba a kortárs (nő)művészeten, (nő)művészeken" [Contemporary (women's) art and (women) artists on water ordeal]. In *Vízpróba* [Water ordeal], ed. Edit András and Gábor Andrási, pp. 25–43. A Series of Exhibitions at the Óbuda Club Gallery and at the Cellar Gallery in Óbuda. Budapest: Óbudai Társaskör.

———. 1999. "Gender Mine Field: The Heritage of the Past." Paper presented at the symposium "After the Wall: Art and Culture in Post-Communist Europe," Moderna Museet, Stockholm, October 15–16.

Apor, Péter. 1994. "Századvégi utóirat anarchizmusról és rockzenéről" [End-of-the-century epigraph on anarchism and rock music]. *Valóság* 37, no. 3: 30–40.

Arato, Andrew. 1993. *From Neo-Marxism to Democratic Theory: Essays on the Critical Theory of Soviet-Type Societies.* Armonk, N.Y.: M. E. Sharpe.

———. 1994. "Revolution, Restoration, and Legitimization: Ideological Problems of the Transition from State Socialism." In *Envisioning Eastern Europe: Postcommunist Cultural Studies,* ed. Michael D. Kennedy, pp. 180–246. Ann Arbor: University of Michigan Press.

Aronowitz, Stanley. 1994. *Dead Artists, Live Theories, and Other Cultural Problems.* New York: Routledge.

Attali, Jacques. (1977) 1985. *Noise: The Political Economy of Music.* Trans. B. Massumi. Minneapolis: University of Minnesota Press.

Bahry, Romana. 1994. "Rock Culture and Rock Music in Ukraine." In *Rocking the State: Rock Music and Politics in Eastern Europe and Russia,* ed. Sabrina P. Ramet, pp. 243–97. Boulder, Colo.: Westview.

Bakács Settenkedő, Tibor. 1995. "Az alternatív kultúra vége, a párhuzamos kultúra, születése" [The end of alternative culture and the rise of parallel culture]. *Magyar Narancs,* July 13, pp. 32–33.

Balassa, Péter. 1994. "Ahogy esik, időszerűtlenül" [Without claims for timeliness]. *Kritika,* no. 12 (December).

Barber-Keršovan, Alenka. 1989. "Laibach." In "Ljubljana: A Symbolic Challenge to the System of Socialist Self-Government." Paper presented at the meeting of the International Association for the Study of Popular Music, "Music, History, Democracy, 1789–1989," Paris.

———. 1996. Review of Rajko Muršič et al., *Bili ste zraven: O rock kulturi v severovzhodni Sloveniji* [You have been involved: On rock culture in northeast Slovenia]. *Popular Music* 15, no. 1: 127–29.

Barker, Adele Marie, ed. 1999. *Consuming Russia: Popular Culture, Sex, and Society Since Gorbachev.* Durham: Duke University Press.

Barthes, Roland. 1977. "The Grain of the Voice." In *Image-Music-Text,* ed. S. Heath, pp. 179–89. Glasgow: Fontana.

Becker, Howard. 1963. "The Culture of a Deviant Group: The 'Jazz' Musician." In *The Subcultures Reader,* ed. K. Gelder and S. Thornton, pp. 55–56. New York: Routledge, 1997.

———. 1982. *Art Worlds.* Berkeley and Los Angeles: University of California Press.

Beilharz, Peter. 1992. "Between Bolshevism and Democracy." In *Between Totalitarianism and Postmodernity,* ed. P. Beilharz, G. Robinson, and J. Rundell. Cambridge: MIT Press.

Beke, László, and Annamária Szőke, eds. 1984. *Jó világ* [Good world]. Budapest: Bölcsész Index, ELTE Bölcsészettudományi Kar.

Benjamin, Walter. 1968. "The Work of Art in the Age of Mechanical Reproduction." In *Illuminations,* ed. Hannah Arendt, trans. H. Zohn, pp. 219–55. New York: Harcourt, Brace & World.

Bennett, Tony, et al., eds. 1993. "Series Editor's Preface." In *Rock and Popular Music: Politics, Policies, Institutions,* pp. x–xi. Culture: Politics and Policies, no. 1. New York: Routledge.

Berdahl, Daphne, Matti Bunzl, and Martha Lampland, eds. 2000. *Altering States: Ethnographies of Transition in Eastern Europe and the Former Soviet Union.* Ann Arbor: University of Michigan Press.

Berger, Bennett. 1981. *The Survival of a Counterculture: Ideological Work and Everyday Life Among Rural Communards.* Berkeley and Los Angeles: University of California Press.

Bohlman, Philip V. 2000. "To Hear the Voices Still Heard: On Synagogue Restoration in Eastern Europe." In *Altering States: Ethnographies of Transition in Eastern Europe and the Former Soviet Union,* ed. Daphne Erdahl, Matti Bunzl, and Martha Lampland, pp. 70–96. Ann Arbor: University of Michigan Press.

Bohn, Chris. 1981. "Hungarian Rhapsody and Other Magyar Melodies." *New Musical Express* 17, no. 16: 18.

Born, Georgina. 1993. "Afterword: Music Policy, Aesthetic and Social Difference." In *Rock and Popular Music,* ed. Tony Bennett et al., pp. 266–93. New York: Routledge.

———. 1995. *Rationalizing Culture: IRCAM, Boulez, and the Institutionalizing of the Musical Avant-Garde.* Berkeley and Los Angeles: University of California Press.

Bourdieu, Pierre. 1980. "The Aristocracy of Culture." Trans. R. Nice. *Media, Culture, and Society* 2. no. 3: 225–354.

———. 1984. *Distinction: A Social Critique of the Judgement of Taste.* New York: Routledge.

———. 1993. *The Field of Cultural Production: Essays on Art and Literature.* Ed. R. Johnson. New York: Columbia University Press.

Boym, Svetlana. 1994. *Common Places: Mythologies of Everyday Life in Russia.* Cambridge: Harvard University Press.

Bozóki, András. 1993. "Hungary's Road to Systemic Change—The Opposition Roundtable." *East European Politics and Societies* 7, no. 2: 276–308.

Brace, Tim, and Paul Friedlander. 1992. "Rock and Roll on the New Long March: Popular Music, Cultural Identity, and Political Opposition in the People's Republic of China." In *Rockin' the Boat: Mass Music and Mass Movements,* ed. Reebee Garofalo, pp. 115–28. Boston: South End Press.

Brooks, William. 1982. "On Being Tasteless." *Popular Music* 2: 9–19.

Broun, Janice. 1988. *Conscience and Captivity: Religion in Eastern Europe.* Washington, D.C.: Ethics and Policy Center.

Chambers, Iain. 1985. *Urban Rhythms: Pop Music and Popular Culture.* London: Macmillan.

———. 1992. Discussion of Simon Frith, "The Cultural Study of Popular Music." In *Cultural Studies,* ed. Lawrence Grossberg, Cary Nelson, and Paula A. Treichler, pp. 182–86. New York: Routledge.

———. 1994. *Migrancy, Culture, Identity.* New York: Routledge.

Cipriani, Roberto. 1994. "Traditions and Transitions: Reflections on the Problems and Prospects for Religions in Eastern and Central Europe." In *Politics and Religion in Central and Eastern Europe,* ed. William H. Swatos Jr., pp. 1–17. Westport, Conn.: Praeger.

Clifford, James. 1992. "Traveling Cultures." In *Cultural Studies,* ed. Lawrence Grossberg, Cary Nelson, and Paula A. Treichler, pp. 96–112. New York: Routledge.

Cohen, Jean, and Andrew Arato. 1992. *Civil Society and Political Theory.* Cambridge: MIT Press.

Cohen, Leonard. 1975. "Chelsea Hotel No. 2." In *The Best of Leonard Cohen* (1968–75). Sony/Columbia, ASIN B00000256G.

Cohen, Sara. 1991. *Rock Culture in Liverpool.* Oxford: Oxford University Press.

———. 1994. "Identity, Place, and the Liverpool Sound." In *Ethnicity, Identity, and Music: The Musical Construction of Place,* ed. Martin Stokes, pp. 117–35. New York: Berg.

Comisso, Ellen. 1997. "Is the Glass Half Full or Half Empty? Reflections on Five Years of Competitive Politics in Eastern Europe." *Communist and Postcommunist Studies* 30, no. 1: 1–21.

Corrigan, Philip. 1990. "Masculinity as Right: Some Thoughts on the Genealogy of 'Rational Violence.' " In *Social Forms/Human Capacities: Essays in Authority and Difference.* London: Routledge.

Csengey, Dénes. 1983. *És mi most itt vagyunk* [And now we're here]. Budapest: Magvető.

Csörsz, István. 1986. *Elhagyott a közérzetem* [I dunno how I am]. Budapest: Magvető.

Cushman, Thomas. 1991. "Rich Rastas and Communist Rockers: A Comparative Study of the Origin, Diffusion, and Defusion of Revolutionary Musical Codes." *Journal of Popular Culture* 25, no. 3: 17–58.

———. 1995. *Notes from Underground: Rock Music Counterculture in Russia.* Albany: State University of New York Press.

Dalos, György. 1991. "A kisfiú válasza: Avagy lehet-e hinni a demokráciában?" [The boy's answer; or, Is it possible to have faith in democracy?]. *Magyar Narancs*, September 11, pp. 18–19.

Dám, László. 1987. *Rockszámla* [Rock account]. Budapest: IRI, Reflex.

Downing, John. 1996. *Internationalizing Media Theory: Transition, Power, Culture.* London: Sage.

Durkheim, Emile. 1951. *Suicide.* New York: Free Press.

———. (1915) 1965. *The Elementary Forms of the Religious Life.* New York: Free Press.

Eagleton, Terry. 1996. *Literary Theory: An Introduction.* Minneapolis: University of Minnesota Press.

Esbenshade, Richard. 1995. "Remembering to Forget: Memory, History, National Identity in Postwar East-Central Europe." *Representations* 49 (Winter): 72–96.

Esterházy, Péter. 1994. "Az idő városa" [The city in time]. In *Egy kékharisnya följegyéšseiből* [From the notes of a bluestocking], pp. 174–80. Budapest: Magvető.

Eyal, Gil, Iván Szelényi, and Eleanor Townsley. 1998. *Making Capitalism Without Capitalists: Class Formation and Elite Struggles in Post-Communist Central Europe.* New York: Verso.

Feuer, Gábor. 1984. "Beszélgetés Menyhárt Jenővel" [A conversation with Jenő Menyhárt]. In *Jó világ* [Good world], ed. László Beke and Annamária Szőke, pp. 103–7. Budapest: Bölcsész Index, ELTE Bölcsészettudományi Kar.

Fiori, Umberto. 1985. "Popular Music: Theory, Practice, Value." In *Popular Music Perspectives* 2, pp. 13–24. Reggio Emilia: International Association for the Study of Popular Music.

Forgács, Éva. 1994. "A valóság fogalmának változása a 80-as évek magyar művészetében" [The shifting concept of reality in the Hungarian arts of the '80s]. In *A modern posztjai: Esszék, tanulmányok, dokumentumok a 80-as évek magyar képzőmuűvészetéről* [The Posts of Modernity: Essays, studies, and documents about the fine arts of the '80s in Hungary], ed. K. Keserű, pp. 15–27. Budapest: ELTE BTK.

Fornäs, Johan. 1995. "The Future of Rock Discourses That Struggle to Define a Genre." *Popular Music* 14, no. 1: 111–26.

Fráter, Zoltán. 1994. "Legendaszervíz." [Legend repair]. *Élet és irodalom*, no. 28: 51–52.

Frigyesi, Judit. 1996. "The Aesthetic of the Hungarian Revival Movement." In *Retuning Culture: Musical Changes in Central and Eastern Europe,* ed. Mark Slobin, pp. 54–76. Durham: Duke University Press.

Frith, Simon. 1981. *Youth, Leisure, and the Politics of Rock'n'Roll.* New York: Pantheon.

———. 1987. "Towards an Aesthetic of Popular Music." In *Music and Society: The Politics of Composition, Performance, and Reception,* ed. R. Leppert and S. McClary, pp. 133–49. New York: Cambridge University Press.

———. 1996. *Performing Rites: On the Value of Popular Music.* Cambridge: Harvard University Press.

Frith, Simon, and Howard Horne. 1987. *Art into Pop.* New York: Methuen.

Frith, Simon, and Angela McRobbie. (1978) 1990. "Rock and Sexuality." In *On Record: Rock, Pop, and the Written Word,* ed. Simon Frith and Andrew Goodwin, pp. 371–89. New York: Pantheon.

Funk, Nanette, and Magda Mueller, eds. 1993. *Gender Politics and Postcommunism: Reflections from Eastern Europe and the Former Soviet Union*. New York: Routledge.

Gal, Susan. 1991. "Bartók's Funeral: Representations of Europe in Hungarian Political Rhetoric." *American Ethnologist* 18, no. 3 (August): 440–58.

Garton Ash, Timothy. 1989. "Reform or Revolution?" In *The Uses of Adversity: Essays on the Fate of Central Europe,* pp. 218–74. Cambridge: Granta.

George, Nelson. 1999. *Hip Hop America*. New York: Penguin.

Goehr, Lydia. 1994. "Political Music and the Politics of Music." *Journal of Aesthetics and Art Criticism* 52, no. 1 (Winter): 99–112.

Goldfarb, Jeffrey C. 1992. *After the Fall: The Pursuit of Democracy in Central Europe.* New York: Basic Books.

———. 1998. *Civility and Subversion: The Intellectual in Democratic Society.* New York: Cambridge University Press.

———. 2000. "Drawing Distinctions, Finding Correlations: Tasks for a Critical Dialogic Sociology of Culture." Paper presented at the Culture and Theory Workshop of the Culture Section Miniconference "Millennial Issues in Sociology," Washington, D.C., Aug. 10–11.

Goodwin, Andrew. 1992. "Rationalization and Democratization in the New Technologies of Popular Music." In *Popular Music and Communication,* ed. J. Lull, pp. 75–100. Newbury Park, Calif.: Sage.

———. 1998. "Drumming and Memory: Scholarship, Technology, and Music Making." In *Mapping the Beat: Popular Music and Contemporary Theory,* ed. Thomas Swiss, John Sloop, and Andrew Herman. Malden and Oxford: Blackwell.

Gordy, Eric. 1997. "The Destruction of Alternatives: Everyday Life in Nationalist Authoritarianism." Ph.D. dissertation, University of California, Berkeley.

———. 1999. *The Culture of Power in Serbia: Nationalism and the Destruction of Alternatives.* University Park: Pennsylvania State University Press.

Goven, Joanna. 1993. "Gender Politics in Hungary: Autonomy and Antifeminism." In *Gender Politics and Postcommunism: Reflections from Eastern Europe and the Former Soviet Union,* ed. Nanette Funk and Magda Mueller, pp. 224–40. New York: Routledge.

Gramsci, Antonio. 1972. *Selections from the Prison Notebooks of Antonio Gramsci.* Ed. and trans. Quintin Hoare and Geoffrey Nowell Smith. New York: International Publishers.

Grandpierre, Attila. 1984. "Punk as a Rebirth of Shamanist Folk Music." Unpublished paper.

Gray, Herman. 1988. *Producing Jazz: The Experience of an Independent Record Company.* Philadelphia: Temple University Press.

Grossberg, Lawrence. 1984a. "Another Boring Day in Paradise: Rock and Roll and the Empowerment of Everyday Life" *Popular Music* 4: 225–58.

———. 1984b. "I'd Rather Feel Bad than Not Feel Anything at All: Rock and Roll, Pleasure and Power." *Enclitic* 8, no. 1/2: 95–111.

———. 1992. *We Gotta Get Out of This Place: Popular Conservatism and Postmodern Culture.* New York: Routledge.

Habermas, Jürgen. 1984–87. *The Theory of Communicative Action.* Trans. Thomas McCarthy. 2 vols. Boston: Beacon.

Hadas, Miklós. 1983. "'Úgy dalolok, ahogy én akarok': A popzenei ipar működésének vázlata" [I sing as I want to: The outline of the workings of the pop music industry]. *Valóság* 26, no. 9: 71–78.
Hajnóczy, Csaba. 1983a. *Voice of Hungary*. Vol. 1. Vienna: Rittn Tittn.
———. 1983b. "Rockandroll." M.A. thesis, Liszt Ferenc Academy of Music, Budapest.
Hankiss, Elemér. 1989. *Kelet-európai alternatívák*. Budapest: Közgazdasági és Jogi Könyvkiadó. Published in English as *East-European Alternatives: Are There Any?* Oxford: Oxford University Press, 1990.
Haraszti, Miklós. 1987. *The Velvet Prison: Artists Under State Socialism*. Trans. K. and S. Landesmann with the help of S. Wasserman. New York: Basic Books.
Harris, David. 1992. *From Class Struggle to the Politics of Pleasure: The Effects of Gramscianism on Cultural Studies*. New York: Routledge.
Hebdige, Dick. 1979. *Subculture: The Meaning of Style*. New York: Methuen.
Hennion, Antoine. 1983. "The Production of Success: An Anti-Musicology of the Pop Song." *Popular Music* 3: 159–95.
Hobbs, Nick. 1993. "The Live Rock Music Scene in Hungary." Unpublished paper.
Howard, Jay, and John Streck. 1996. "The Splintered Art World of Contemporary Christian Music." *Popular Music* 15, no. 1: 37–53.
Hunter, Ian. 1992. "Aesthetics and Cultural Studies." In *Cultural Studies*, ed. Lawrence Grossberg, Cary Nelson, and Paula A. Treichler, pp. 347–73. New York: Routledge.
Huyssen, Andreas. 1990. "Mapping the Postmodern." In *Feminism/Postmodernism*, ed. L. J. Nicholson, pp. 234–77. New York: Routledge.
Jenkins, Robert, and Edie Gorman. 1994. "Contesting Images: Parties and Media in Democratic Hungary." Paper presented at the Annual Conference of the American Sociological Association, Los Angeles.
Jones, Andrew F. 1992. *Like a Knife: Ideology and Genre in Contemporary Chinese Popular Music*. Ithaca: East Asia Program, Cornell University.
Juno, Andrea. 1996. *Angry Women in Rock*. Vol. 1, *Interviews by Andrea Juno*. New York: Juno.
Kamarás, Ferenc, and István Monigl. 1984. "A demográfiai folyamatok és az ifjúság" [Demographic processes and youth]. In *A magyar ifjúság a nyolcvanas években* [Hungarian youth in the '80s], pp. 69–119. Budapest: Kossuth.
Kennedy, Michael D. 1994. "An Introduction to East European Ideology and Identity in Transformation." In *Envisioning Eastern Europe: Postcommunist Cultural Studies*, ed. Michael D. Kennedy, pp. 1–46. Ann Arbor: University of Michigan Press.
Klíma, Ivan. 1994. "Progress in Prague." *Granta*, no. 47, pp. 249–55.
Kloet, Jeroen de. 2000. "Audiences in Wonderland: The Reception of Rock Music in China." In *Changing Sounds: New Directions and Configurations in Popular Music, IASPM 1999 International Conference Proceedings*, ed. Tony Mitchell and Peter Doyle with Bruce Johnson. Sydney: Faculty of Humanities and Social Sciences, University of Technology.
Kőbányai, János. 1979. "Biztositótű és bőrnadrág" [Safety pin and leather]. *Mozgó Világ* 5, no. 2: 64–77.
Konrád, György. 1989. *Antipolitika—az autonómia kísértése* [Antipolitics: The temptation of autonomy]. Budapest: Codex RT.

Körösényi, András. 1992. "The Decay of Communist Rule in Hungary." In *Post-Communist Transition: Emerging Pluralism in Hungary,* ed. A. Bozóki, A. Körösényi, and G. Schöpflin, pp. 1–13. New York: St. Martin's Press.

Kruse, Holly. 1993. "Subcultural Identity in Alternative Music Culture." *Popular Music* 12, no. 1: 33–43.

Kürti, László. 1991a. "Rocking the State: Youth and Rock Music Culture in Hungary, 1976–1990." *East European Politics and Societies* 5, no. 3: 483–513.

———. 1991b. "The Wingless Eros of Socialism—Nationalism and Sexuality in Hungary." *Anthropological Quarterly* 64, no. 2: 55–67.

———. 1994. "How Can I Be a Human Being? Culture, Youth, and Musical Opposition in Hungary." In *Rocking the State: Rock Music and Politics in Eastern Europe and Russia,* ed. Sabrina P. Ramet, pp. 73–103. Boulder, Colo.: Westview.

Laing, Dave. 1985. *One-Chord Wonders: Power and Meaning in Punk Rock.* Milton Keynes: Open University Press.

Lange, Barbara Rose. 1996. "Lakodalmas Rock and the Rejection of Popular Culture in Post-Socialist Hungary." In *Retuning Culture: Musical Changes in Central and Eastern Europe,* ed. Mark Slobin, pp. 76–92. Durham: Duke University Press.

Leitner, Olaf. 1983. *Rockszene DDR: Aspekte einer Massenkultur im Sozialismus* [Rock Scene DDR: Aspects of a mass culture under socialism]. Reinbek bei Hamburg: Rowohlt.

———. 1994. "Rock Music in the GDR: An Epitaph." In *Rocking the State: Rock Music and Politics in Eastern Europe and Russia,* ed. Sabrina P. Ramet, pp. 17–40. Boulder, Colo.: Westview.

Levine, Lawrence. 1988. *Highbrow/Lowbrow: The Emergence of Cultural Hierarchy in America.* Cambridge: Harvard University Press.

Levy, Claire. 1998. "Old New Sounds: Ethno Revival in Bulgaria." Paper presented at the U.K. Branch Conference of the International Association for the Study of Popular Music, Liverpool, September 11–13.

Lipsitz, George. 1990. *Time Passages: Collective Memory and American Popular Culture.* Minneapolis: University of Minneapolis Press.

———. 1994. *Dangerous Crossroads: Popular Music, Postmodernism, and the Poetics of Place.* New York: Verso.

LiPuma, Edward. 1993. "Culture and the Concept of Culture in a Theory of Practice." In *Bourdieu: Critical Perspectives,* ed. C. Calhoun, Edward LiPuma, and M. Postone, pp. 14–35. Chicago: University of Chicago Press.

Lopes, Paul. 1996. "Pierre Bourdieu's Fields of Cultural Production: A Case Study of Jazz." Paper delivered at the Annual Meeting of the American Sociological Association, New York City.

Lukács, György. 1982. " 'Szakadék Nagyszálló' " [Grand Hotel "Abyss"]. In *Esztétikai írások, 1930–1945* [Aesthetic Writings, 1930–1945], ed. László Sziklai, trans. Ottó Beöthy. Budapest: Kossuth Könyv Kiadó.

Manuel, Peter. 1995. "Music as Symbol, Music as Simulacrum: Postmodern, Premodern, and Modern Aesthetics in Subcultural Popular Musics." *Popular Music* 14, no. 2: 227–39.

Marcus, George. 1993. "Introduction to the Series and to Volume 1." In *Perilous States: Conversations on Culture, Politics, and Nation,* ed. George Marcus. Chicago: University of Chicago Press.

Marcus, Greil. 1989. *Lipstick Traces: A Secret History of the Twentieth Century.* Cambridge: Harvard University Press.

Melucci, Albert. 1996. *The Playing Self: Person and Meaning in the Planetary Society.* New York: Cambridge University Press.

Merkel, Ina. 1994. "From a Socialist Society of Labor into a Consumer Society? The Transformation of East German Identities and Systems." In *Envisioning Eastern Europe: Postcommunist Cultural Studies,* ed. Michael D. Kennedy, pp. 55–65. Ann Arbor: University of Michigan Press.

Meštrović, Stjepan G., with Slaven Letica and Miroslav Goreta. 1993. *Habits of the Balkan Heart: Social Character and the Fall of Communism.* College Station: Texas A&M University Press.

Middleton, Richard. 1990. *Studying Popular Music.* Philadelphia: Open University Press.

Milun, Kathryn. 1992. "Rock Music and National Identity in Hungary." *Surface.* 24 pp. Internet: <http://www.pum.umontreal.ca/revues/surfaces/vol1./milun.html>

———. 1993. "Returning to Eastern Europe." In *Perilous States: Conversations on Culture, Politics, and Nation,* ed. George Marcus, pp. 53–81. Chicago: University of Chicago Press.

Mitchell, Tony. 1992. "Mixing Pop and Politics: Rock Music in Czechoslovakia Before and After the Velvet Revolution." *Popular Music* 11, no. 2: 187–205.

Modleski, Tania. 1986. "A Feminist Approach to Mass Culture." In *High Theory/Low Culture: Analyzing Popular Television and Film,* ed. Colin MacCabe, pp. 37–53. New York: St. Martin's Press.

Mukerji, Chandra, and Michael Schudson. 1991. "Introduction." In *Rethinking Popular Culture: Contemporary Perspectives in Cultural Studies,* ed. Mukerji and Schudson. Berkeley and Los Angeles: University of California Press.

Nagy, Gyula. N.d. "A Fekete Lyuk története" [The history of the Black Hole]. Unpublished paper.

Negus, Keith. 1992. *Producing Pop: Culture and Conflict in the Popular Music Industry.* New York: Routledge.

Pekacz, Jolanta. 1992. "On Some Dilemmas of Polish Post-Communist Rock Culture." *Popular Music* 11, no. 2: 205–8.

———. 1994. "Did Rock Smash the Wall? The Role of Rock in Political Transition." *Popular Music* 13, no. 1: 41–51.

Ramet, Sabrina P. 1991. *Social Currents in Eastern Europe.* Durham: Duke University Press.

———, ed. 1994. *Rocking the State: Rock Music and Politics in Eastern Europe and Russia.* Boulder, Colo.: Westview.

Ramet, Sabrina P., Sergei Zamascikov, and Robert Bird. 1994. "The Soviet Rock Scene." In *Rocking the State: Rock Music and Politics in Eastern Europe and Russia,* ed. Sabrina P. Ramet, pp. 181–218. Boulder, Colo.: Westview.

Rimmer, Dave. 1985. *As If Punk Never Happened: Culture Club and the New Pop.* London: Faber & Faber.

Robinson, Deanna, Elizabeth Buck, and Marlene Cuthbert. 1991. *Music at the Margins: Popular Music and Global Cultural Diversity.* Newbury Park, Calif.: Sage.

Róna-Tas, Ákos. 1994. "The First Shall Be Last—Entrepreneurship and Communist Cadres in the Transition from Socialism." *American Journal of Sociology* 100, no. 1: 40–69.

Rose, Tricia. 1994. *Black Noise: Rap Music and Black Culture in Contemporary America.* Hanover, N.H.: University Press of New England.

Ryback, Timothy. 1990. *Rock Around the Bloc.* New York: Oxford University Press.

Sátántangó. 1994. *Sátántangó: Krasznahorkai László regénye alapján Tarr Béla filmje* [*Satan's Tango:* Béla Tarr's film based on László Krasznahorkai's novel]. Budapest: Budapest Film Rt.

Schiach, Morag. 1989. *Discourse on Popular Culture: Class, Gender, and History in the Analysis of Popular Culture, 1730 to Present.* Cambridge: Polity.

Schudson, Michael. 1992. *Watergate in American Memory: How We Remember, Forget, and Reconstruct the Past.* New York: Basic Books.

Schwartz, Barry. 1996. "Introduction: The Expanding Past." *Qualitative Sociology* 19, no. 3 (special issue, *Collective Memory*).

Scott, James. 1990. *Domination and the Arts of Resistance: Hidden Transcripts.* New Haven: Yale University Press.

Sebők, János. 1983–84. *Magya-Rock.* 2 vols. Budapest: Zeneműkiadó.

Slobin, Mark. 1993. *Subcultural Sounds: Micromusics of the West.* Hanover, N.H.: University Press of New England.

———, ed. 1996. *Retuning Culture: Musical Changes in Central and Eastern Europe.* Durham: Duke University Press.

Starr, Frederick. 1983. *Red and Hot: The Fate of Jazz in the Soviet Union.* New York: Limelight.

Stewart, Tony, ed. 1981. *Cool Cats: Twenty-five Years of Rock'n'Roll Style.* London: Eel Pie.

Stokes, Martin, ed. 1994. *Ethnicity, Identity, and Music: The Musical Construction of Place.* New York: Berg.

Straw, Will. 1991. "Systems of Articulation, Logics of Change: Communities and Scenes in Popular Music." *Cultural Studies* 5, no. 3: 368–88.

Sükösd, Miklós. 1993. "Helyzeti alternatívok" [Positional alternatives]. *Mozgó Világ* 19, no. 11: 79–91.

Survilla, Maria. 1994. "Rock Music in Belarus." In *Rocking the State: Rock Music and Politics in Eastern Europe and Russia,* ed. Sabrina P. Ramet, pp. 219–43. Boulder, Colo.: Westview.

Szemere, Anna. 1992a. "Bandits, Heroes, the Honest, and the Misled: Exploring the Politics of Representation in the Hungarian Uprising of 1956." In *Cultural Studies,* ed. Lawrence Grossberg, Cary Nelson, and Paula A. Treichler, pp. 623–50. New York: Routledge.

———. 1992b. "The Politics of Marginality: A Rock Musical Subculture in Socialist Hungary in the Early 1980s." In *Rockin' the Boat: Mass Music and Mass Movements,* ed. Reebee Garofalo, pp. 93–115. Boston: South End Press.

———. 1993. "The Limits of Rationality: A Critique of Habermas' Theory of Communicative Action." Unpublished paper.

———. 1996. "Subcultural Identity and Social Change: The Case of Postcommunist Hungary." *Popular Music and Society* 20, no. 2: 19–42.

Szilágyi, Ákos. 1995. "A temetés temetése: A szovjet temetés mint totalitárius életünnep, 1924–1985" [The burial's burial: The Soviet burial as totalitarian life festivity]. *ABCD Interactive Magazine* 2, no. 4. CD-ROM.
Szőnyei, Tamás. N.d. "Óriások törpeországban: A majorok bejövetele" [Giants in dwarf country: The arrival of the majors]. Unpublished paper.
———. 1992. *Az új hullám évtizede* [The decade of the new wave]. Vol. 2. Budapest: Katalizator Iroda.
———. 1993. " 'A zene mindenkié': A független zenekiadók" [Music is for everyone: The independent record companies]. *Mozgó Világ,* no. 11, pp. 103–10.
———. 1994. "Szomorú szimfónia" [Sad symphony]. Unpublished paper.
Thornton, Sarah. 1996. *Club Cultures: Music, Media, and Subcultural Capital.* Hanover, N.H.: University Press of New England.
Tipton, Steven. 1982. *Getting Saved from the Sixties: Moral Meaning in Conversion and Cultural Change.* Berkeley and Los Angeles: University of California Press.
Tismaneanu, Vladimir. 1992. *Reinventing Politics: Eastern Europe from Stalin to Havel.* New York: Free Press.
Tomasi, Luigi. 1994. "The New Europe and the Value Orientations of Young People: East-West Comparisons." In *Politics and Religion in Central and Eastern Europe,* ed. William H. Swatos Jr., pp. 47–64. Westport, Conn.: Praeger.
Troitsky, Artemy. 1987. *Back in the USSR: The True Story of Rock in Russia.* London: Omnibus Press.
Turner, Victor. 1990. "Are There Universals of Performance in Myth, Ritual, and Drama?" In *By Means of Performance: Intercultural Studies of Theatre and Ritual,* ed. Richard Schechner and Willa Appel, pp. 8–19. New York: Cambridge University Press.
Varga, Ivan. 1994. "Churches, Politics, and Society in Postcommunist East Central Europe." In *Politics and Religion in Central and Eastern Europe,* ed. William H. Swatos Jr., pp. 101–18. Westport, Conn.: Praeger.
Verdery, Katherine. 1991. *National Ideology Under Socialism: Identity and Cultural Politics in Ceauşescu's Romania.* Berkeley and Los Angeles: University of California Press.
———. 1996. *What Was Socialism and What Comes Next?* Princeton: Princeton University Press.
Vermorel, Fred, and Judy Vermorel. 1978. *Sex Pistols: The Inside Story.* London: W. H. Allen.
———. 1985. *Starlust: The Secret Fantasies of Fans.* London: W. H. Allen.
Vidić Rasmussen, Ljerka. 1996. "The Southern Wind of Change: Style and the Politics of Identity in Prewar Yugoslavia." In *Retuning Culture: Musical Changes in Central and Eastern Europe,* ed. Mark Slobin, pp. 99–117. Durham: Duke University Press.
Vulliamy, Graham. 1977. "Music and the Mass Culture Debate." In *Whose Music? A Sociology of Musical Languages,* ed. J. Shepherd, P. Virden, G. Vulliamy, and T. Wishart, pp. 179–200. London: Latimer.
Walker, John. 1987. *Cross-Overs: Art into Pop, Pop into Art.* New York: Methuen.
Wallis, Roger, and Krister Malm. 1984. *Big Sounds from Small Peoples: The Music Industry in Small Countries.* London: Constable.

Walser, Rob. 1992. "Eruptions: Heavy Metal Appropriations of Classical Virtuosity." *Popular Music* 11, no. 3: 263–308.

Weber, Max. (1930) 1989. *The Protestant Ethic and the Spirit of Capitalism.* Trans. Talcott Parsons. London: Unwin Hyman.

Wicke, Peter. 1990. "The Influence of Rock Music on Political Changes in East Germany." First Annual Public Lecture, Centre for Research on Culture and Society, Carleton University, Ottawa.

———. 1992. "'The Times They Are A-changing': Rock Music and Political Change in East Germany." In *Rockin' the Boat: Mass Music and Mass Movements,* ed. Reebee Garofalo, pp. 81–92. Boston: South End Press.

——— 1998. " 'Born in the GDR': Ostrock Between Ostalgia and Cultural Self-Assertion." *Debatte: Review of Contemporary German Affairs* 6 (November): 148–55.

Williams, Raymond. 1977. *Marxism and Literature.* New York: Oxford University Press.

Willis, Paul. 1978. *Profane Culture.* London: Routledge and Kegan Paul.

———. 1979. *Learning to Labor: How Working-Class Kids Get Working-Class Jobs.* New York: Columbia University Press.

———. 1990. *Common Culture: Symbolic Work at Play in the Everyday Cultures of the Young.* Boulder, Colo.: Westview.

Wolff, Janet. 1987. "Foreword: The Ideology of Autonomous Art." In *Music And Society,* ed. R. Leppert and S. McClary, pp. 1–13. New York: Cambridge University Press.

———. 1992. "Excess and Inhibition: Interdisciplinarity in the Study of Art." In *Cultural Studies,* ed. Lawrence Grossberg, Cary Nelson, and Paula A. Treichler, pp. 706–17. New York: Routledge.

———. 1995. *Resident Alien: Feminist Cultural Criticism.* New Haven: Yale University Press.

Wuthnow, Robert. 1989. *Meaning and Moral Order: Explorations in Cultural Analysis.* Berkeley and Los Angeles: University of California Press.

Yurchak, Alexei. 1999. "Gagarin and the Rave Kids: Transforming Power, Identity, and Aesthetics in Post-Soviet Nightlife." In *Consuming Russia: Popular Culture, Sex, and Society Since Gorbachev,* ed. Adele Marie Barker, pp. 76–110. Durham: Duke University Press.

Zolberg, Vera. 1990. *Constructing a Sociology of the Arts.* New York: Cambridge University Press.

INTERVIEWS

(All conducted in Budapest unless otherwise indicated.)
Bárdos Deák, Ágnes, June 1995.
Bornai, Tibor, November 1993.
Bródér, Ferenc, July 1995.
FeLugossy, Laca, November 1993, Szentendre.
Grandpierre, Attila, November 1993.
György, Péter B., November 1993, May 1995.
Hajnóczy, Csaba, November 1993, May 1995.
Kamondy, Ágnes, November 1993.
Kiss, László, October 1993.
Kistamás, László, October 1993.
Kocsis, Tamás, May 1995.
Magyar, Péter, October 1993.
Máriás, Béla, May 1995.
Márton, András, December 1993.
Menyhárt, Jenő, February 1984 (with András Bozóki), November 1993.
Müller, Péter Iván (with Ágnes Bárdos Deák), February 1984, December 1993, Szentendre.
Nagy, Kriszta, June 1995.
Rácz, Mihály, June 1995.
Siklós, András, November 1993.
Szőnyei, Tamás, November 1993, June 1995.
Víg, Mihály, May 1995.
Wahorn, András, November 1995.
Zámbó, ef. István, November 1993.

Uncited personal interviews were also conducted with the following musicians, musical entrepreneurs, and music fans: Mária Bán (Bizottság and Takács Tamás Dirty Blues Band); Sándor Gecse (Ápolók); János and Anna Hanák; Ferenc Jávori (Budapest Klezmer Band); Endre Kardos (Sziámi); Gabi Kenderesi (Kampec Dolores); members of Korai Öröm; Tamás Kovács (Centrál Station); András Lovasi (Kispál és a Borz); Marietta Méhes (Trabant); Mihály Rácz (Hidegroncs/Trottel Records); Zsuzsa Ujj (Csókolom); Orsolya Varga (Európa Kiadó); Simi Wahorn and Imánuel Oláh (Balaton); László "Gazember" Waszlavik.

Index